AF541435

CONSTRUCTING NUCLEAR STRATEGIC DISCOURSE

THE SOUTH ASIAN SCENE

Dr MOHAMMED B. ALAM et. al.

India Research Press

India Research Press
Flat-6, Khan Market, New Delhi – 110 003.
Ph.: 24694610; Fax : 24618637
bahrisons@vsnl.com; contact@indiaresearchpress.com
www.indiaresearchpress.com

2007

ISBN thirteen : 978-81-8794-394-5
ISBN ten : 81-8794-394-7

Cataloging in Publication Data
Dr MOHAMMED B. ALAM *et al*
CONSTRUCTING NUCLEAR STRATEGIC DISCOURSE :
The South Asian Scene
by Dr MOHAMMED B. ALAM et al

Includes end note references and index.
1. Security 2. Politics 3. South Asia 4. Nuclear.
I. Title. II. Author

Printed in India at Focus Impressions, New Delhi – 110 003.

Contributors

Dr Mohammed Badrul Alam, Professor of Political Science, Jamia Millia Islamia University, New Delhi, India.

Prof. Ramamurti Rajaraman, Professor of Theoretical Physics, School of Physical Sciences, Jawaharlal Nehru University, New Delhi, India.

Dr Jozef Goldblat (Sweden/Switzerland), Vice President, Geneva International Peace Research Institute (GIPRI), Geneva, Switzerland; Consultant, United Nations, Geneva (former Director, Arms Control & Disarmament Programme, SIPRI).

Prof. Abdul H. Nayyar, Sustainable Development Policy Institute, Islamabad, Pakistan; on leave from the Physics Department, Quaid-i-Azam University, Islamabad.

Prof. Maurizio Martellini, Secretary-General, Landau Network-Centro Volta (LNCV), Como, Italy; Professor of Physics, University of Insubria, Como, Italy.

Dr Farah Zahra, independent Security Analyst, (former Fellow of the John F. Kennedy School of Government, Harvard University, US).

Dr Zafar Iqbal Cheema, Quaid-i-Azam Fellow, Oxford University, UK.

Dr Zafar Nawaz Jaspal, Assistant Professor at the Department of International Relations, Quaid-i-Azam University, Islamabad, Pakistan.

Dr Rafi uz Zaman Khan Researcher at the Strategic Plans Division, Government of Pakistan.

Dr Moeed Pirzada, Britannia Chevening Scholar, London School of Economics and Political Science.

Dr Subrata K. Mitra, Professor of Political Science and Director, South Asia Institue, University of Heidelberg, Heidelberg, Germany.

Prof. Andrew C. Winner, Senior Staff Member at the Institute of Foreign Policy Inc., an affiliate of Tufts University, US.

Acknowledgements

This book has its origin from teaching a wide range of students in India, the US and Japan. My students at Nimapara College (Utkal University, Bhubaneswar, India) were the early inspirations for sharpening my writing skills. Later in New Delhi where I earned my M.Phil degree in American Studies at Jawaharlal Nehru University, my professors, Dr B.K. Shrivastava, Dr M.S. Venkatramani and Dr R.P. Kaushik taught me aspects of nuclear security studies and its implications. My long stint at the American Center library in New Delhi opened my eyes to the scope and breadth of literature on almost all important facets of security studies.

While at Cornell University in Ithaca, New York, where I earned my MA and PhD degrees in International Studies, many professors revealed to me the intricacies and complexities of issues related to nuclear proliferation and their impact in the shaping of South Asian society. The professors are: Dr Richrad Polenberg, Dr Mary Fainshod Katzenstein, Dr Milton Jacob Esman, Dr Walter Lafeber, Dr Martin Shefter, Dr Benjamin Ginsburg, Dr Peter Katzenstein, Dr Richard Rosecrance, Dr Ami Ayalon, Dr Stewart Blumin, Dr Joel Silbey, Dr Myron Rush, Dr George Kahin, Dr Norman Uphoff, Dr Steven Jackson. From the Cornell University Library, Ved Kayastha was of invaluable help in providing input and feedback whenever needed.

I am grateful to Dr Bryan Reddick, Dean of Elmira College, New York, Dr Anthony Layng, Professor of Anthropology, Dr Robert Park, Professor of Political Science,

Dr Myra Glenn, Professor of History and Professor Peter Ladley, Department of English all from the same institution, for encouraging me at all times. Dr Frank Czerwinski of the State University of New York at Cortland offered me useful advice whenever I sought it. My colleagues at Midway College, Kentucky, namely, Dr Robert Miller, Professor of Religion, Dr Judith Hatchet, Professor of English, Dr Glenna Graves, Professor of History, provided me with useful research assistance.

In Japan, where I have been teaching at Miyazaki International College in Southern Kyushu since January 1998, the following people helped me in shaping my ideas and bringing in the right focus on South Asian security discourse. Among the colleagues who helped me are: Dr Kate Greenfield, Dean; Dr. Getachew Felleke, Professor of Economics; Prof. Jun Maeda, Professor of Japanese Literature; Dr Daniel Bratton, Professor of English Literature; Dr Scott Davis, Professor of Anthropology; Prof. Amanda Bradley, Professor of English Language; Dr Jeong Pyong-Hong and Dr.Yasu Izumikawa, Professors in Political Science as well as faculty secretaries: Rumi Matsuda and Kenta Imanishi. My students at the Miyazaki International College in the course, "South Asian Societies and Cultures", provided interesting glimpses from the security literature as India and Pakistan evolved the nuclear security doctrine. My friends working at other institutions in Japan also offered useful comments on this book project. Among those are: Dr Joel Campbell (Professor of Political Science, Osaka University), Dr Mika Mervioe (Professor of Political Science, University of Shimane), Dr Jeffrey Folks (Professor of American Literature, Doshisa University at Kyoto).

From the Pugwash International, Dr Jeffrey Boutwell and from the Islamabad Peace Research Institute, Ahmad Ejaj Malik, were instrumental in giving me the necessary permission in re-printing some of the publications that were under their outfits.

The greatest gratitude is owed to my mother, Hedatun Nisa and brothers Dr Mohammed Shamsul Alam and Mohammed Aminul Alam, and sisters: Dr (Mrs) Swaleha Khatun, Rahima Khatun, Sofia Khatun; my wife: Gahartaj Rokeya and my children: Saira Alam, Zubair Alam, Sadaf Alam and Munawar Alam. Although quite demanding and at times frustrating, everyone allowed me the time and necessary emotional support I needed to complete my work. Much of my success is due to their love and affection at all times.

Dr Mohammed B. Alam
New Delhi, India

Contents

Preface

The primary purpose of this book is to analyze, examine, evaluate and critique contemporary works on South Asian security order encompassing aspects of nuclear doctrines of India and Pakistan, impact of nuclear South Asia in the regional context as well as the viability of various confidence building measures both in the conventional and non-conventional areas. The book offers a number of scenarios under which a stable security regime may evolve in South Asia in the not so distant future.

Chapter One deals with key elements of India's draft nuclear doctrine including the changes and transformations that has taken place within the last few years. Mohammed Badrul Alam also looks at and examines some workable and plausible confidence-building measures both at the military and non-military levels that could be experimented in the context of India-Pakistan relations.

Chapter Two looks at recent conciliatory overtures and peace initiatives between India and Pakistan. R. Rajaraman explains how this call for peaceful dialogue from Pakistan has not found immediate acceptance from the Indian side for a variety of reasons including the presence of China as a nuclear neighbor - a factor that introduces a major asymmetry between India and Pakistan in their security requirements.

Chapter Three focuses on the objectives of confidence building among nations that has been practised for many years. Jozef Goldblat outlines how CBMs translate certain principles of international law into positive action so as to provide credibility to states' affirmations of their peaceful intentions.

Chapter Four analyses elections in Pakistan to the National Assembly, and in India to the state assembly of the state of Jammu and Kashmir that took place in the first week of October 2002 and its ramifications for the peace process. Pran Chopra also offers concrete suggestions for improving relations between India and Pakistan in resolving the long standing Kashmir conflict.

Chapter Five addresses the origin of militancy in Kashmir and the extent to which it affects the overall security situation in the Kashmir valley. A.H.Nayyar and M.Martelini also analyze the pros and cons of a limited confrontation and whether or not that can lead to an all out nuclear war in the Indian sub-continent.

Chapter Six examines nuclear confidence building measures (NCBMs) in light of the Strategic Restraint Regime (SSR) suggested by Pakistan and the Lahore Memorandum of Understanding signed between India and Pakistan. It will also examine the technological limitations of NCBMs, and consider the role of the United States and the international community in managing proliferation in South Asia. Farah Zahra offers plausible suggestions and makes policy recommendations in the above context.

Chapter Seven attempts to list Pakistan's threat perceptions. Zafar Iqbal Cheema also describes Pakistan's nuclear capabilities and delivery systems, analyses the nuclear doctrine and stability factor and offers some suggestions and envisages the likely future trends

Chapter Eight evaluates the anticipated impacts of India-Pakistan's nuclear strategies on the geo-political and geo-economic environment of the Indian Ocean. Zafar Nawaz Jaspal also discusses the anticipated repercussions of the overt nuclear weaponization of the sub-continent and makes recommendations for tackling and decreasing the evolving danger to the regional security arrangements.

Chapter Nine examines the merits and demerits of establishing nuclear risk reduction centers(NRRCs) for South Asia and what could be the likely apprehensions of the citizens. Rafi uz Zaman also analyzes how NRRCs be successfully operationalized given the dissolution of previous Indo-Pak security agreements.

Chapter Ten looks at the challenges faced by Indian strategic thinking after 9/11, vis-à-vis Pakistan; options available to it and responses offered. Moeed Pirzada also examines the convergence of external and internal imperatives that now drive US strategic alliance with New Delhi and whether Washington can prevent it from becoming a "zero sum game" in South Asia.

Chapter Eleven discusses Lahore Declaration and Kargil crisis as two different ways of conceptualizing India-Pakistan relations between a non-dichotomous model and a dichotomous model that could work towards the containment and solution of other conflicts. Subrata Mitra evaluates the origin of the two models and examines their implications for regional security in South Asia.

Finally, Chapter Twelve outlines how and why US policy treats India and Pakistan differently and to what extent national interests of the United States dictate its policy toward South Asia. Andrew Winner also analyses Bush administration's priorities as it tries to deal with broader issues such as terrorism, democracy and stability within its core decision making process.

This book attempts to have a balanced, objective assessment of nuclear strategies of India and Pakistan and provides a rationale from a state centric paradigm. The book also discusses in cogent details various critical viewpoints of prominent scholars who have tried to address South Asian nuclear discourse using content, empirical and analytical approaches.

Between Dominance and Confidence-building Measures: A Study of India's Nuclear Doctrine and the Current Regional Environment in South Asia

Dr Mohammed B. Alam

India's response to global nuclear non-proliferation measures has been a dominant theme in the country's overall evolution of nuclear policy since the country gained independence from British colonial rule in 1947. In 1974, India conducted a nuclear test that it termed a 'peaceful nuclear explosion', and in 1998 a full-scale nuclear test subsequently claiming to attain nuclear capability. Soon after, its neighbour Pakistan took the same nuclear route.

The purpose of this article is to critically evaluate key elements of India's draft nuclear doctrine including the transformations that have taken place within the last few years. The paper also examines plausible confidence-building measures (CBMS) that could be experimented upon in the context of India-Pakistan relations.

Background

The draft on nuclear doctrine was presented in August 1999 to the Indian Prime Minister, Atal Behari Vajpayee, and the Cabinet and was released later for public debate by the National Security Advisory Board (NSAB).

The nuclear doctrine of India was perhaps the first of its kind among the known nuclear weapon states of the world, and India prepared the draft nuclear doctrine document before obtaining capability mentioned in it. Since August 1999, when the doctrine was pronounced by India's national security advisor, the document has not been put before any parliamentary committee or been given a formal title. It was not clear whether the doctrine as presented was a set of recommendations or just simply a set of formulations based on reasoned judgement made by a select group of India's leading academics, bureaucrats, diplomats mostly based in New Delhi's power corridor.

Certain key assumptions, accepted by consecutive governments in New Delhi, guide the nuclear doctrine paper that was submitted by the National Security Advisory Board to the Cabinet Committee for Security Affairs (CSA). First, there is a belief that nuclear weapons remain key instruments for national and collective security. Nuclear weapons do have utility. The selective possession of these weapons has been legitimized and perpetuated by the indefinite extension of the Nuclear Non-Proliferation Treaty (NPT). Second, the de jure nuclear weapon states have essentially abandoned their commitment towards disarmament. Third, autonomy of decision-making on development and defense issues is the right of democratic India.[1]

The timing of the release of the Draft Nuclear Doctrine (DND) raises questions as in August 1999, the Vajpayee government was in a caretaker capacity after losing its majority in the lower house of Indian parliament. Re-elections had already been called for in October 1999. Some might argue that the draft doctrine was released to the media to bolster the Bharatiya Janata Party's (BJP) electoral advantage. It might also be suggested that the nuclear doctrine was formulated only to formalize BJP's nuclear policy declared after the nuclear tests conducted in May 1998.

According to Jaswant Singh, a BJP member and Minister for External Affairs (1999-2004), "Nehru's policies provided continuity within India's strategic culture. However, Nehru's legacies consisted of little more than negative attributes like veneration of the received wisdom; an absence of iconoclastic questioning; a still continuing lack of institutional framework for policy formulation; lack of a sense of history and geography; an absence of a sufficient commitment to territorial impregnability and tendency to remain static in yesterday's doctrines."[2]

Yet, another view might be that it was to legitimize India's nuclear weapons through the formulation of DND arising out of "the reciprocal fear of surprise attack" on the part of political leaders, military planners and strategic analysts in India.[3] This has been summed up as: "The bomb has many fathers. The Congress conceived it, the United Front nurtured it, the BJP delivered. Let us not give the obstetrician any more credit than is due."[4]

India's Nuclear Doctrine within the Realm of Discourse on Deterrence

When the draft document was released, it included statements that fell within the purview of the notion and practice of deterrence. It stated that India would not conduct more nuclear tests, join the Comprehensive Test Ban Treaty (CTBT) with some modifications and enter negotiations to stop fissile materials production without conditions. It was also proclaimed by India's official spokesperson of pursuing a "no-first-use" (NFU) policy vis-à-vis non-nuclear weapon states and, finally, establish a "credible, minimum nuclear deterrent". (This core policy was also reinforced by the new Congress-led government when Prime Minister Manmohan Singh, in a speech to the nation on June 24, 2004, supported it). However, an Indian government official, in 2001, said that a no-first strike policy did not mean India would not have a first strike capability and added that how this option would be exercised was a political decision within the "no- first-strike" policy.[5]

One of India's leading defense analysts, C. Raja Mohan, was quite forthright in articulating India's rationale for going for the nuclear tests in the summer of 1998. According to him, "India has taken too long to come to terms with the nuclear revolution and its impact on world affairs. But the technology underlying the atomic revolution is fifty years old, and a continuing obsession with it will prevent India from making crucial investments and policy decisions on the new revolution in military affairs. The dramatic advances in information and communication technologies and their application to warfare will increasingly determine the locus of military power in the coming century. Worship of the old nuclear gods and the reluctance to pay attention to the impact of (information technology) on the conduct of future wars will put India back in the position of global irrelevance with or without nuclear weapons... Nuclear weapons are certainly important. And India's decision to acquire them was long overdue. But in the flush of becoming an atomic power, India could easily overstate the significance of nuclear weapons. They can only serve a limited purpose for India – of preventing the use or threat of nuclear weapons by its adversaries against it. There is little else that nuclear weapons can do ... Even the most sophisticated and expansive nuclear arsenal will not propel India into the ranks of great powers. Mindless obsession with nuclear weapons will instead push India down the ruinous path that the Soviet

Union went. Having acquired an insurance policy through nuclear weapons, India must now pursue the arduous domestic agenda of economic modernisation, political reform, and social advancement ... The productive economic and political engagement of the world must remain the bedrock of nuclear India's diplomacy. A paranoid reading of external threats to security and an over-determination of the role of nuclear weapons in national strategy will drive India into a needless confrontation with most nations and undermine New Delhi's efforts to expand its regional influence and global standing."[6] It echoes Prime Minister Atal Behari Vajpayee's statement made in the Indian Parliament that "India does not intend to use these weapons for aggression or for making threats against any country, these are weapons of self-defense, to ensure that India is not subjected to nuclear threats or coercion."[7]

The defense establishment of India also supported this notion of the absoluteness of nuclear weapons when Raja Ramanna, one of the early pioneers of India's Atomic Energy Commission, concurred with Bernard Brodie's work published in 1946 a year after the atomic explosion in Hiroshima and Nagasaki as well as with Glenn Snyder's 1961 seminal piece on deterrence.[8]

According to Raja Ramanna, "Since the end of the Second World war, the problem of security has become aggravated because of two reasons: military power has become synonymous with technological and industrial power, and new developments in technology have brought the situation to a state where weapons of destruction have not merely been improving in potency in some linear manner, but a fundamental change in overall capability has taken place. Besides being assisted by automaton, never dreamt of before, some of them have reached the status of what is known as 'ultimate' weapons, that is, their individual destructive power is more than what the world can bear. The 'ultimate' weapon has the power of destroying vast areas of the Earth and making them uninhabitable in a matter of a few seconds. In spite of this, the 'ultimate' nature of modern weapons does not by itself seem sufficient for countries to give up further development of more efficient weapons. Greater effort is being put on defense research and the testing of weapons continues as before. In some countries the burden of deterrence has messed up not only their entire economic structures, but even their very integrity as nations."[9] Using similar language, George Perkovich writes of a strategic enclave, and in a detailed and comprehensive study examines the history not just of Bhabha's influence on India's political leaders, but of the efforts of Bhabha's successors, such as Vikram Sarabhai, Homi Sethna, Raja Ramanna, V. Arunachalam and others.[10]

Unlike China, which has made clear its policy of "negative security assurances" in respect to non-nuclear countries and adherence to "no-first-use" except using the nuclear weapons within its territory against an adversary, India has yet to formulate a coherent policy in this regard.[11]

No First Use versus First Use: Strategic Dilemma

While officially India has adhered to a "no-first-use" policy in its nuclear doctrine, President A.P.J Kalam has pronounced that despite the "no-first-use" policy, India will use nuclear weapons when peace is threatened and some other country uses such weapons against it (India).[12]

It is a matter of debate as to how to define when exactly

and under what conditions peace is threatened or purported to have been threatened.

According to Kanti Bajpai, a South Asian security analyst, the Indian government and most of the Indian strategic community tend to support the idea of NFU. At least four considerations seem to be behind Indian thinking on the subject.[13]

First of all, there is possible diplomatic advantage for India in an NFU commitment. The NFU offer to Pakistan and the other nuclear powers is a sign of moderation and responsibility in nuclear matters. It is consistent with India's pre-1998 policy and, therefore, shows continuity in Indian policy – another sign that India is a conservative and incrementalist power and not a revolutionary and unpredictable one. Pakistan's opposition to NFU was always anticipated, and the contrast to India's position is expected to enhance India's image as a restrained power and to reinforce Pakistan's image as a troublesome one.

Secondly, a moderate, restrained nuclear weapons programme, without tactical weapons and complicated command and control (both of which are implied by first-use doctrines), is an economically rational choice. A minimum deterrent will be an affordable deterrent from India's point of view.

Thirdly, NFU has military-strategic utilities. The military advantage of a NFU with Pakistan is rarely articulated publicly, but one can see readily enough that if Pakistan also could be persuaded to agree to NFU, then India's conventional superiority could be used against Pakistan, particularly in a situation of asymmetric warfare such as in Jammu and Kashmir. On the other hand, New Delhi hopes that an Indian commitment to NFU will serve to reassure Pakistan and its public that it does not wish to threaten the existence of its neighbour, that war will not be a war of conquest and domination. Reassuring Pakistan is in India's interest since an edgy nuclear Pakistan would be a recipe for further instability in the region.

Fourth, and this is more speculative, as Kanti Bajpai argues, an NFU commitment gives India time to sort out a number of technological, doctrinal, institutional, and even political issues. Technologically, it gives India time to figure out if it can produce tactical nuclear weapons, which would be vital to any first-use posture, particularly in relation to a superior conventional power such as China. Doctrinally, the NFU allows India to debate what the real threats and challenges are and, therefore, what its nuclear use postures should be. Institutionally, the NFU may buy enough time for rival inter-service claims on nuclear weapons to be dealt with. Politically, no first use is helpful in solidifying domestic support for nuclear weapons and increasing civilian control over nuclear weapons. A no first use policy helps bridge the divide between those who are not enthusiastic advocates of nuclear weapons and those who are more supportive of nuclearization. The former are more likely to support nuclear weapons if India's posture remains a more defensive, no first use one. In addition, a no first use policy may be useful to civilians in retaining as much control over nuclear weapons as possible. If no first use translates into a de-mated posture in which Indian scientists control the nuclear warheads or cores, then such a posture will preserve the very highest degrees of civilian control over it. Thus, NFU may give India more time to establish command and control.

Pakistan's Thinking on No First Use/First Use

Pakistan has thus far shown little interest in the idea of NFU. Perhaps the closest Pakistan has officially come to accepting the language of no first use was in the summer of 2002 when India and Pakistan confronted each other in the wake of the Kaluchak massacre in Jammu and Kashmir. In response to Indian threats to retaliate conventionally to the massacre, Pakistan stated that it would respond forcefully in turn, hinting that it was prepared to use nuclear weapons. Shortly thereafter Islamabad publicly clarified, apparently under US pressure, that responding to an Indian attack did not mean nuclear use, presumably first use, against India.

Among non-officials, those who oppose weaponization as well as those who support a minimum deterrent would probably support NFU, the former as an interim confidence-building measure in the transition to nuclear renunciation and the latter in order to keep the arsenal small and to signal moderation and restraint. Most prominently, Dr Pervez Hoodbhoy (Professor of Physics at Quaid-e-Azam University in Islamabad, Pakistan) has suggested that India and Pakistan should, as part of a bilateral nuclear treaty, agree to no first use. Hoodbhoy argues that NFU would actually benefit Pakistan. NFU would be an investment in stability and survival. In case of nuclear war, Pakistan would lose much more than India since New Delhi can inflict much greater nuclear damage (and presumably absorb much greater loss).

Pakistani skepticism or opposition to NFU seems to arise from the following concerns. In contrast to India, Pakistan's thinking on a no first use/first use policy is almost completely military-strategic. First of all, as in India and elsewhere in the world, there are those in Pakistan who doubt the efficacy and practicality of an NFU. In extremis, can Pakistan rely on India's leadership to abide by a no first use commitment? Is there any way of verifying that an adversary is committed to no first use?

Secondly, even if NFU were credible, acceptance of it would mean permanent Pakistani strategic inferiority and vulnerability. Given Pakistan's inferiority in conventional forces, the threat of first use is vital to deter its use against India, while the actual use of nuclear weapons first may be vital for the defence if and when deterrence fails.

Thirdly, there is a school of more offense-oriented Pakistani thinking that opposes an NFU. According to this view, first use is intrinsic to Pakistan's exploitation of the "stability-instability" situation in South Asia. Protected by nuclear weapons, Pakistan is free to choose sub-conventional conflict with India, as in Kashmir: fearing first use by Pakistan, India cannot cross the line of control (LoC) in Kashmir or the international boundary further south to punish Pakistan for its interference in Kashmir. These Pakistani strategists regard Pakistan's support of cross-border terrorism in Kashmir since the late 1980s, the Kargil war in 1999 and the crisis of May-June 2002 as validating the correctness of their analysis. In spite of Pakistani provocations, India chose not to retaliate across the line of control or the international boundary.

Pakistan's interest in first use may in part be supported by a calculation that there are first uses of nuclear weapons against India that would not necessarily invite nuclear retaliation. Stephen P. Cohen suggests that the Pakistani army has conceived of a five-rung escalation ladder. Four of these involve the threat of first use or actual first use:

- Private and public warnings to India not to move its forces threateningly
- A demonstration explosion on Pakistani territory to deter India from a conventional attack
- The use of a "few" nuclear weapons on Pakistani territory against intruding Indian forces
- Nuclear strikes against "critical" Indian military targets, preferably in areas with low population and without much by way of infrastructure.

Of these four, the first two could well avoid Indian retaliation altogether since they would be carried out in Pakistan and would not target Indian assets. The second two, Pakistani planners might calculate, would be more provocative but might still not cause India to unleash a full retaliatory strike.

The three broad segments among nuclear analysts in India, namely, the "rejectionists, the pragmatists, and the maximalists" opine that nuclear issues have not been articulated adequately in the draft nuclear doctrine.[14] It leaves open to question whether it considers the notion of "logic of non-proliferation"[15] to be preponderant in security considerations, meaning a clear advantage in pursuing a proactive policy towards non-proliferation regime, or whether or not India should rely on the "logic of deterrence"[16]. The latter suggests that proliferation has stabilizing effects and nuclear weapons could and would deter war between India and an adversary that has functional utilities. Similarly, some scholars find merit in the "existential deterrence"[17] involving the 1990 near nuclear flash point between India and Pakistan which envisaged both countries to convert their nuclear weapon programme rapidly into actual weapons. In July of 1999, in the aftermath of the Kargil crisis as the recently declassified papers suggest, both India and Pakistan were eyeball to eyeball with Pakistan having already decided to raise the stake to the nuclear level in order to force India to back down from the strategic forward positions in Kargil and its adjoining areas.[18] Yet, the dominant view has been towards a general definition of deterrence that looks at the situation in which "one side (the defender) threatens the other side (the challenger) with some form of punitive retaliation if the other side takes certain action."[19] It can also be argued that in case of nuclear asymmetry, deterrence can be resorted to in the face of nuclear blackmail and hegemony and possible use of the nuclear arsenals by the other side.[20] It is inconceivable for a nuclear power to hope for a total disarming strike of its nuclear adversary and, therefore, escape retaliation. The Indian arsenal will be dispersed, mobile and camouflaged with various deception measures to make the adversary's task more difficult.[21]

The public opinion among the Indian elite was sharply divided in its assessment on the viability of going in for nuclear weapon capability. The elite in the economic affairs believed that "supporting nuclear weaponization undercuts the prospects for growth and investment."[22] In contrast, those in the political and strategic establishment argued that, "India's size and capabilities allowed it to pursue further nuclearization with minimal damage to the prospects for continued growth."[23]

In this context, the stand taken by the anti-nuclear lobby deserves special mention. According to Booker Prize winner Arundhati Roy, "Who the hell conducted those opinion polls? Who the hell is the Prime Minister to decide whose finger will be on the nuclear button that could destroy everything we love – our earth, our skies, our mountains, our rivers, our cities and villages? Who the hell is he to reassure us that there would be no accidents? How does he know? Why should we trust him? What has he ever done to make us trust him? The nuclear bomb is the most anti-democratic, anti-national, anti-human, outright evil thing that man has ever made. If you are religious, then remember that this bomb is man's challenge to God."[24]

The anti-nuclear movements that include politicians, citizens' movements, environmentalists, feminists and progressive activists have put forward different rationales for building up a strong case against Indian nuclearization. They have based their arguments on three major premises. First, that nuclear weapons are strategically irrational weapons of mass destruction and hence cannot provide security – no matter who possesses them and how many. Second, that the concept of nuclear deterrence cannot stand on moral, political, legal, and cultural grounds; and third, that the Indian government's nuclear policy is "inseparably linked to a belligerent and male supremacist notion of militarized nationhood, which is not only anti-pluralist, communal, and masculinist, but also creates an unacceptably dangerous situation in escalating an arms race in South Asia."[25]

Long time India watchers find it ironic that India – the land of Gandhi, Mahavira, Mother Teresa, Buddha (ironically, the nuclear test that India conducted in May 1998 was code named "Buddha is smiling") who espoused the cause of non-violence in its long history of over five thousand years – chose to shun its oft-stated goals of global disarmament in favour of going nuclear in the summer of 1998. That India decided to use the permanent extension of the nuclear Nuclear Non-Proliferation Treaty in May 1995 as a rationale for joining the nuclear weapon states only diluted its stand at various international forums which strive for a genuine non-nuclear world (1.1. Draft Doctrine).

As if to provide a rationale for the shift in India's policy on nuclear issues, Jaswant Singh said in a parliamentary debate held on December 15, 1998, "Look at it as a crowded railway compartment. When you are trying to come into it, your perspective is one. When you are in it, you want the rules that will keep you in and keep the others out."[26]

It is to be remembered, however, that under the Indian political system, it is the prime minister who has the ultimate say in major policy matter such as on the crucial nuclear issue. "The actual policy choices are determined by the autonomous interests of the prime minister in office, who while taking into account the preferences of the strategic enclaves, the political elite, and various political parties has generally been acutely sensitive to the impact of the nuclear issue on economic development and foreign relations precisely because these variables must affect the living conditions of the large voting populace and, by implication, the political survival of the politician."[27]

Possible Cost Factor and its Ramification

India now has a nuclear weapon capability. However, one can argue as to whether India can maintain overall economic growth rate in the face of the stupendous costs involved in researching and developing a nuclear programme (1.2. Draft Doctrine). Although it is difficult to make an accurate prediction of likely expenditures for both ongoing and planned expansion of India's nuclear programme, one study quotes a figure between 15 and 150 billion US dollars for achieving a minimum deterrence capability assuming India does maintain 30-50 bombs.[28] If India decides to increase the number to 400 or more, the costs will be even more prohibitive. To put it within a comparative perspective, the United States nuclear programme has cost an excess of 5.5 trillion dollars and India's neighbour in the north, China, has spent over 100 billion dollars. For a country such as India, where over 30 per cent of the people live below the poverty line and the per capita income is $382 (1998 estimate), the exorbitant costs may be too high for the country's limited resources. Instead of enhancing peace, stability and security, a disproportionate level of expenditures on nuclear weapons may have the opposite effect. Nuclear weapons may bring in more instability and insecurity in spite of the prestige and status factors that are usually ascribed to possession of such capabilities.

Politically, too, India's overall security in the South Asian region may be less stable today and headed towards "ugly stability" with the acquisition of nuclear weapons than with the overwhelming conventional forces India has had since independence. Also, in the coalition-based Indian politics of today, it is more than likely that one or more constituents of India's government may play the nuclear card close to its chest purely for political gains and considerations. As the leading partner of the ruling NDA government in New Delhi, BJP was also under increasing pressure to raise the nuclear rhetoric and Pakistan baiting due to a number of internal developments, such as the attack on India's parliament in December 2002, bombing of Kashmir state secretariat in October 2001 and the upsurge of communal violence in the Hindi heartland of

Gujarat.[29] Even the Congress Party wanted to dispel the notion about the party being "soft on national security" issues. This view also has been reinforced in May 2004 by the new government in New Delhi led by Dr Manmohan Singh of the Congress Party.[30] On a societal level, too, in a country which Economist John Kenneth Galbraith termed the world's only "functioning anarchy", the unstable political environment and the staggering economic cost of a nuclear programme is likely to trigger more social unrest and turbulence along caste and religious lines, and thus may offset any gains India might have in terms of enhanced status. Cumulatively, what would have been the sequence of events had an actual war broken out? According to Dr Chris Smith, "First, India would launch air strikes on the training ground used by insurgents who crossed into Kashmir. In retaliation, Pakistan would attack somewhere along the border between the two countries. India, with its much superior conventional forces, would then counter-attack. Presumably at that critical point, there will be enormous potential for a nuclear counterstrike from Pakistan, followed by retaliation from India."[31]

Other Ambiguities in the Nuclear Doctrine

The draft doctrine also mentions the notion of entity, which in the strategic literature implies "non-state actors"(2.4. Draft Doctrine) and more plainly, "terrorists". With the breakdown of the old Soviet Union, there is a growing fear in intelligence circles that terrorists and some rogue elements in and around the South Asian region may acquire fissile materials. If so, can India go after these entities, for example, against remnants of former Taleban and Al Qaeda forces of Afghanistan as well as other foreign mercenaries and Pakistan based mujahideen outfits such as Hizbullah, Lashkar-i-Toiba and Jaish-i-Mohammed who are believed by Indian intelligence officials to have crossed over to Pakistan-occupied Kashmir valley along the LoC and even termed as "freedom fighters" by forces supporting autonomy for the people of India-occupied Kashmir? There needs to be some clarity in this regard in the draft document.

According to a report published by New Delhi-based Institute of Peace and Conflict Studies (IPCS), an influential thinktank, there are significant discrepancies in India's nuclear doctrine. Some of the highlights of the IPCS report are:[32]

- No first use of nuclear weapons is beset with problems about how India would respond if it were attacked with CBWs by a non state actor, given the volatile situation in South Asia.
- Moratorium on nuclear tests has not addressed tests in laboratories.
- While there is need to have some level of transparency about command and control, some remnant of ambiguity could strengthen deterrence. The non-identification of the chain of political and military succession brings out the issue of its positive/negative impact on nuclear deterrence in South Asia.
- A pivotal role has been accorded to the National Security Advisor (NSA), who heads the Executive Council (EC) and would function as a conduit between the political and military wings of the NCA and also function as the Principal Secretary to the prime minister. He remains busy tackling both domestic and international crises. In addition he travels a lot.

- Other options also need to be explored. The Kargil Review Committee called for a full time National Security Advisor, and grooming a second line of leadership, which as anathema for New Delhi's bureaucracy, driven by personality factors.

- An important question that remains unclear is who will exercise military control over the Strategic Forces during peacetime – Chairman, Chiefs of Staff Committee/SFC or some other committee. The Strategic Forces Command will perforce have to be a tri-service command. The real problem is that the nuclear arsenal might be weaponized, but not deployed, thereby reflecting a demated status. Nuclear weapons assemblies are with the Defence Research & Development Organisation (DRDO), the weapon cores are with the Atomic Energy Commission (AEC), and delivery systems are with the services.

- How these dispersed assets would be brought together and the system worked in a wartime situation when communications could get affected and quick decision-making is needed, has not been clarified. The issue of how the SFC would integrate the nuclear weapons with the delivery vehicles during a conflict situation remains unanswered, but greater transparency would have implications for the stability of Indo-Pakistan ties.

- The Political Council, Executive Council do not conform to a command structure hence raising doubts about its efficacy during a nuclear attack.

- The civil bureaucratic structure has diffused accountability and does not reveal who is accountable to whom, or what would be the line of succession if a decapitating strike succeeds.

- The command authority must be transparent, and the chain of command for the use of nuclear weapons should be made transparent. An increased level of transparency strengthens credibility and has implications for stability in South Asia.

One can play with numbers regarding credible minimum deterrence. Who will determine what should constitute minimum deterrence remains unresolved between the scientific and strategic community, while no requirement seems to have been forwarded by the armed forces.

- There have to be clear "red-lines" or thresholds to launch a nuclear strike or retaliate or to cross the LoC. There was no response, except to deploy the troops after the attack on the Indian Parliament. There has to be a clear message regarding an assured response or retaliatory strike, which needs to be provided for.
- The threat of use of CBWs will generate an ambiguous situation if there is an outbreak of disease like plague. Should India respond with a nuclear strike? If it does not, then what would be the implications for its credibility as a nuclear power? There are additional questions on verifiability of a suspicious outbreak of disease.
- When deconstructed "credible minimum deterrence" raises three pertinent points – credibility raises the issue of transparency versus ambiguity and the question of survivability; minimum is a function of numbers – minimum against China might exceed the maximum for Pakistan, since deterrence is a psychological game. The requirement of a triad is a maximalist response in this situation and will be viewed as such in the neighbourhood.

- A limited war under the nuclear shadow should be confined to limited objectives. Limited war cannot remain limited as it carries the seeds of escalation. A losing side will always want to use all the weapons at its disposal. As a concept this doctrine has been discarded in the West but has found adherents in India.
- Security in the present context is being discussed from the state-centric viewpoint. In this perspective human security has been relegated to the background and internal security not given any significance. It does not take into account the emergence of non-state actors. Nuclear deterrence is futile against terrorists and religious extremists.
- The issue of nuclear stockpile numbers remains problematic, as it is dependent on the strategic calculations of the adversary. What deters is a state of mind. India needs to formulate a policy, whilst its adversarial state is run by an autocratic, risk-taking, adventurist regime.

In the section 2.5 of the draft nuclear doctrine, the document states, "India will not resort to the use or threat of use of nuclear weapons against states which do not possess nuclear weapons, or are not aligned with nuclear weapon powers"(See Annex).

Does this imply that "India could conceivably use its nuclear weapons against countries such as Japan and Germany, who are aligned or receive security cover from the United States either through bilateral treaty or through NATO?"[33] As another sign of seeming contradictions, India's official government spokesman dissociated itself from remarks on India's nuclear doctrine and nuclear programme targeted against big powers, especially the US and China, made by Bharat Karnad, a former member of the National Security Advisory Board, saying it "Appears to reflect his personal view."[34]

Even with an overwhelming conventional superiority in its armed forces, India has had a series of low intensity conflicts with its neighbours, China and Pakistan, with some glaring examples such as in Aksai Chin in the Ladakh region and Kargil along the Line of Control in the Kashmir valley as was witnessed in the summer of 1999. The introduction of nuclear weapons along with maintaining a strong, viable conventional force will have an enormous cost which India can ill afford.

India at the present time has only land to air ballistic missiles such as Agni, Prithvi and Dhanaush that can deliver a 20-kilotonne device. With some additional technical prowess, India may also be able to deploy a nuclear device from a MIG, Mirage or Jaguar aircraft that are under its Air Force's domain. On Pakistan's side, it can use Abdali, Ghauri, Ghaznavi and fit it with nuclear capable missiles aiming at Indian targets. India cannot retaliate effectively against its adversaries when it is just in the process of having mobile launchers, hardened silos, submarine-based nuclear weapon storage. The new government in New Delhi only on May 27, 2004, has appointed a task force to work on the indigenous nuclear submarine project, code-named the Advanced Technology Vessel (ATV), to give it a kick-start. The Strategic Air Command is required to keep some of its aircrafts on nuclear alert at all time, as does the United States, has recently been implemented. The decision that has been made so far indicates the following: [35]

In a cabinet meeting chaired by Prime Minister Atal Bihari Vajpayee on September 1, 2003, the government reviewed the arrangements in place for the strategic forces programme including the chain of command and transfer of nuclear assets to it. On the basis of the recommendations made by the Executive Council, the Political Council also undertook a number of important policy decisions on further development and management of the programme. These decisions upon implementation are likely to consolidate India's nuclear deterrence. This high-powered meeting was attended among others by Deputy Prime Minister L.K. Advani, Union Defence Minister George Fernandes, Union Finance Minister Jaswant Singh and National Security Advisor Brajesh Mishra, besides some top government and defence officials.

The Council, which met for the first time after the Nuclear Command Authority was set up on January 4, 2003, examined all the aspects of the nuclear programme of the country.

Special stress was laid on the chain of command, transfer of nuclear assets and the relationship between the three services, the institution of Chief of Integrated Defence Staff (CIDS) and the Strategic Forces Command.

The transfer of assets including ballistic missiles and nuclear weapons from the Army, Navy and Air Force, and the scientific establishment, to the Strategic Forces Command, and the drill to be followed, came under scrutiny of the Political Council, it was learnt. The Council also reviewed the preparedness of the Strategic Command vis-a-vis the platforms to carry the weapons including air, land and under-sea, and the doctrines adhered to by the Strategic Forces Command.

The security scenario in the Indian subcontinent with regard to the nuclear threat, the nuclear capabilities of the neighbouring countries and the developments in some parts of the world in this sphere were also discussed.

The Political Council was formed to lay down the political principles and administrative arrangements to manage the country's nuclear arsenal, which is under civilian control with the final authority resting with the Prime Minister. This Council comprises members of the Cabinet Committee on Security (CCS) and the National Security Advisor.

While Brajesh Mishra was the first National Security Advisor from 1999 to 2004, in the new Congress-led government that was formed in late June 2004 in India, former Foreign Secretary, J.N. Dixit, was appointed as the new National Security Advisor.

The Executive Council includes the Chairman, Chiefs of Staff Committee of the three services, the three service chiefs, heads of intelligence agencies, the scientific establishment engaged in the nuclear programme and the National Security Advisor. While the Political Council and the NCA is headed by the Prime Minister, the Executive Council is headed by the National Security Advisor.

Even the United States, which originated the concept of "massive retaliation" in the early 1950s, shifted to a more "flexible response" and "mutual assured destruction" strategies in the 1960s and 1970s. US defense policy went through further transformation during the Reagan years from the "deployment of cruise missiles" to the "Strategic Defense Initiative" in the 1980s. Under President George W. Bush, who assumed office in January 2001, the United States has made the National Missile Defense (NMD) programme as its major policy plank. With India's limited resources and in the absence of any tactical weapons and the absence of the position of Chief of Defense Staff to administer the nuclear arsenal and act as a single point military advisor, it is doubtful that it can have a sound nuclear mechanism in place in the immediate near future.[36] In order to maintain "strategic balance" Pakistan, taking note of India's overwhelming superiority in conventional arms and manpower, may be tempted to go in for a first-strike option. Pakistan is very likely to exercise this option to counter India should the latter pose a serious threat to Pakistan's territorial integrity, leading to its dismemberment and further fragmentation.[37] Pakistan's President General Pervez Musharraf while proclaiming to be in full control of his nation's strategic assets did not hesitate to threaten India to use nuclear weapons in the event of the latter violating the "line of control or the international border."[38] In this context, it is worth mentioning the comments made by General Khalid Kidwai, Head of the Strategic Plan Division of Pakistan's Army:

"Nuclear weapons are aimed solely at India. In case deterrence fails, they will be used, if,

a. India attacks Pakistan and conquers a large part of its territory (space threshold)

b. India destroys a large part either of its land or air forces (military threshold)

c. India proceeds to the economic strangling of Pakistan (economic threshold)

d. India pushes Pakistan into political destabilization or creates a large internal subversion in Pakistan (domestic destabilization)"[39]

Pakistan, however, is acutely aware of asymmetry in military balance in South Asia. In the words of General Jehangir Karamat, a former Chief of Army of Pakistan, "Pakistan accepts the imbalance inherent in the equation with India and will not seek to match capabilities. Pakistan will, therefore, modernise and upgrade its military power in carefully selected areas so that its deterrent and defense capability are not degraded and it never faces a scenario of overwhelming strategic superiority from India. This deterrence is the best guarantee of stability because an unacceptable imbalance can have serious implications."[40]

Even limited war, in conventional sense, between India and Pakistan can lead to nuclear conflict. Four factors can turn any conventional conflict, however "limited" in nature, into acquiring a nuclear dimension.[41]

a. The politico-military objectives which India considers limited, might be considered unlimited and unacceptable by Pakistan. Islamabad plans to use nuclear weapons in the event of a deep military offensive by India. How "deep" would be deep enough for India to obtain its objective, and how "deep" would be too much for Pakistan, is unclear and will always remain so. Issues of extent of loss of territory, image, legitimacy are important.

b. Pakistan's military has shown a greater inclination towards a possible use of nuclear weapon. In Pakistan, nuclear command and control are exclusively in the hands of the military.

c. In the case of India and Pakistan, inadequate command and control structures, deficient early warning arrangements and perceptions about a doubtful capacity to launch a retaliatory "second strike" send mixed signals which enhance the risk of a nuclear exchange.

d. A possible reappraisal of India's operational doctrine following the nuclear tests can further encourage Pakistan to take recourse to atomic weapons.

It is not clear in the document whether "launch-on-warning" will be followed. Does it mean India will endure repeated nuclear attacks before it retaliates in a way unacceptable to the aggressor in the belief that the threat of massive retaliation will deter the attacker? (2.7. Draft Doctrine). But then, from a logical point of view, will there be anything left to defend after a first massive nuclear attack on India and whether the adversary will misperceive and miscalculate in the absence of any dialogue? Also, there are no identified "red lines", the crossing of which would trigger a nuclear conflict between India and Pakistan.

"Hawks in India think they can manage a limited war with Pakistan without either side resorting to nuclear arms. Pakistan's hardliners believe that demonstrating the will to use nuclear weapons is important in containing an Indian threat. If the hawks on both sides carry out their threats, India could start a limited conventional war, and Pakistan would take it to the nuclear stage."[42]

What is worrisome are the increased levels of indulgence in nuclear brinkmanship by both countries. In response to former Chief of Pakistan Army, General Mirza Aslam Beg's declaration to make a first strike, Indian Prime Minister Vajpayee of India stated that no weapon would be spared in self-defense and "Whatever weapon is available, it would be used no matter how it wounded the enemy"[43].

The "hot line" that was restarted among the leaders at the highest level in both Islamabad and New Delhi following a twenty-year gap, in 1997, is in disuse now. Although some movement has been made in this regard during the June 19-20, 2004, meeting at the foreign secretary level, yet no firm timetable has been set as to when the hot lines might be activated and operational. According to Dr Pervez Hoodbhoy "Should a nuclear war occur, it may well be that the order is not given by the Chief Executive or the Prime Minister or whoever. That decision may be taken by a Brigadier, who will decide whether you and I live or die. Any missiles fired by India or Pakistan would take four to eight minutes to hit its target. This means both countries are prepared to launch a nuclear strike on the basis of a warning. In a few hundred seconds, the credibility of the warning must be gauged. Is the blip on the radar screen really a missile? If so, is it likely to be carrying a nuclear warhead? An alert must then be flashed to the strategic command centre. And, if necessary, a launch order transmitted to the missile site."[44]

The problem of managing these nuclear weapons in the real world poses unprecedented challenges. As one description explains it aptly: managing nuclear weapons "involves the unpredictability of circumstances and human behaviour interacting with complex sensors, communications systems, command centres and weapons. The smallest details can assume central importance and range widely in substance, from the legitimacy of presidential succession to computer algorithm, from the psychology of stress to the physics of electromagnetic pulse ... even the most advanced experts and the most experienced practitioners are narrowly and incompletely informed. No one understands the whole."[45]

It is also doubtful whether posture control vis-a-vis nuclear weapons has been set in place by India. "Posture control involves a set of interlocked technological and administrative systems, with associated procedures and plans to ensure nuclear weapons that can be used by a national authority when it decides to do so. These systems include: 1. An early warning system, 2.

The procedure to assess the nature and extent of an attack that may be taking place, 3. The command and decision centres, 4. Communication between leaders and nuclear-armed units; and 5. Military units equipped with nuclear armed missiles or other delivery systems. "[46]

If Pakistan perceives that it will be going downhill in a conventional conflict, it may use nuclear weapons to deter India. Pakistan's Minister for Railways and Communications, Javed Ashraf Qazi's comments are quite telling in this regard; "Pak will not hesitate to use nukes against India. If it ever comes to annihilation of Pakistan, than what is this damned nuclear option for, we will use against the enemy. If Indians destroy most of us, we too will annihilate parts of the adversary. If Pakistan is being destroyed through conventional means, we will destroy them by using the nuclear option … as they say if I am going down the ditch, I will also take my enemy with me."[47]

Debating the Issue of Credibility in the Nuclear Doctrine

How can an adversary know what is credible (see 4.1 & 4.3. Draft Doctrine)? Supposing the adversary is in an irrational state or does not believe in rational thinking or discourse. It may very well tolerate massive destruction of all its major cities with the belief that it will be able to knock out at least one major Indian city either in a first attack or in a retaliatory attack. Will that be acceptable to Indian political leaders? It goes back to the central element of DND (Draft Nuclear Doctrine), which is "Credible, Minimum Deterrence". What is credible may not be minimal and India may have to adopt maximalist position in order to maintain minimum deterrence. Also, by the same logic, deterrence will fail by coaxing the adversary to take advantage of India's minimum nuclear deterrence policy and inflict a nuclear attack on India which India's adversary may think to be acceptable and tolerable on India's part. Deterrence should be credible, otherwise it cannot deter. What is credible to one leader at the top of the chain of command might not be so for a commander who is at the actual operational level. Deterrence is after all a mind game. As per India's defense equation with Pakistan, the dilemma is obvious. If India submits to Pakistan's irrationality, it risks being blackmailed into inaction. If India chooses to call the bluff, it invites a pre-emptive strike by Pakistan.[48] Without going into specifics, K. Subrahmanyam, a leading member of India's National Security Advisory Board, which authored India's Draft Nuclear Doctrine, has argued for one hundred and fifty nuclear warheads for an effective Indian deterrent against Pakistan and China.[49] General K. Sundarji, India's former Army Chief of Staff, however, has opined that India needed a minimum of twenty nuclear weapons of twenty kilotons each to deter a small country such as Pakistan and about fifty such weapons to provide a credible nuclear deterrence against a large country such as China.[50] Estimates of the nuclear warheads belonging to India and Pakistan vary. Defense experts at Jane's speculated, in 2002, that Pakistan could have as many as one-fifty against an Indian arsenal of two-hundred to two-fifty. However, the Washington-based Centre for Strategic and International Studies provides a lower estimate, suggesting that India has about sixty nuclear warheads and the Federation of American Scientists suggests that Pakistan possesses about twenty-five warheads.[51]

The concept of nuclear deterrence was first evolved by US Joint Chiefs of Staff who argued that the "Threat of the use of atomic bombs would be a great deterrent to any aggressor who might be considering embarking upon an atomic war."

Moreover, "minimal" deterrence might not be achieved, when it has been stated in the draft doctrine that it is India's intent to develop nuclear weapons based on a "triad of aircraft, mobile-based missiles and sea-based assets". (3.1 Draft Doctrine). The annual report (2003-2004) of India's Department of Atomic Energy has not stated what the "minimum" is in terms of research, development and manufacturing of nuclear weapons as determined by India's nuclear policy.

Questions on India's Tenuous Chain of Command

Under India's constitutional system, the prime minister is the head of government and the president is the head of state. It is also mentioned in India's constitution that it is the duty of the president to aid and advise the prime minister and the cabinet. In a nuclear stand-off, who advises whom, to what degree and to what consequence (5.1. Draft Doctrine)?

Also, unlike in the American system, where there is a clear chain of command should the president be temporarily incapacitated due to death, resignation or impeachment, there is no such provision in the existing Indian constitution other than following the official protocol in order of precedence. On a comparative note, in the US on 9/11[52], the president was taken to the strategic forces headquarters and the vice-president whisked away to a secret location. Whenever a threat is anticipated, the vice-president is separated and kept in an unknown destination in constant touch with the president and other members of the National Security Council through safe and uninterrupted communication channels. The US law provides for succession of up to more than twenty. Military succession is also well defined. The command chain runs in normal times from the president, to the defense secretary, the chairman, joint chief of staff and the strategic forces both in the US and NATO. There is also the danger of conflict between the civilian and military units battling over control of nuclear button. While India's air force feels it has the capability to deliver nuclear weapons, the navy feels the ultimate nuclear decision making in the operational arena belongs to it as it had both maritime and aviation roles. On June 23, 2004, the Indian Navy announced maritime doctrine that envisaged primacy among the armed forces by arguing that it was the most potent force of the nuclear triad to launch an attack with nuclear weapons if circumstances warranted.[53] Belatedly, the government of India is experimenting with the idea of creating a cabinet sub-committee on national security matters as well as a chief of defense staff in order to provide a single point of military advice to the government.[54] Defense Minister George Fernandes on October 5, 2003, has declared that a nuclear command chain, including alternative nerve centres, was in place, giving India an effective retaliatory capability. He disclosed that other nuclear command and control structures, like nuclear command shelters including one in Delhi's underground metro rail tunnels and VVIP shelters around the presidential palace, prime minister's office and the Indian Parliament building have also been built.[55] What is also needed is to create a tri-service strategic forces command for maintaining functional control over the nuclear weapons and related matters such as surveillance, early warning, intelligence, targeting, and damage assessment system. The strategic triad in the strike force should also make sure that the "command and control chain from the political level to the implementing level should also reflect its survivability under the worst conditions of decapitation attack. This is the essence of deterrence."[56]

An ideational system for India must:

a. enunciate nuclear deterrence doctrine

b. continue development of testing doctrine, methodology, and staff

c. articulate war termination concepts

d. acquire supporting infrastructure such as intelligence and warning system, meteorological system, secure communications network, physical command and control infrastructure, damage assessment system, develop procedural system such as posture negative control system, national command authority, civil-military coordination arrangements, nuclear planning structure."[57]

India's nuclear doctrine also claims that "space-based and other assets shall be created to provide early warning"(5.6. Draft Doctrine). Apart from the stupendous costs and technical challenges needed to develop such assets, the proximity of Pakistan and China will make nuclear early warning systems almost meaningless. Once launched, missiles would take somewhere between 4-8 minutes to fly to Delhi, India's capital. This is too short a time to determine "early warning". One can compare this period with the 20-30 minute flight time in the case of ICBM flying from Russia to the United States or vice versa, which allows a greater window of maneuverability to check signal and other technical systems. Even with the sophisticated early warning system, it is known that between 1972 and 1984, the US early warning system showed over 20,000 false alarms of a missile attack. Over 1,000 of them were considered serious enough for bombers and missiles to be placed on alert. In the Indian case, a crisis of similar nature might lead to a nuclear launch."[58]

Sometimes, in a crisis situation, two nations at the forefront of conflict learn different lessons. During the India-

Pakistan crisis of 2002, from the Indian point of view, its nuclear deterrent neutralised Pakistan's and the former could successfully call Pakistan's bluff and thus brinkmanship was used as a viable policy. From Pakistan's perspective, the combination of conventional and nuclear deterrence worked in sending India a strong message and in calling India's bluff.[59]

The doctrine states explicitly that unauthorized access or use of nuclear weapons will not take place (6.1. Draft Doctrine). What happens if the Prime Minister or the designated successor(s) and the entire communication systems are wiped out in a first strike? Who controls the nuclear button? Will it be political operatives in the prime minister's office or the field commander in actual charge of the nuclear weapons or the civilian bureaucracy? How will the coordination in policy formulation and rapid response mechanism be maintained in the National Security Council that was formed in the aftermath of the 1998 nuclear test by the BJP- led government? Would it be possible for a lower ranked officer to launch a weapon without authorization in the atmosphere of mixed signals and/or political vacuum emanating from New Delhi? Even at the highest level, there may be moments of rash decision-making and recklessness. "The former US president, Richard Nixon, under the strain of his final days in the presidency, is said to have sobbed, beaten his fists on the power of his office and brooded over his ability to release the forces of nuclear disaster."[60] Also, in a surprise first attack by the other side, could India retaliate with rapid, punitive response when some of the missiles may be submarine-based or in mobile launcher status and which require safe and secured communication lines? India would also need "a massive investment in surveillance and target acquisition infrastructure by way of satellite, aerial reconnaissance and human intelligence" which it clearly lacks at this juncture due to its limited resources.[61] There have been some transparent steps taken in this regard. As per new directions taken by Indian Cabinet me, "once the attack is verified through an alternative source, the Nuclear Command Authority comes into play. It has two components: the Political and Executive councils. The Political Council need not meet physically in New Delhi. If by chance, the Political Council is eliminated in the initial attack, India has an alternative system, made up of specially designated constitutional authorities, to authorize retaliation. The government will also convert the Prime Minister's plane into a fully operational centre, like the United States' Air Force One. Once the political council orders retaliation, the EC conveys it to the SFC (Strategic Force Command). The SFC is capable of taking decisions within minutes and all it needs is time to mat the warheads into the platforms."[62]

Furthermore, as former Army Chief of Staff, V. P. Malik has elaborated, "the escalation ladder would be carefully climbed in a carefully controlled ascent by both protagonists."[63]

Are the Provisions related to Disaster Management Adequate?

The open-ended assertion (6.3. Draft Doctrine) that an appropriate disaster control system shall be developed to deal with potential accidents is open to criticism. Given India's extremely dismal record in disaster management from the super cyclone of 1999 in Orissa to the earthquake in Gujarat, it is indeed doubtful if India, at the present time, has anything even close to the capabilities of managing a nuclear disaster, should it occur either from a nuclear first strike or from a retaliatory strike by the adversary.

In a chilling report published by Britain-based *New Scientsts*, it was reported that a massive loss of men and materials would occur should a nuclear exchange take place between India and Pakistan. As per this report, "At least 2.9 million people would be killed and another 1.4 million severely injured, based on 10 Hiroshima-type bombs. Five in India (Bangalore, Mumbai, Kolkata, New Delhi, Chennai) and 5 in Pakistan (Karachi, Lahore, Faisalabad, Islamabad, Rawalpindi), India side: 1.5 million dead and 900,000 injured. And, Pakistan side: 1.2 million dead and 600, 000 injured. If the bomb explodes on the ground instead of in the air, resulting radioactive dust could kill more people.

Due to prevailing winds from west to east, India would incur more casualties than Pakistan. This is just 10 bombs, which is 1/10th of estimated nuclear bombs both countries are believed to have possessed."[64]

Another report provided a scarier picture. "Nuclear exchange could kill up to 12 million people in one stroke plus injure up to 7 million. Even a so-called 'limited war' would have, cataclysmic effect, overhauling hospitals across Asia and requiring vast foreign assistance to battle radioactive contamination, famine and disease. More deaths would occur later caused by urban firestones, ignited by the heat of a nuclear exchange, deaths from longer term radiation, or the disease and starvation expected to spread."[65]

Lately, however, India's Union Home Ministry is raising eight battalions to tackle natural disasters and combat nuclear, biological and chemical warfare. As per its report, "The National Emergency Response Force battalions will be deployed in strategic locations under the supervision of the Director-

General of Civil Defense. It would be a special force like the Rapid Action Force to be under the overall control of Central Reserve Police Force. The Bhabha Atomic Research Centre will train select officers of the Central Industrial Security Force (CISF) and the Indo-Tibetan Border Force (ITBF) on responding to nuclear disasters, and these officers will in turn train their subordinates in disaster management. Four battalions will gain expertise only in nuclear, biological and chemical warfare. Capsules on disaster management are being included in the training schedules of all central para-military forces, the Indian Administrative Service, the Indian Police Service, The Indian Foreign Service and State Police Forces so that government officers are equipped with the basic knowledge on how to respond in cases of emergency."[66]

Present Nuclear Capabilities of India and Pakistan: A Profile

At the present time, India's nuclear delivery system consists of assault aviation French Mirage 200 H fighters, which will be supplemented by Russian Sukhoi SU-30 MIC multi role fighters, along with a limited number of Prithvi-I and II short-range ballistic missiles as well as Agni and Dhanaush medium range ballistic missiles.[67] While none of the nuclear delivery systems it possesses is capable of providing deterrence against China, India has been developing a long range ICBM version of Agni with a range of 5,000 km in early 2001 and 12,000 km by 2003 to fill the vacuum. *Jane Intelligence Review's* report published in March 26, 2001, has stated that Pakistan, India's traditional adversary, has nearly completed development of a solid fuel missile that could strike key Indian cities from deep within Pakistan territory through Ghauri-series of liquid propelled missiles in a offensive operation and Shaheen-series weapons as defensive measures.

On May 24, 2002, Pakistan also tested Ghauri missiles that has a range of 1,500 kilometers (1,000 miles) that can hit most populous cities of northern, central and western India. The father of the Pakistan bomb, Dr A. Q. Khan, in a declaration has asserted that Ghauri missiles could "wipe out thrice, all the big cities of India."[68] Pakistan has also established the nuclear command authority in February 2000 with three components: an Employment Control Committee, the Development Control Committee and the Strategic Plans Division. Pakistan also has set up a nuclear regulatory authority to bring coordination in its nuclear programme.

India also successfully test fired Brahmos, the supersonic cruise missile with a range of 290 km, for the first time on November 9, 2003, that can travel at Mach 2.823 and has been configured to be launched from either land, ship, sub-marine and aircraft using liquid ramjet technology.[69]

Furthermore, India has developed capability to test fire Agni-III which can hit objects from a range of 300 miles and thus the entire territorial space of Pakistan can be within India's missile range. In addition, India's Armed forces have formulated joint war doctrine to ensure that individual combat capabilities of Army, Navy and Air Force can come together in the event of war. It remains to be seen whether and when Pakistan will match India's cruise missile and related capabilities so as not to provide its rival a strategic edge.

Status of Nuclear Non-Proliferation Regimes

In the present environment, with India having its draft nuclear doctrine widely circulated in the aftermath of the nuclear blasts in May 1998, some people may voice support for India to sign CTBT in order to see the entire gamut of economic sanctions and other restrictions imposed upon India lifted. Countries such as the United States very much hope that India will comply with CTBT and abide by other international safeguards.[70] Although it (US) no longer insists India to sign either CTBT or NPT, the United States is fully aware that the effectiveness of a carrot and stick strategy "will depend on sanctions and incentives that are carefully targeted, vigorously monitored and enforced and sustained. Such a strategy requires cohesion within the enforcing state or coalition of states and must, above all, serve a coherent policy and consistent goals."[71]

In the United States itself, there has been a growing support in favour of ratification of CTBT after the US Senate voted against it in October 1999.[72]

However, the basic rationale for India not signing the CTBT still remains the same. India's concern was conveyed on June 20, 1996, when the Indian representative rejected the text presented by the Chairman at the Conference on Disarmament "The CTBT that we see emerging...(is) not the CTBT India envisaged in 1954. This cannot be the CTBT that India can be expected to accept ... Our capacities are demonstrated but, as a matter of policy, we exercise restraint. Countries around us continue their weapons program, either openly or in a clandestine manner. In such an environment, India cannot accept any restraints on its capability, if other countries remain unwilling to accept the obligation to eliminate their nuclear weapons. Such a treaty is not conceived as a measure towards universal nuclear disarmament and is not in India's national security interest. India, therefore, cannot subscribe to it in its present form."[73] Even Russia supports India's nuclear weapons as those are "based on its dire necessity to ensure national security and such weapons playing a positive role in ensuring peace and stability in South Asia."[74] Unless the situation at the international and regional level changes drastically, this may very well be India's position for the foreseeable future.

Confidence-building Measures and the Issue of Kashmir

The escalating situation in Kashmir, the bone of contention between India and Pakistan since 1947, may yet provide a flash point and may induce both countries to come to the negotiating table and to opt for nuclear deterrence and quick implementation of "enforceable and verifiable" confidence-building measures which may include simultaneous signing of CTBT and other international safeguards and ushering in of citizens diplomacy. The statement made by General Pervez Musharraf on December 18, 2003 to be flexible on Kashmir issue and be ready to bend on his UN Kashmir baggage by keeping aside UN Security Council Resolution is a welcome sign and should be explored further.[75] Elaborating his vision for the resolution of the long tangled Kashmir problem, Musharraf outlined a four-step approach. It involves recognition of the centrality of Kashmir for the settlement of all disputes between India and Pakistan, commencement of a dialogue on that basis, elimination of solutions not acceptable to India, Pakistan and Kashmiris, and initiating the process for finding a solution acceptable to all parties.[76]

On Kashmir, both India and Pakistan have realised an urgent need in developing a structured dialogue.[77] This may include the following in terms of ushering CBMs:

- Formalizing structure of dialogue, in terms of mechanisms and issues involved in the dispute
- Formal recognition by tne two sides that there is no military solution to the Kashmir dispute

- In determining the wishes of the Kashmir's population, representatives of all different constituents and faiths of J&K need to be effectively involved in the dialogue process
- Encouraging and initiating intra-Kashmir dialogue on both sides of the LoC on the final status of Kashmir
- Involving people of Kashmir in the bilateral dialogue process of Kashmir
- Setting a timeframe for structured dialogue on Kashmir
- The resolution of the Kashmir conflict and restoration and development of mutual trust should be treated as interdependent processes
- Kashmir solution must be based on the principle of mutual respect India and Pakistan have for each other and dignity and justice for the people of Kashmir
- The pursuit of solution around zero-sum game needs to be avoided
- The process of de-escalation of hostilities needs to be initiated and efforts should be made to de-link Kashmir from point-scoring domestic agendas
- The hostile domestic propaganda around Kashmir in both electronic and print media needs to be stopped
- Unofficial dialogue through Track-II should be encouraged by the two governments to assist official-level talks between India and Pakistan
- The heads of governments of both sides should meet twice a year to assess the progress of the dialogue and sort out the deadlocks around various points

On the more immediate issue of de-escalation along the Line of Control in Kashmir, some of the CBMs suggested along these lines can also be pursued.[78]

- Relocation of heavy weapons which are considered a major cause of tension-escalation across the LoC
- Exercises along the LoC and working boundary may not exceed one division involving 12,500-15,000 troops, and the number of combat vehicles must not exceed 100 and 50 artillery pieces
- Continuous scheduled and unscheduled visits to forward areas by journalists, representatives of various national and international human rights organizations, diplomats, defence and UN military observers
- Commitment not to violate airspace across the LoC/ Working Boundary and military commanders of India and Pakistan to meet and explore the reduction of troops in both Indian and Pakistan administered Kashmir.

Pakistan's General Pervez Musharraf's visit to India on July 14-16, 2001, provided a window of opportunity to bring India and Pakistan closer to some kind of negotiated settlement on the Kashmir, CTBT and other related issues. However, domestic constraints in both India and Pakistan prevented Vajpayee and Musharraf in making more tangible progress on confidence-building measures beyond what the two countries agreed in 1988 that included not to attack each other's nuclear facilities, establish a hotline between the two nation's general headquarters and work towards a "strategic restraint regime."[79] Similarly, a mutually agreed formula between India proposed no-first use of nuclear weapons and Pakistan proposed non-aggression pact and in declaring South Asia as a nuclear weapon free zone can also be pursued by interested parties. General Pervez Musharraf on May 5, 2003, made a grand gesture of peace, mooting a no-war pact with India, followed by the de-nuclearization of South Asia, provided, of course, the Kashmir issue was resolved first.[80] In this context, the June 19-20, 2004, meeting at the foreign secretaries level between India and Pakistan generated more confidence-building measures including setting up of a hot line at the respective ministerial level as well. This meeting also held preliminary discussions on India's ex-foreign minister, K. Natwar Singh's proposal to evolve and study the feasibility of a common nuclear doctrine between India, China and Pakistan in order to bring peace and stability to the region.[81] During February 2004 meeting, it was decided by the respective foreign secretaries that talks on Siachen, Tulbul Navigation Project, Sir Creek, Terrorism, Drug Trafficking, Economic and Commercial Cooperation and promotions of friendly exchanges in various fields would be held at different levels in July 2004.[82] Another measure that can be tried is a concerted effort on the part of the permanent members of the UN Security Council to act as honest facilitators "to help in ushering a common, strategic dialogue and language on arms control in South Asia"[83] and foster open communications among the parties concerned. But then, the concept of nuclear deterrence for two South Asian rival countries with deep rooted historical animosities and regional ambitions may be an uphill task unlike the case of the United States and former Soviet Union during the Cold War years who stayed broadly within the perimeter of deterrence. Even in the case of US and the Soviet Union, they almost came to the brink of nuclear war on more than one occasion including the now famous Cuban missile crisis of 1962. For more transparency in communication and ushering in a meaningful dialogue between the India and Pakistan, one can examine the feasibility of establishing an international university located in the border area between Lahore in Pakistan and Amritsar in India which would be devoted to sustaining peace and security and conflict resolution under the aegis of the United Nations.[84]

It is fair to surmise that neither India nor Pakistan has developed an acceptable command and control system of their new found nuclear arsenals at this time. Nor have any concrete contingency plans been envisaged for the day after as other declared nuclear powers have done. Even a preliminary study of basic nuclear risk reduction measures (NRRM) in the four key areas of potential risks such as miscalculation, unauthorized use, accidents and panic behaviour as proposed by members of an influential peace group, MIND (Movement in India for Nuclear Disarmament), are yet to be initiated by either India or Pakistan.[85] According to Praful Bidwai and Achin Vanaik, "the role of NRRM should not be exaggerated. NRRMs can make South Asia less unsafe in nuclear terms. But they cannot make it nuclear safe. NRRMs or kindred confidence-building measures have another limitation. They become most effective when located in a cooperative context. But that is no excuse for not beginning a process to negotiate NRRMs for the safety and security of South Asian peoples."[86] Separately, Washington DC based think-tank (Henry L. Stimson Center) has proposed establishment of nuclear risk reduction centers (NRRCs) in New Delhi and Islamabad to build mutual trust between India and Pakistan. As per this report, setting up nuclear risk reduction centers may be promptly negotiated and implemented without waiting for the resolution of the Kashmir dispute, which might take time due to its own dynamics and complexity. NRRCs, may, thus become the highest level central coordinating institutions for the implementation of confidence-building measures.[87] Another major step which can take India and Pakistan towards nuclear risk reduction and confidence building would be a bilateral agreement what can be termed as a posture of "paused deployment".[88] By a Paused Deployment Posture (PDP), it may mean deliberate, mutually verifiable built-in-delay of about a day in the arming of delivery vehicles with nuclear weapons, agreed upon by both countries. Sometimes, called 'de-alert', delay could be by a full day or more or just few hours and by precluding instanteous deployment, it will greatly diminish the probability of hasty, emotionally driven or accidental use of nuclear arms and provide much needed breathing space to respective decision makers on both sides for finding ways and means of diffusing an impending crisis.

Nature of CBMs in South Asia

(a) Military CBMs

Between India and Pakistan, at the military level, several CBMs have been initiated with varying scopes and limitations. Here are some of these military CBMs.

Communication Measures: Military Hotlines

Following the 1971 war between India and Pakistan, a secured communication link, or 'hotline,' between the Pakistani and Indian director generals of military operations (DGMOs) was established. In December 1990, India and Pakistan agreed to reestablish the DGMO hotline and to use it on a weekly basis, if only to exchange routine information. At the February 1999 Lahore Summit, India and Pakistan agreed to review all existing communication links with a view to upgrade and approve the DGMO and other hotlines.

Hotline between Prime Ministers

The first hotline was installed in 1989 by prime ministers Benazir Bhutto and Rajiv Gandhi of Pakistan and India, respectively. Since then, hotlines have been in disuse for the most part. The June 19-20, 2004, foreign secretaries level meeting in New Delhi, however, has provided some hopeful sign in this regard.

Declarations on Non-Use of Force, Bilateral Resolution of Differences

The 1966 Tashkent Declaration facilitated by the Soviet Union, formally concluded the 1965 Indo-Pak war. It stipulated that relations between India and Pakistan shall be based on the principle of non-interference in the internal affairs of the other. The 1972 Simla Accord followed the 1971 Indo-Pak war which obliges both countries to renounce the use of force as a means of settling outstanding disputes between the two countries. In addition, both sides agreed to resolve their disputes in bilateral forums only.

Notification Measures: Military Exercises

An Agreement of Prior Notification of Military Exercises was completed in April 1991. Notification is required for exercises comprising two or more divisions in specified locations.

Non-intrusion of Air Space

An Agreement on the Prevention of the Violation of the Air Space was signed in April 1991, and entered into force in August 1992. It stipulates that combat fixed-wing aircraft are not to fly within 10 km of foreign airspace.

Transparency Measures

Pakistan invited observers to watch major military exercises (*Zarb-e-Momin*) in 1989 while India in 1990 in order to diffuse tension arising from a major 1990 military exercise, invited US observers to monitor troop and equipment deployment as an assurance of non-hostile intent.

Constraint Measures: Non-Attack of Nuclear Facilities

An Agreement on the Non-Attack of Nuclear Facilities was signed by Indian Prime Minister Rajiv Gandhi and Pakistani Prime Minister Benazir Bhutto in December 1988. It was ratified by both countries and implemented in January 1992. The agreement requires an annual exchange of lists detailing the location of all nuclear-related facilities in each country. The measure further pledges both sides not to attack listed facilities.

Bilateral Accord on Chemical Weapons

A Joint Declaration on the Prohibition of Chemical Weapons was concluded in August 1992. Both countries agreed not to develop, produce, acquire, or use chemical weapons.

Non-Military CBMs at Track-II Levels

As in the case of military CBMs, non-military CBMs at Track-II, non-governmental levels among interested individuals and informed citizens are also germane in diffusing tension between the two adversaries, India and Pakistan.

Non-military CBMs cover areas such as the following:[89]

- Collaboration in science and technology
- Dialogue on art and culture including reciprocal visits by

Bollywood/Lollywood stars and other entertainment artists

- Free movement of people and ideas (easing of visa restrictions for the nationals of adversarial countries)
- Exchange of information, views and analyses, that is, newspapers, books, magazines
- Commerce and trade such as having a Free Trade Agreement, granting most favored nations status, evolving a common currency, etc
- Strengthening democracy.

Goodwill Measures

Although termed as short term by analysts and observers, both India and Pakistan since their independence in 1947, have embarked on number of peace-making steps as goodwill measures.[90] These measures adopted by the two countries exist in the form of:

- Transfer of official assets (1948)
- Prevention of an even larger exodus of refugees (1948)
- Protection of rights of minorities (1950)
- Maintenance of places of worship (1953,1955)
- Resolution of some lingering territories claim (1958,1959, 1960, and 1963)
- Indus Water Treaty (1960)
- Tashkent Agreement (1966)
- Agreement relating to the Rann of Kutch dispute (1968)

- Some provisions in the Simla Agreement (1972)
- Joint Commission agreement signed in March 1983 to cooperate in areas other than military and political matters.

Some of the more contemporary CBMs initiated and undertaken by India and Pakistan in the non-military arena are the following:[91]

1. Various military goodwill measures (1993).
   - i) Participation of senior military and civilian officials in various seminars in each other's country (1993).
   - ii) Inviting guest speakers at each other's national defence colleges.
   - iii) Participation and visits of various sports teams particularly cricket and hockey (which received a set back when BJP, the ruling government in New Delhi decided to disallow sporting contact but it has now been allowed in late 2003).
2. Visits of parliamentarians.
3. Visits of businessmen.
4. In May 1984 and followed by another meeting of Indo-Pakistan Joint Commission held in July 1989, decisions were made to promote tourism, easing visa difficulties.
5. Opening of the regular bus service between Indian-administered Srinagar and Pakistan-administered Muzaffarabad in April 2005 and between Poonch and Rawalakote in June 2006.
6. Resumption of Amritsar (India)-Lahore (Pakistan) bus service

7. Khokrapar-Munabao rail link at an advance state of completion

8. Family re-union and meetings planned along the Line of Control in Mendhar, Poonch, Suchetgarh, Uri, Tangdhar

9. Trade and commerce across Jammu-Sialkot line

10. Promotion of Pilgrimage centers and Open Visa systems on both sides

Paradoxes in pursuing the CBM Modality

Proceeding further, three unresolved paradoxes can be identified in South Asian region concerning the applicability and viability of CBMs. These steps have relevance for other conflict-prone regions in other parts of the world as well.

- First, CBMs admittedly "provide the atmospherics for improving inter-state relations, and providing the instrumentality to proceed further with an arms control and disarmament process."[92] They can establish trust between adversarial states; but the paradox remains that trust is required before CBMs can be negotiated. The need for some limited confidence between adversarial states is, therefore, essential before CBMs can be negotiated.

- Second, CBMs are difficult to establish, but easy to disrupt and abandon. Continued adherence to them requires adversarial states to perceive the balance of advantage to lie in not abrogating them, particularly during periods of deep crises. Experience reveals, on the contrary, that the hotline established between the director generals of military operations became non-functional during the

Indo-Pak war of 1971 due to telephones being either left unattended or manned by junior officers with no real authority. In addition, during the Brasstacks crisis (1987), "... information shared through the hotline was deemed unreliable because of mutual suspicions; hence, information supplied on Pakistani request was only minimally complied with".[93] Obviously, hotlines can only be relevant in crises if trust is evident on both sides. They are known to work satisfactorily in times of peace. Hence the paradox that states may abide by CBMs in normal times, but ignore them in emergency situations.

- Third, public declarations can serve as useful CBMs to alleviate tensions and promote stability; they "can take the form of joint summit statements, negotiated agreements of a declaratory nature–such as non-attack pledges–and/or unilateral statements."[94] The historical record shows that national leaders in India and Pakistan routinely make conciliatory statements, but they are meant either for domestic consumption or to impress international audiences or lower the other's guard. The paradox then emerges: "Rather than promote security and confidence building, such declarations have often exacerbated existing regional tensions."[95]

Conclusion

It may be that the real choice before the international community is not to treat India and Pakistan's nuclear tests as an isolated regional problem but rather to commence serious negotiations to draft a treaty for limiting nuclear warheads at its absolute minimum level within a set time. It will be counterproductive if the international community resorts to unilateralism such as the plans made by the current US president George W. Bush with the National Missile Defense program and selective morality on the part of Big Five nuclear weapon states in maintaining the existing status quo of nuclear powers prior to India and Pakistan's explosion and not work towards a genuine nuclear arms control agreement. Although US and Russian leaders have shown willingness to drastically cut their nuclear arsenals to a historic 2,000 warheads, START III is yet to pick up the right momentum. According to Ashley J. Tellis, a Rand corporation analyst, "Several critical impediments are still there in the arena of global nuclear reform, despite all the other beneficial developments that have occurred on the aftermath of the Cold War. For example, neither Russia nor the small nuclear powers, the United Kingdom and France, appear willing to contemplate reductions in nuclear capabilities as part of some larger process that will eventually culminate in nuclear abolition. Even US has demurred about carrying nuclear arms reduction to its logical terminus, preferring instead to pursue a 'lead and hedge" policy well into the future.'[96]

In this context, India's views for a genuine nuclear reduction sounds credible and plausible. "Indian government called all nuclear weapon states to join with it in opening early negotiations for a nuclear weapons convention so that these weapons can be dealt with in a global, non-discriminatory framework as other weapons of mass destruction have been – dealt with in the past. While it appears self-serving, coming as it did on the heels of the 1998 nuclear tests, it is certainly consistent with India's past proposals and represented a continuation of traditional Indian policy which has always held out the threat of overt nuclearisation so long as the global nuclear order remained unreformed."[97] What should be the best strategy and policy option for India to maximize its national interests. According to S.D. Muni, "A strategy of forging differential and issue-based coalitions with the major concerned players is the best option for India to deal with the unfolding strategic reality in Asia at present."[98] Air Commodore Jasjit Singh complements that view by saying, "India's strategic interests would be served better through sustaining a non-hegemonic polycentric world which leaves it with greater flexibility to pursue its national interest."[99] From India's perspective, "reconstructing and redefining the confines of its national interest beyond its militaristic focus (in order) to make it meet the sustainable well-being of humans in economic, cultural, and political terms... may help to settle tensions between the realist and the anti-nuclear groups within India's domestic politics and subsequently to reconfigure India's national interest in terms of a broader regional security agenda."[100]

Six elements are critical to sustain this process of dialogue. One, preservation of agreements and CBMs (military and non-military) institute so far between India and Pakistan. Two, promoting resolution of disputes so that peace process gains momentum into a conflict resolution mode. Three, a problem-solving proactive approach applied by both sides. Four, principle of reciprocity and goodwill guiding the dialogue process. Five, political contacts sufficiently at high level to the highest level are needed to discuss issues critically and keep the engagement process moving. Six, evolving a convergent vision for a future of peace and cooperation in the entire South Asian region. What is more important in this regard is the perception of risk which appear to be only limited regional perceptions of the shared bilateral risks of nuclear war and avoidance of possible catastrophe. There is also a compelling need to recalibrate other national strategic priorities-national defence, Kashmir, etc. The issue is complicated further by the profound asymmetry between Pakistan's obsession with India in its security thinking and India's focus on a range of security imperatives of which Pakistan is but one.[101]

Perhaps that day is not far off when all the nuclear weapon states can sit together and work towards a genuine new world order based on a reasonable nuclear arms reduction package commensurating with the defined national interests of individual nation-states.

Appendix

Preamble

1.1 The use of nuclear weapons, in particular, as well as other weapons of mass destruction constitutes the gravest threat to humanity and to peace and stability in the international system. Unlike the other two categories of weapons of mass destruction, biological and chemical weapons which have been outlawed by international treaties, nuclear weapons remain instruments for national and collective security, the possession of which on a selective basis has been sought to be legitimized through permanent extension of the nuclear Non Proliferation Treaty in May 1995. Nuclear weapon states have asserted that they will continue to rely on nuclear weapons, with some of them adopting policies to use them even in a non-nuclear context. These developments amount to virtual abandonment of nuclear disarmament. This is a serious setback to the struggle of the international community to abolish weapons of mass destruction.

1.2 India's primary objective is to achieve economic, political, social, scientific and technological development within a peaceful and democratic framework. This requires an environment of durable peace and insurance against potential risks to peace and stability. It will be India's endeavour to proceed towards this overall objective in cooperation with the global democratic trends and to play a constructive role in advancing the international system towards a just, peaceful and equitable order.

1.3 Autonomy of decision making in the developmental process and in strategic matters is an inalienable democratic right of the Indian people. India will strenuously guard this right in a world where nuclear weapons for a select few are sought to be legitimized for an indefinite future, and where there is growing complexity and frequency in the use of force for political purposes.

1.4 India's security is an integral component of its development process. India continuously aims at promoting an ever-expanding area of peace and stability around it so that development priorities can be pursued without disruption.

1.5 However, the very existence of offensive doctrines pertaining to the first use of nuclear weapons and the insistence of some nuclear weapon states on the legitimacy of their use even against non-nuclear weapon countries constitute a threat to peace, stability and sovereignty of states.

1.6 This document outlines the broad principles for the development, deployment and employment of India's nuclear forces. Details of policy and strategy concerning force structures, deployment and employment of nuclear forces will flow from this framework and will be laid down separately and kept under constant review.

Objectives

2.1 In the absence of global nuclear disarmament India's strategic interests require effective, credible nuclear deterrence and adequate retaliatory capability should deterrence fail. This is consistent with the United Nations Charter, which sanctions the right of self-defense.

2.2 The requirements of deterrence should be carefully weighed in the design of Indian nuclear forces and in the strategy to provide for a level of capability consistent with maximum credibility, survivability, effectiveness, safety and security.

2.3 India shall pursue a doctrine of credible minimum nuclear deterrence. In this policy of "retaliation only", the survivability of our arsenal is critical. This is a dynamic concept related to the strategic environment, technological imperatives and the needs of national security. The actual size, components, deployment and employment of nuclear forces will be decided in the light of these factors. India's peace time posture aims at convincing any potential aggressor that:

a. Any threat of use of nuclear weapons against India shall involve measures to counter the threat; and

b. Any nuclear attack on India and its forces shall result in punitive retaliation with nuclear weapons to inflict damage unacceptable to the aggressor.

2.4 The fundamental purpose of Indian nuclear weapons is to deter the use and threat of use of nuclear weapons by any state or entity against India and its forces. India will not be the first to initiate a nuclear strike, but will respond with punitive retaliation should deterrence fail.

2.5 India will not resort to the use or threat of use of nuclear weapons against states which do not possess nuclear weapons, or are not aligned with nuclear weapon powers.

2.6 Deterrence requires that India maintain:

a. Sufficient, survivable and operationally prepared nuclear forces.

b. A robust command and control system.

c. Effective intelligence and early warning capabilities.

d. Comprehensive planning and training for operations in line with the strategy, and

e. The will to employ nuclear forces and weapons.

2.7 Highly effective conventional military capabilities shall be maintained to raise the threshold of outbreak both of conventional military conflict as well as that of threat or use of nuclear weapons.

Nuclear Forces

3.1 India's nuclear forces will be effective, enduring, diverse, flexible, and responsive to the requirements in accordance with the concept of credible minimum deterrence. These forces will be based on a triad of aircraft, mobile land-based missiles and sea-based assets in keeping with the objectives outlined above. Survivability of the forces will be enhanced by a combination of multiple redundant systems, mobility, dispersion and deception.

3.2 The doctrine envisages assured capability to shift from peace time deployment to fully employable forces in the shortest possible time, and the ability to retaliate effectively even in a case of significant degradation by hostile strikes.

Credibility and Survivability

The following principles are central to India's nuclear deterrent:

4.1 *Credibility:* Any adversary must know that India can and will retaliate with sufficient nuclear weapons to inflict destruction and punishment that the aggressor will find unacceptable if nuclear weapons are used against India and its forces.

4.2 *Effectiveness:* The efficacy of India's nuclear deterrent be maximized through synergy among all elements involving reliability, timeliness, accuracy and weight of the attack.

4.3 *Survivability:*

i. India's nuclear forces and their command and control shall be organized for very high survivability against surprise attacks and for rapid punitive response. They shall be designed and deployed to ensure survival against a first strike and to endure repetitive attrition attempts with adequate retaliatory capabilities for a punishing strike, which would be unacceptable to the aggressor.

ii. Procedures for the continuity of nuclear command and control shall ensure a continuing capability to effectively employ nuclear weapons.

Command and Control

5.1 Nuclear weapons shall be tightly controlled and released for use at the highest political level. The authority to release nuclear weapons for use resides in the Prime Minister of India, or his designated successor(s).

5.2 An effective and survivable command and control system with requisite flexibility and responsiveness shall be in place. An integrated operational plan, or a series of sequential plans, predicated on strategic objectives and a targeting policy shall form part of the system.

5.3 For effective employment, the unity of command and control of nuclear forces including dual capable delivery systems shall be ensured.

5.4 The survivability of the nuclear arsenal and effective command, control, communications, computing, intelligence and information (C412) systems shall be assured.

5.5 The Indian defense forces shall be in a position to execute operations in an NBC environment with minimal degradation.

5.6 Space-based and other assets shall be created to provide early warning, communications, damage/detonation assessment.

Security and Safety

6.1 *Security:* Extraordinary precautions shall be taken to ensure that nuclear weapons, their manufacture, transportation and storage are fully guarded against possible theft, loss, sabotage, damage or unauthorized access or use.

6.2 *Safety* is an absolute requirement and tamper-proof procedure and systems shall be instituted to ensure that unauthorized or inadvertent activation/use of nuclear weapons does not take place and risks of accident are avoided.

6.3 *Disaster Control:* India shall develop an appropriate disaster control system capable of handling the unique requirements of potential incidents involving nuclear weapons and materials.

Research and Development

7.1 India should step up efforts in research and development to keep up with technological advances in this field.

7.2 While India is committed to maintain the deployment of a deterrent which is both minimum and credible, it will not accept any restraints on building its R&D capability.

Disarmament and Arms Control

8.1 Global, verifiable and non-discriminatory nuclear disarmament is a national security objective. India shall continue its efforts to achieve the goal of a nuclear weapon-free world at an early date.

8.2 Since no-first use of nuclear weapons is India's basic commitment, every effort shall be made to persuade other states possessing nuclear weapons to join an international treaty banning first use.

8.3 Having provided unqualified negative security assurances, India shall work for internationally binding unconditional negative security assurances by nuclear weapon states to non-nuclear weapon states.

8.4 Nuclear arms control measures shall be sought as part of national security policy to reduce potential threats and to protect our own capability and its effectiveness.

8.5 In view of the very high destructive potential of nuclear weapons, appropriate nuclear risk reduction and confidence building measures shall be sought, negotiated and instituted.

Endnotes

1. "Nuclear Weapons Challenges In Asia", Position paper, Asia Pacific Center for Security Studies, April 22, 2000. Honolulu, Hawaii, p.16, available at http://www.apcss.org.

2. Singh, Jaswant, *Defending India*, New Delhi: India, MacMillan , 1999, p.58.

3. Vanaik, Achin, "India's Draft Nuclear Doctrine-A Doctrine", The Online Archives, available at http://www.tni.org/archives/vanaik/critique.htm

   See also, Schelling, Thomas C, The Strategy of Conflict, New York, Oxford University Press, 1963, pp.207-229. see also, Alam, Mohammed B, "India's Nuclear Doctrine: Context and Constraints", Working Paper No. 11, South Asia Institute, University of Heidelberg, Germany, October 2002.

4. Surya Prakash, A, "All were Party to the nuclear gatecrash", *The Pioneer*, Chandigarh, India, May 25, 1998.

5. Ahmedullah, M, "Indian Air Force advocates first strike capability", Defence News, January 2, 2001, p.1. also, see, *The Times of India*, New Delhi, June 25, 2004.

6. Raja Mohan, C, "Beyond the Nuclear Obsession", *The Hindu*, Chennai, India, November 25, 1999.

7. See, *The Times of India*, New Delhi, India, May 28, 1998, available at http://timesofindia.com/ Also see, Ashley J. Tellis; *India's Emerging Nuclear Posture*, Santa Monica: CA, Rand Corporation, 2001, p. 266.

8. Brodie, Bernard, *The Absolute Weapon: Atomic Power and World Order*, New York, Harcourt Brace, 1946. Also see Snyder, Glenn; *Deterrence and Defense*; Princeton, Princeton University Press, 1961.

9. Ramanna, Raja Dr, "Security, Deterrence, and the Future", Journal of the United Services Institution of India, 122:509, July-September 1992. Also see Alam, Mohammed B; *Essays on Nuclear Proliferation*, New Delhi, Vikas Publishing House, 1995.

10. Perkovich, George, *India's Nuclear Bomb*, Berkeley, University of California Press, 2000. Also see Alam, Mohammed B; *India's Nuclear Policy*, New Delhi, Mittal Publications, 1988.

11. "China Denies Posing Threat to India, Calls for Dialogue", *The Times of India*, New Delhi, India, March 22, 1999. See also Singh, Swaran "China's Nuclear Weapons and Doctrine", *Nuclear India*, New Delhi, Knowledge World, in association with Institute of Defense Studies and Analyses, 1998, p.152

12. See *The Hindustan Times*, New Delhi, November 14, 2002, available at *http://www.hindustantimes.com.*

13. Pugwash Meeting No.279, Bajpai Kanti, "No First Use of Nuclear Weapons", available at *www.pugwash.org/reports/nw/bajpai.htm.* Also see Cohen, Stephen P; *The Pakistan Army*, Karachi: Oxford University Press, 1998, pp.177-79.

14. See Bajpai Kanti, "The Great Indian Debate", *The Hindu*, Chennai, India, November 12, 1999.

15. See, Dunn, Lewis A *Controlling the Bomb*, New Haven, Connecticut, Yale University Press, 1982; Sagan, Scott "The Perils of Proliferation: Organization Theory, Deterrence Theory, and the Spread of Nuclear Weapons", *International Security*, Vol.18, No.4, Spring 1994, pp.83-99.

16. See, Waltz, Kenneth "The Spread of Nuclear Weapons: More may Be Better", Adelphi Papers, No.171, London: International Institute of Strategic Studies, 1981; Weltman, John, "Managing Nuclear Multipolarity", *International Security*, Vol.6, No.3, Winter 1981/82, pp.182-194.

17. Hagerty, Devin T, "Nuclear Deterrence in South Asia: the 1990 Indo-Pakistani Crisis", *International Security*, Vol.20, No.3, Winter 1995. See also Hersh, Seymour M, "On the Nuclear Edge", *New Yorker*, March 29, 1993, pp.56-73. McGeorge Bundy, "Existential Deterrence and its Consequences", in Douglas MacLean(ed.) *The Security Gamble: Deterrence Dilemmas in the Nuclear Age*, Totowa: NJ; Rowman and Allanheld, 1984, Trachtenberg, Marc; "The Influence of Nuclear Weapons in the Cuban Missile Crisis", *International Security*, 10:1, Summer 1985, p.139

18. "Musharraf brought region to the brink of nuclear war", The Times of India, New Delhi, India, May 16, 2002. Also, see, Reidel, Bruce; "American Diplomacy and the 1999 Kargil Summit at the Blair House", Policy Paper Series, 2002, Center for the Advancement Study of India, University of Pennsylvania

19. Morgan, Patrick M, Deterrence: A Conceptual Analysis, 2nd ed, Beverly Hills, California, Sage Publications, 1983, p.30.

20. Subrahmanyam, K, "Nuclear Policy: Arms control and Military Cooperation", Paper presented at the Carnegie Endowment of international Peace-India International Center Conference on India and the United States after the Cold War, New Delhi, March 7-9, 1993, p.7.

21. Subrahmanyam, K, "Triple Deterrent: India must stick to No-First-Use", *The Times of India*, New Delhi, New Delhi, January 27, 2003; also see, Sen, Amartya "India and the Bomb" in Smitu Kothari and Zia Mian(ed.), *Out of the Nuclear Shadow*, London, Zed Books, 2001, p.117-123.

22. Ghosh, Jayati, "The Bomb and the Economy", Frontline, Chennai, India, May 8-11, 1999, available at http://www.frontlineonnet.com/

23. Karnad, Bharat, "Going Thermo-Nuclear: Why, With What Forces, at What Cost", pp. 327-330. *Journal of the United Services* Institutions of India, 127:533, July-September 1998

24. Roy, Arundhati "The End of Imagination", in Smitu Kothari and Zia Mian(ed.); *Out of the Nuclear Shadow*, London, Zed books, 2001, p.69

25. .ibid, p.69-70

26. Ram, N, "Dreaming India's Nuclear Future", *Frontline*, Chennai, India, Issue 18, August 28-September 10, 1999, available at http://www.frontlineonline.com/fl1618/16180210.htm27.

27. Tellis, Ashley; Ibid, p. 106

28. Vanaik, Achin; Ibid

29. *The Japan Times*, Editorial, May 23, 2002

30. See, *The Times of India*, New Delhi, March 22, 2004

31. "India and Pakistan: Attempts at Rapprochement", Lecture Series, The Emirates Center for Strategic Studies and Research, Abu Dhabi, UAE, A speech by Dr Chris Smith, available at http://www.ecssr.ac.ae/CDA/en/FeaturedTopics/DisplayTopic/0,1670,276,00.html

32. "Nuclear Command Authority and Strategic Forces Command", Institute of Peace and Conflict Studies, New Delhi, February 8, 2003, available at www.ipcs.org

33. Chari, P.R, "The BJP's Nuclear Doctrine", *The Deccan Chronicle*, Hyderabad, India, August 27, 1999, p.6, available at http://www.deccan.com/

34. See, *The Times of India*, New Delhi, April 26, 2004

35. See, The Pioneer, Chandigarh, India, September 2, 2003, available at http://www.dailypioneer.com/, see, also, "Nuclear submarine project may get a kick-start", *The Hindu*, Chennai, India, May 27, 2004

36. See, *The Times of India*, New Delhi, March 30, 2004

37. "India's Nuclear Command to be in place", *The Times of India*, New Delhi, India, May 23, 2002

38. "Pakistan's Nuclear Gamble: A Deadly Ploy", Institute of Peace and Conflict Studies, January 17, 2003, New Delhi, available at www.ipcs.org

39. Lieutenant General Sardar Lodhi, F.S, (Retd; Pakistan Army). "Pakistan's Nuclear Doctrine", Pakistan Defense Journal, 1999. See, also, Brigadier Ismat, Saeed; (Retd; Pakistan Army), "Strategy for Total Defense: A Conceptual Nuclear Doctrine", Pakistan Defense Journal, March 2000

40. General Jehangir Karamat, "South Asian Stability- A Pakistan Perspective", Pugwash Meeting No.277, Pugwash Group on South Asian Security, Geneva, Switzerland, November 1-3, 2002.

41. See, Albright, David, "Securing Pakistan's Nuclear Weapons Complex", October 2001, www.isis-online/publications/terrorism/stanleypaper.html. Also, see, Landau Network. http://www.mi.infn.it/~landnet and cotta@mi.infn.it

42. "Limited war between India, Pakistan can lead to nuclear conflict", *The Hindu*, Chennai, India, May 26, 2002

43. See, *The Hindu*, Chennai, India, January 3, 2002, available at http://www.hinduonnet.com, also, quoted by M.V.Ramana and C.Rammanohar Reddy(ed.), Prisoners of the Nuclear Dream, London, Orient Longman, 2003, p.21

44. "Deterrence, did someone say?," *Indian Express*, New Delhi, India, June 11, 2002

45. Carter, Ashton; Steinbrunner, John and Zraket, Charles; Managing Nuclear Operations, Washington, DC, The Brookings Institution Press, 1987, p.3

46. Blair, Bruce, *Strategic Command and Control, Washington, DC*, The Brookings Institution Press, 1985, p.10

47. "Finger on nuclear button is not Musharraf's", The Daily Telegraph, London, June 7, 2002, also, see, Alam, Mohammed B; "Stepping back from nuclear brinkmanship", *National Herald*, New Delhi, June 24, 2002, p.4

48. "Pakistan will not hesitate to use nukes against India," rediff.com, May 23, 2002

49. "Desperate Pak ready to nuke India", *The Times of India*, New Delhi, India, May 20, 2002. Also see, Landesman, Peter; *The Atlantic Monthly*, March 2002

50. Proliferation News and Resources, Carnegie Endowment for International Peace, available at http://www.ceip.org/files/nonprolif/templates/articles.asp?NewsID=125

51. BBC News, February 19, 2003, available at http://news.bbc.co.uk/1/hi/south_asia/

52. K.Subrahmanyam, "Essence of Deterrence; Put in Place the strategic Triad", *The Times of India*, January 7, 2003, p.10

53. "Maritime doctrine made public", The Hindu, Chennai, June 24, 2004; also, see, Kamath, P.M; "Indian Nuclear Strategy: A Perspective for 2020", available at http://www.idsa-india.org/an-mar9-9.html

54. Ibid, no.52

55. See, *The Asian Age*, Kolkata, India, October 6, 2003, available at http://www.asianage.com/

56. Ibid, no.52

57. "Three Services Squabble Over Nuclear Button", May 16, 2001, available at http://www.thenewspapertoday.com/india/inside.phtml?News-ID=13976

58. See, Dean Wilkening and Kenneth Watman, Nuclear Deterrence in a Regional Context, MR-500-A/AF, Santa Monica; ca, Ran Corporation, 19940, pp.1-30 Also, see, Tellis, Ashley; Ibid, p.220

59. "The Lessons Learned—The India, Pakistan Crisis on 2002", Report from The Henry L. Stimson Centre, Washington, DC, available at http://www.stimson.org/southasia/pubs.cfm

60. Russett, Bruce, *The Prisoners of Insecurity; Nuclear Deterrence, the Arms Race, and Arms Control*, San Francisco: W.H.Freeman and Co, 1983, p.121, also, quoted by Ramana and Reddy, ibid, no.60, p.66-67

61. Ramana, M.V, "A Recipe for Disaster", *The Hindu*, Chennai, India, September 9, 1999, p.6

62. Available at: www.rediff.com, May 12, 2003

63. "Limited War can erupt any time", *The Times of India*, New Delhi, January 7, 2000

64. Kanwal, Gurmeet; "India's Nuclear Doctrine and Policy", available at http://www.idsa-india.org/an-feb1-01.html

65. www.sify.net, May 25, 2002. Also see, *New Scientist*, England, May 24, 2002

66. See, *The Telegraph*, Kolkata, India, February 16, 2004, available at http://www.telegraphindia.com/section/frontpage/index.asp

67. "The Day After in India,Pak:12 million dead", *Indian Express*, New Delhi, India, May 28, 2002

68. See, www.reditt.com, October 5, 2001

69. See, *The Times of India*, New Delhi, November 10, 2003

70. *Indian Express*, New Delhi, March 26, 2001, p.4, available at http://www.expressindia.com

71. See, *Mid-Day*, Mumbai, July 3, 2003, available at http://web.mid-day.com

72. Ahmed, Samina and David Cortright, South Asia at the Nuclear Crossroads, Working Paper, Joan B. Kroc Institute for International Peace Studies, University of Notre Dame, March 2001, p.6, also, see, Baldwin, David; "The Power of Positive Sanctions", World Politics, Vol.24, October 1971, p.25

73. Shalikasvili, John M, "The Test Ban Solution", *The Washington Post*, January 6, 2001.

74. See, *Indian Express*, New Delhi, November 23, 2002

75. See, *Indian Express*, New Delhi, December 19, 2003

76. See, *The Hindu*, Chennai, December 19, 2003

77. "The beginning of the future", Regional Perspective, Islamabad: Institute of Regional Studies, September 2000.

78. Ahmar, Moonis(ed.), *Paradigms of Conflict Resolution in South Asia*,. Dhaka: Bangladesh, The University Press Limited, 2003, p.56-57

79. Statement by Ambassador Ms. Ghose, Arundhati; Conference on Disarmament, Document CD/PV .740, Geneva, 20 June 1996

80. See, *The Hindustan Times*, New Delhi, May 6, 2003

81. Available at www.sify.com, May 6, 2003, see, also, "Common N-doctrine needed", *The Hindustan Times*, June 2, 2004

82. See, The Pioneer, Chandigarh, India, April 22, 2004

83. Statement by Ambassador Akram, Akram, Pakistan in the Conference on Disarmament, August 19, 1999, available at http://www3.itu.int/pakistan/CD-Indian%20Nuclear%20Doctrine-19%20 August % 2099.htm

84. For details, see, Singh, Ravinder Pal, "Some Cooperative Initiatives for India-Pakistan Dialogue and Risk Reduction", Pugwash Meeting, No.277, Geneva, Switzerland, November 1-3, 2002.

85. Available at *http://news.indya.com/newshtml/india1506nuke.htm.* "India, Pakistan shouldn't get nuclear recognition", A Report from the Stanley Foundation, Iowa.

86. Bidwai, Praful; "From the Worlds' Most Dangerous Place", June 3, 2002, available at *www.antiwar.com/bidwai/particleid=607*

87. *News India-Times*, New York City, September 2, 2002, available at *www.newsindia-times.com.*

88. Rajaraman, R, "Delayed Deployment: Towards Nuclear Risk Reduction", *The Times of India*, October 1, 1999.

89. P.R.Chari, Navnita Chadda, Maroof Raja, *Confidence-Building Measures in South Asia*, New Delhi: Center for Policy Research, January 1995, p.4.

90. Ahmar, Moonis, Ibid, p.166. also see, Gulab Mishra Prahar; *Indo-Pakistan Relations: From Tashkent Agreement to the Simla Agreement*, New Delhi: Sheetal Printing Press, 1987.

91. Pervaiz Iqbal Cheema, "Assessing the Role of Confidence-Building Measures in the India, Pakistan Tangle", Islamabad: Pakistan, Islamabad Policy Research Institute(IPRI), Winter 2004, p.22.

92. R. Rajaraman, "Delayed Deployment: Towards Nuclear Risk Reduction", *The Times of India*, October 1, 1999; also see, P.R.Chari, Navnita Chadda, Maroof Raja: Ibid, p.10.

93. Kanti P. Bajpai, P.R.Chari, Pervaiz Iqbal Cheema, Stephen P. Cohen, Sumit Ganguly, *Brasstacks and Beyond: Perception and Management of Crisis in South Asia*, New Delhi: Manohar, 1995, p.41.

94. Michael Krepon and Jerry S. Drezin, "Inroduction", in Michael Krepon, Jerry S. Drezin, Michael Newbill, eds; *Declaratory Diplomacy: Rhetorical Initiatives and Confidence-Building*, Report No. 27, April 1999, p.11.

95. P.R.Chari, "Declaratory Statements and Confidence-Building in South Asia", in *Newer Sources of Insecurity: The Crisis of Governance in India*, Ibid, p.130.

96. See, Tellis, Ashley, Ibid, p.240, also, see, Stuart Croft and Phil Williams, "The United Kingdom", and Klaus Schubert, "France", in Regina Cowen Karp (ed.), *Security with Nuclear Weapons?*, Oxford: UK, Oxford University Press, 1991, pp.145-188.

97. Burns, John F, "India calls for talks on New Treaty limiting nuclear arms", *The New York Times*, June 1, 1998.

98. Muni, S.D, "The Cold War in Asia: India's Options", *Strategic Analysis*, New Delhi, March 1997, Vol.19, No.12, p.1609.

99. Singh, Jasjit, *India's Defence Spending; Assessing Future Needs*, New Delhi, Knowledge World, 2000, p.271, also, see, Budania, Rajpal; "The Emerging International Security System; Treats, Challenges and

opportunities for India", Institute of Defence and Strategic Studies, New Delhi, also available at *www.idsa-india.org*.

100. Das, Runa, "Engendering Post-Colonial Nuclear Policies Through the Lens of Hindutva: Rethinking the Security Paradigm of India", *Comparative Studies of South Asia, Africa and Middle East*, Vol. XXII, No.1 &2, 2002, p.90.

101. See, Maleeha Lodhi, "Nuclear Cloud over South Asia", The Times of India, New Delhi, May 1, 2006.

Towards De-Nuclearisation of South Asia

R. Rajaraman

It augurs well for the second Pugwash workshop on May 16-18, 2003, in Geneva, Switzerland, on South Asian Security that it has been preceded by the recent volley of conciliatory overtures between India and Pakistan. The peace initiative by the Indian Prime Minister Atal Bihari Vajpayee was met with a warm response from the Pakistani Prime Minister Zafarullah Khan Jamali, who had invited the former to visit Islamabad.

It is too early to be overly optimistic about where these initiatives might lead. But any thaw in Indo-Pak relations must be used, apart from other things, as an opportunity to reduce the danger of nuclear weapons in South Asia. Pakistani President Pervez Musharraf has already upped the ante in the recent round of initiatives by calling for a no-war pact with India followed by steps towards de-nuclearisation of the subcontinent. But in its present form this call has not found immediate acceptance from the Indian side for a variety of reasons including the presence of China as a nuclear neighbour – a factor that introduces a major asymmetry between India and Pakistan in their security requirements.

Therefore full de-nuclearisation of South Asia is perhaps still a distant goal. But in the present atmosphere of conciliatory moves, some early steps would be conducive to eventual de-nuclearisation. The first step, in our view, is to put a cap on the size of the nuclear arsenal on both sides. At present, most reports suggest that each side already has several dozen weapons.

Nevertheless they see themselves as being only at some incomplete phase in the build-up of their respective nuclear arsenals.

Apart from establishing full-fledged command and control structures and missile detection systems, each side is continuing to enlarge its inventory of nuclear weapons and the missile systems to deliver them. In this they seem to be going ahead as fast as resources and technology allow. There is, understandably, no precise information available in the public domain about the ultimate levels of nuclear capability that each country in the subcontinent is aiming for. But one can get some idea by looking at the objectives listed in the Draft Report of India's Nuclear Doctrine. Section 3 of the doctrine declares that "India's nuclear forces will be … based on a triad of aircraft, mobile land-based missiles and sea-based assets…" with "… multiple redundant systems …" Such a spread out arsenal in all three sectors of the services, with redundancy built in, would lead one to expect an arsenal of over a hundred nuclear weapons. While Pakistan has not put out a formal nuclear doctrine it is likely, if one goes by statements of their governmental and military leadership that they will, in their own way, aim for a similar nuclear build-up.

As a first step towards eventual de-nuclearisation, one must stop this continuing growth in the number of weapons in South Asia. Needless to say, this can only be done by a broad consensus between people with different shades of opinion on the nuclear issue. There are many in the subcontinent who, like me, believe that nuclear weapons are not essential for national security. But there are others, perhaps many more, who genuinely feel that nuclear weapons are a necessary evil. Their concerns must be addressed if such a consensus is to be evolved to stop and reverse the onward march of nuclearisation.

Let me begin with the Indian side. The Indian government has declared that its nuclear arsenal is meant only for purposes of deterrence. The logical underpinnings of the concept of nuclear deterrence are shaky. Nevertheless let us overlook that for a moment and broadly accept the notion, just for the sake of argument. But even those who believe in the importance of deterrence must re-examine the question of whether such a large arsenal of over a hundred bombs is really needed. The strategy of deterrence relies in possessing an assured and convincing nuclear capability to inflict unacceptable damage to the other side which, it is argued, would deter them from attempting a nuclear first strike. But such deterrence does not require that your arsenal matches that of your adversary, but only that it be capable of inflicting damage which is unacceptable to any rational leadership. Now, just a couple of modest 15-20 kiloton weapons dropped on Lahore or New Delhi would kill lakhs of people in either city. Surely, that should already be "unacceptable damage" to even a remotely responsible leadership. A leadership that finds this "acceptable" is beyond the pale of rationality and cannot be relied upon to feel deterred by the prospect of even a larger attack. In other words, a successful attack on a major city with a couple of twenty-kiloton weapons should already inflict unacceptable damage. It is not clear why meaningful deterrence calls for dozens, let alone hundreds of weapons, even after taking into account some redundancy to offset survivability and missile defense factors. It is far better to spend money and technology on survivability and accuracy of a small truly minimal arsenal than to just go ahead and keep making more weapons just because the required fissile material and technology is available.

The situation with regard to the Pakistani nuclear agenda is even more worrisome in that they have not, unlike India, foresworn first use. There is also the oft-heard view that the Pakistani nuclear program is meant not just to deter an Indian attack, but also to offset India's superiority in conventional military strength. Whether such superiority exits in any significant sense can be debated, but even if it were to be true, going nuclear was a very dangerous way to go about compensating for it. It is as much in Pakistan's interests as it is in India's to stop further growth in their nuclear capability and eventually work for a nuclear free South Asia.

The fact that China, France and the UK have weapons in the hundreds is no reason for us in South Asia to aspire for the same. The size of their arsenal was determined decades back during the Cold War in the context of the tens of thousands of weapons that the US and USSR had, which in turn was based not on deterrence alone but mixed with wild ambitions of winning nuclear wars and decimating entire continents.

To return briefly to the China factor in South Asia, the presence of neighbouring China as a major nuclear power certainly makes full de-nuclearisation a complicated matter for India. Much more time will be needed to work out an acceptable and viable formula. But as far as capping the arsenal to a small size is concerned, the preceding arguments about it being sufficient to inflict unacceptable damage should hold just as much with regard to China as it does for India and Pakistan.

Lastly, some people who abhor nuclear weapons may be unhappy with the suggestions made above on the grounds that we seem to be endorsing a nuclear arsenal in South Asia, as long as it is small. That is not so. Our view is that having no nuclear weapons at all anywhere is the safest alternative. But it is a fact of life that there are already dozens of weapons in both India and Pakistan and more are in the pipeline. They will not disappear overnight and cannot be wished away. Before eliminating them totally one must first work towards curbing their growth.

Confidence-building Measures in Asia

Jozef Goldblat

Although confidence building among nations has been practised for many years, the term "confidence-building measure" (CBM) entered the vocabulary of international relations only in the early 1970s. Since the CBMs subsequently discussed and agreed upon have come to accentuate security aspects, they are also referred to as "confidence- and security-building measures" (CSBMs).

The objective of CSBMs is to translate certain principles of international law into positive action so as to provide credibility to states' affirmations of their peaceful intentions. Such action means implementing measures aimed at: (a) reassuring states of the non-aggressive intentions of their potential adversaries and reducing the possibility of misrepresentation of certain activities; (b) narrowing the scope of political intimidation by the forces of stronger powers; and (c) minimizing the likelihood of inadvertent escalation of hostile acts in a crisis situation.

In general, CSBMs do not directly affect the strength of armed forces or arms inventories, but in facilitating progress towards disarmament they constitute a separate category of arms control measures. They also make less likely the use of force for settling disputes. To have the intended effect, CSBMs must be significant in scope and binding. A mere exchange of solemn declarations is rarely sufficient.

For a great majority of states, threats to national security arise from conditions within their own region. Hence attention is most often devoted to regional approaches. For confidence-building purposes, a region could embrace states, which do not meet the geographical criteria of a "region" but are linked economically or politically. Arrangements initiated by neighbouring states may subsequently attract more distant states as well. Regional confidence-building measures cannot be imposed by outsiders; they must be freely negotiated and agreed to by states in the region. It is only these states that can address the causes of their specific security problems and determine the type, scope and area of application of the required undertakings. In one region, distrust and tension could be generated by a lack of reliable information about the military activities of neighbouring states and the inadequacy of channels of communication among political decision-makers. In another region, distrust and tension could be generated by the absence of agreed restraints on the behaviour of the armed forces and uncertainty about compliance with international obligations.

Confidence building to promote better communication and understanding among the parties may include: (a) exchange of information about military expenditures, strength of armed forces, arms production and arms transfers; (b) open presentation and clarification of defence doctrines; (c) prior notification of military manoeuvres and major military movements, including their scope and extent; (d) the establishment of a mechanism to check the accuracy of the data provided; (e) the presence of foreign observers at military exercises; (f) exchanges of visits by military officers; (g) exchanges of cadets between military academies; and (h) the establishment of direct, rapid communication links – "hotlines" – for crisis management.

Confidence-building measures that impose military constraints may include: (a) abstaining from certain specified military activities in border areas; (b) disengagement of armed forces by establishing zones between neighbouring countries that are partly or fully demilitarised; (c) voluntary submission to inspections to demonstrate compliance with agreed standards of behaviour; and (d) formalized commitment to the peaceful settlement of disputes.

Security cannot be obtained by promoting measures solely in the field of military affairs; it embraces economic and social factors as well. However, the military factor is of prime importance, as the absence of war constitutes a prerequisite for non-military CSBMs. Since the 1980s CSBMs have been adopted in relations among several Asian states, mainly in order to diminish military tensions along the disputed borders. Those considered most important are described below.

The 1988 Indian-Pakistani Nuclear Agreement

On December 31, 1988, India and Pakistan reached an agreement not to cause the destruction of or damage to each other's nuclear installations. The parties exchange annually information about the location of their nuclear-related facilities.

The 1992 Indian-Pakistani Chemical Weapons Agreement

On August 19, 1992, India and Pakistan adopted a joint declaration, by which they committed themselves not to develop, produce, or otherwise acquire, or use chemical weapons. They also undertook not to assist, encourage or induce anyone to engage in development, production, acquisition or use of these weapons.

The 1996 Shanghai Agreement

On April 26, 1996, Russia and three Central Asian republics bordering on China – Kazakhstan, Kyrgyzstan and Tajikistan – constituting the Joint Party and China signed, in Shanghai, the Agreement on Confidence Building in the Military Field in the Border Area. The signatories committed themselves not to attack the other party or carry out any military activity threatening the other party and disturbing the tranquillity and stability in the border area between Russia, Kazakhstan, Kyrgyzstan and Tajikistan, on the one hand, and China, on the other. They decided to exchange information on the agreed components of the armed forces and the border troops; not to conduct military exercises directed against the other party; to limit the scale, geographical scope and number of military exercises; to give notification of any large-scale military activity and troop movements resulting from emergency situations; to give notification of the temporary entry of troops and weapons into the hundred-kilometre geographical zone on both sides of the border between the Joint Party territories and China; to invite observers to military exercises on a reciprocal basis; to give notification of the temporary entry of the parties' river-going combat vessels of navies or naval forces into the hundred-kilometre geographical zone on both sides of the eastern part of the Russian-Chinese border; to take measures to prevent hazardous military activity; to make inquiries about unclear situations; to strengthen friendly contacts between military personnel of the armed forces and the border troops in the border area and carry out other confidence-building measures agreed upon by the parties.

Moreover, the border troops should not use inhuman or rough treatment in dealing with border violators. The use of weapons by the border personnel would be determined by the domestic legislation of the parties and the corresponding agreements of Russia, Kazakhstan, Kyrgyzstan and Tajikistan with China.

The Agreement was concluded for an indefinite period of time, but each party has the right to terminate it. Also each state of the Joint Party has the right to withdraw from the Agreement, but the Agreement will remain in force as long as at least one state of the Joint Party and China remain parties to it.

The 1996 Sino-Indian Agreement

On November 26, 1996, China and India signed the Agreement on Confidence-Building Measures in the Military Field along the Line of Actual Control in the India-China Border Areas. It was a follow-up to their Agreement on the Maintenance of Peace and Tranquillity along the Line of Actual Control in the India-China Border Areas, signed on September 7, 1993.

The signatories to the 1996 Agreement agreed that neither side should use its military capability against the other side. No armed forces deployed by either side in the border areas along the line of actual control, as part of their respective military strength, may be used to attack the other side or engage in military activities that threaten the other side or undermine the peace, tranquillity and stability in the India-China border areas. The two sides reiterated their determination to seek a fair, reasonable and mutually acceptable settlement of the boundary question. Pending an ultimate solution to this question, they reaffirmed their commitment to strictly respect the line of actual control. They also reaffirmed that they would reduce or limit their military forces, within mutually agreed geographical zones along the line of actual control in the border areas, to minimum levels compatible with the friendly and good-neighbourly relations and consistent with the principle of mutual and equal security. Reductions or limitations concerned the number of field army, border defence forces, paramilitary forces and any other mutually agreed category of armed force deployed in mutually agreed geographical zones. The major categories of armament to be reduced or limited were: combat tanks, infantry combat vehicles, guns (including howitzers) with 75-mm or larger calibre, mortars with 120-mm or larger calibre, surface-to-surface missiles, surface-to-air missiles and any other weapon system mutually agreed upon. Data were to be exchanged on the military forces and armaments to be reduced or limited. The ceilings on military forces and armaments to be kept by each side within mutually agreed geographical zones were to be determined with due consideration given to parameters, such as the nature of terrain, road communication and other infrastructure, as well as the time needed to induct troops and armaments.

China and India undertook to avoid holding large-scale military exercises, those involving more than one division (approximately 15,000 troops), in close proximity to the line of actual control in the border areas. However, if such exercises had to be conducted, the strategic direction of the main force involved was not to be towards the other side. If either side conducted a major military exercise, involving more than one brigade group (approximately 5,000 troops), in close proximity to the line of actual control in border areas, it would have to give the other side prior notification with regard to the type, level, planned duration and area of exercise, as well as the number and type of units or formations participating in the exercise.

Both sides must take adequate measures to ensure that air intrusions across the line of actual control do not take place. Combat aircraft (to include fighter, bomber, reconnaissance, military trainer, armed helicopter and other armed aircraft) may not fly within 10 km of the line of actual control. If either side is required to undertake flights of combat aircraft within 10 km, it must give the relevant information to the other side through diplomatic channels. No military aircraft of either side may fly across the line of actual control, except by prior permission. Unarmed transport aircraft, survey aircraft and helicopters are to be permitted to fly up to the line of actual control. Neither side is allowed to open fire, cause biodegradation, use hazardous chemicals, conduct blast operations or hunt with guns or explosives within 2 km of the line of actual control.

Detailed implementation measures were to be decided through mutual consultations in the India-China Joint Working Group on the Boundary Question. The India-China Diplomatic and Military Expert Group was to assist the Joint Working Group in devising implementation measures under the Agreement.

The 1997 Moscow Agreement

On April 24, 1997, as a follow-up to the 1996 Shanghai Agreement, Russia, Kazakhstan, Kyrgyzstan and Tajikistan, constituting the Joint Party, and China signed, in Moscow, the Agreement on the Mutual Reduction of Armed Forces in the Border Area. The signatories agreed on the following measures.

The parties' armed forces stationed in the border area should not be used to attack another party or to conduct any military activity that threatened the other party or disturbed the tranquillity and stability in the border area.

The parties should reduce and limit the number of personnel and the quantities of basic types of armament and military equipment of the ground forces, air forces and air defence aviation, deployed within the geographical zone of application (GZA) of the Agreement, that is, in the geographical area extending to a distance of 100 km from either side of the border between Russia, Kazakhstan, Kyrgyzstan and Tajikistan, on the one side, and China, on the other side. Certain limited areas within the GZA of the Agreement are to be considered sensitive areas. In the Eastern Sector (the eastern part of the state border between Russia and China), on the Russian side, these are the Khabarovsk sensitive area and the Vladivostok sensitive area.

Upon expiration of the reduction period (see below) the maximum level of personnel of ground forces, air forces and air defence aviation remaining for each party in the GZA of the agreement should not exceed 130,400 persons, including 115,400 in ground forces, 14,100 in air forces and 900 in air defence aviation. The maximum level of personnel for the Eastern Sector should not exceed 119,400 persons; for the Western Sector (the western part of the state border between Russia and China, as well as the state borders between Kazakhstan, Kyrgyzstan, Tajikistan and China), 11,000 persons. From the date of entry into force of the agreement, the maximum number of personnel of the border forces for each party within the GZA of the agreement may not exceed 55,000 persons, including 38,500 for the Eastern Sector and 16,500 for the Western Sector.

The maximum levels of armaments and military equipment remaining for each party within the GZA of the agreement should include armaments and military equipment located in combat units as well as in storage. Upon expiration of the reduction period, the maximum levels remaining for each party within the GZA should not exceed: 3,900 battle tanks, 5,890 armoured combat vehicles, 4,540 artillery systems, 96 tactical rocket launchers, 290 combat aircraft and 434 combat helicopters.

The reductions provided for in the agreement had to be brought about within 24 months from the date of its entry into force. The reduction of military personnel was to be carried out by disbanding entire military formations, by reducing the staff size of military formations or by removing military formations from the GZA of the agreement. The reduction of armaments and military equipment was to be carried out by destroying, dismantling, converting to civilian purposes, placing on permanent display, using as ground or aerial targets, reclassifying into training material, or partially removing from the GZA.

In order to reinforce mutual confidence and ensure control over the implementation of the agreement, the parties should exchange information about the troop formations, the number of personnel in these formations, and the quantity of main types of armament and military equipment deployed within the GZA of the agreement. The information exchanged must be treated as confidential. Each party has the right to conduct and the obligation to accept inspections within the GZA, with the exception of the specified sensitive areas. The inspecting party should bear the expenses related to the transportation of the inspectors to the established entry/exit points. The inspected party should bear the expenses related to the visit of the inspectors. A Joint Control Group supervises the implementation of the agreement.

The Agreement does not affect the obligations previously undertaken by the parties in relation to other states and is not directed against third states or their interests. Each party is allowed to terminate the agreement by notifying the other party of its intention to do so at least six months before the date of the agreement's expiration, which was set for December 31, 2020. In the absence of such notification, the duration of the agreement is to be automatically extended for successive five-year periods. Each state belonging to the Joint Party may withdraw from the Agreement by notifying the other party and the other states of the Joint Party of its decision. After such notification the parties should conduct negotiations on the maximum levels of armed forces and border forces in the border area.

The 1997 Sino-Russian Statement

As a result of the meeting held in Beijing on November 10, 1997, the presidents of China and Russia issued a statement on the development of relations between the two countries. In particular, the heads of state stated that all points of contention regarding the demarcation of the Eastern sector of the Sino-Russian border had been resolved and that the demarcation of the Western sector would be completed within an agreed period of time. Hope was expressed that a fair demarcation of the border would enhance friendship and good-neighbourly relations between the two countries and contribute to regional stability.

Exchanges of visits by heads of state, regular meetings between prime ministers and consultations between foreign ministers were found conducive to improving mutual communication and understanding, as well as to expanding and deepening cooperation between the two nations in various fields. It was noted that cooperation in the field of military technology was an important component of Sino-Russian relations and that it was not directed against a third country.

The 1998 Almaty Joint Statement

In the joint statement issued on July 3, 1998 at Almaty as a result of the five-nation meeting of China, Kazakhstan, Kyrgyzstan, Russia and Tajikistan, the participants undertook to take all the necessary measures to ensure the implementation of the 1996 Shanghai Agreement and the 1997 Moscow Agreement. They valued the positive impact of these agreements on the security in their region and the world at large, appreciated the initiative of the Central Asian countries for the establishment of a Central Asian nuclear-weapon-free zone and reaffirmed the importance of holding regular consultations among themselves.

The parties expressed concern over the tensions in Afghanistan and noted that greater effort should be made to promote a peaceful settlement of the conflicts in that country under the auspices of the United Nations and with the participation of the states concerned. They also expressed concern over the growing tension in South Asia following the nuclear test explosions in that region and called for stopping the nuclear arms race there.

The 1999 Lahore Memorandum of Understanding

On February 21, 1999, the foreign secretaries of India and Pakistan signed a Memorandum of Understanding identifying measures aimed at promoting an environment of peace and security between the two countries. The parties undertook to engage in bilateral consultations on security concepts and nuclear doctrines with a view to developing measures for confidence building in the nuclear and conventional fields; to take national measures to reduce the risks of accidental or unauthorized use of nuclear weapons under their control; to notify each other immediately in the event of an incident that could create the risk of a fallout with adverse consequences for both sides or an outbreak of a nuclear war between the two countries; to adopt measures aimed at diminishing the possibility of such incidents being misinterpreted by the other side, and to identify or establish appropriate communication mechanisms for this purpose; to abide by their moratoria on nuclear test explosions, unless either side decided that extraordinary events had jeopardized its supreme interests; to conclude an agreement on the prevention of incidents at sea; to periodically review the implementation of the CBMs and, where necessary, set up consultative mechanisms; and to review the existing communication links with a view to upgrading them. The Lahore Memorandum of Understanding has not been carried into effect.

The 2001 Sino-Russian Good-Neighbourliness Treaty

On July 16, 2001, Russia and China signed, in Moscow, a Treaty of Good Neighbourliness, Friendship and Cooperation. The contracting parties reaffirmed their commitments not to be the first to use nuclear weapons against each other and not to target strategic nuclear missiles on each other; pledged to expand and deepen confidence-building measures in the military field so as to consolidate the security of both countries and strengthen regional and international stability; promised not to be members of any alliance or bloc nor embark on any action which compromises the sovereignty, security or territorial integrity of the other party, nor allow its territory to be used by third countries to the detriment of the other party; and undertook to cooperate in combating terrorism, separatism and extremism and in fighting organized crime, illegal trafficking in drugs, psychotropic substances and weapons. Should a situation arise which, in the view of either party, might endanger or undermine the peace or affect its security interests, or should either party face the threat of aggression, the parties shall immediately contact and consult each other with a view to averting the danger.

The ASEAN Undertakings

In the 1990s the Regional Forum of the Association of South East Asian Nations (ASEAN) adopted a series of CBMs covering, inter alia, military and defence-related issues. In particular, the forum's members have developed bilateral exchanges on security perceptions; expanded high-level defence contacts and military exchange/training; submitted annual defence policy statements; prepared defence white papers; invited observers to and provided notification of select military exercises on a case-by-case basis; and exchanged views on defence conversion programmes. None of these measures is mandatory.

Assessment

Unlike in Europe, the CSBMs in Asia do not cover all the militarily important countries of the continent and have not been followed by substantial, verifiable cuts in the military potential of the participating states. Nonetheless, the CSBMS taken by China, Russia and the Central Asian Republics helped to set aside the disputes over large sectors of their common borders and to put off the final delineation of these borders for an unspecified period of time.

On the other hand, the CSBMs adopted by India and

Pakistan have not helped to resolve the most contentious issues, in particular, the issue of Jammu and Kashmir. The continuous armed clashes between the two countries can lead to a large-scale war fraught with disastrous consequences for both regional and extra-regional states, including a nuclear exchange, whether deliberate or accidental. It appears therefore necessary for both India and Pakistan, to agree on CSBMs more substantial and more binding than those agreed hitherto. In other words, a new security agenda is needed. Such an agenda would have to be incorporated in a formal, duly ratified document and include the following undertakings by India and Pakistan:

- To give up nuclear-test explosions and refrain from test-firing ballistic missiles of any range without prior notification.
- To reduce the conventional armed forces significantly enough to attenuate Pakistan's opposition to adopting the posture of no first use of nuclear weapons.
- To thin out the forces stationed on both sides of the common borders so as to diminish the risks of armed incidents.
- To entrust impartial observers with the determination of facts in case of alleged breaches of the Line of Control in Kashmir.
- To improve communications at both political and military levels.

The above undertakings could prepare the ground for meaningful talks about the settlement of the several-decades old disputes on the basis of the generally recognized principles of international law.

India and Pakistan: Appeal for a Monitoring Mechanism Along the LoC

A.H. Nayyar and M. Martellini

The past conflict in 2004 originated from militants, both Kashmiri insurgents and non-Kashmiri religious armed militias, causing unacceptable harm to India in Kashmir. Pakistan has been accused of nurturing and supporting the militants infiltrating across the LoC. India felt most annoyed with the increasingly potent actions of the militants and felt pushed, also by its domestic dynamics, to retaliate. The only hesitancy towards a war-path was due to the dangers of escalation of a limited confrontation to an all out nuclear war.

It has been usually underlined that the situation has reached a state where the dangers of war could be averted only by the picture of a Pakistan not supporting the militancy in Kashmir by effectively stopping cross-border infiltration. However, it must be understood that there are indigenous insurgents in the Indian part of Kashmir and their activities may not end with the end of cross-border terrorism. Any measure from Pakistan to stop infiltration must, therefore, be accompanied by a monitoring mechanism, necessarily requiring the presence of an external agency, be it the United Nations or European Union (EU) or NATO or anyone else.

Understandably, the United Nations cannot enter into the picture unless consented to by both the parties. India opposes a UN intervention because that internationalizes a bilateral problem. It would be good if the UN found a way to post an international monitoring force on the Pakistani side of the line of control alone, should Pakistan request so. The United Nations Military Observer Group in India and Pakistan (UNMOGIP) has existed in both countries since 1949. Pakistan could be persuaded to ask for an enhanced presence of UNMOGIP monitors placed on its part of the line of control.

It appears that Pakistan is not averse to the idea of a reinforcement of UNMOGIP, even if it is only on the Pakistani side of the LoC. On the other hand, India is not likely to agree to it because UNMOGIP is directly connected with the Kashmir issue, and, in the eyes of India, it is in conflict with the Simla Accord. Unless India agrees, no UN-sponsored mechanisms like UNMOGIP can be put in practice. If the solution has to be such that it caters to the sensibilities of both the parties, then it has to be – paraphrasing a declaration of the Pakistani Ambassador in Washington – a "neutral, impartial [monitoring] mechanism on the LoC", that is outside the UN. Institutions other than the UN – such as the EU, G8 or NATO or any other international organization – may not have such problems of principle and could consider providing a neutral, impartial and multilateral monitoring force.

Such an arrangement should be acceptable to both India and Pakistan for the following reasons:

- Pakistan will need a monitoring mechanism to show that it does not support the infiltration of insurgents.

- The presence of a monitoring external force would ensure that India does not wage a war on that frontier: de-escalation should follow.

- India would also achieve the objective that an external insurgency-based policy may not be pursued in Kashmir, stopping infiltration altogether.
- And above all it would provide the two countries with an exit strategy, always needed in a situation of conflict.

The British Foreign Secretary Jack Straw, during a visit to Pakistan and India, suggested formation of an international helicopter-borne force to monitor infiltration along the LoC. In India it has been suggested that, as long as such a force is specifically for monitoring infiltration of terrorists – meaning that it is not in any way tied to the dispute of Kashmir – India should accept it. It is not clear whether India will readily agree to allow foreign monitors on its side of the LoC. On the other hand, there are reasons to believe that Pakistan can be persuaded to accept an arrangement of this nature on the Pakistani side alone.

In short, the proposal is to build an international helicopter-borne force, on the Pakistani side of the LoC alone, if any other bilateral arrangement is not possible, to monitor any infiltration of terrorists across the LoC, reporting to India and Pakistan and to the relevant international community body involved.

Evolving Nuclear Constructs of Indo-Pak Détente

Farah Zahra

Although India and Pakistan have embarked upon a path to establish peace and stability in the region, they continue to strengthen their military capabilities, as if oblivious of the positive political developments. "Alongside these developments, discussions on Nuclear Confidence Building Measures (NCBMs) began from 1999 onwards after both countries went overtly nuclear in the summer of 1998." Thus, South Asia presents an interesting situation where, despite détente, number of aspects gain significance within the realm of nuclear weapons.

Regarding nuclear weapons, a number of technical stability enhancing measures such as notification of missile tests, moratorium on testing and non-deployment suggestions will form part of the series of discussions to be held between India and Pakistan. However, these NCBMs should not delude us into thinking that India and Pakistan can overcome the nuclear risks involved in maintaining and improving their nuclear arsenals by working towards implementation of NCBMs. Both states might move towards a reduction of nuclear risks – though it is debatable whether specific technological CBMs make us safer or more vulnerable – a poor substitute for a larger vision of the future of nuclear weapons. The majority of us may take for granted that, "Nuclear development is likely to continue in predictable directions in the move towards stable deterrence."[1]

Secondly, the question arises as to what shape a wider, long-term vision the nuclear arsenals of India and Pakistan might take. As the two begin to mend fences and there seems to be enough goodwill on either side, this may be the right time to set a "preamble" to the NCBMs, not a concretely-defined, highly optimistic vision, yet containing some positive ideas for the future, even outside the confines of "stable deterrence". There has to be a preamble to the eventual aims of the NCBMs. In formulating such a preamble, we need to factor in two realities: (a) even if the Kashmir dispute is "resolved", nuclear weapons will still exist in the subcontinent; and (b) the deterrence equation is not static: capabilities and scenarios are changing in the region. A perfect deterrence situation for South Asia perhaps exists only in the realm of dialectical discussions.

Thirdly, the proposal put forward by India's Former External Affairs Minister, K. Natwar Singh, for a "common nuclear doctrine" received an apt response from the Pakistani government – neither acceptance nor rejection; Indian analysts predict that the proposal has a shelf life of about two months.[2] However, Singh's suggestion should be seen as a reiteration by India that its security calculus also includes China, and that India is willing to think in terms of a regional solution (which, for India, also includes China), in contrast to its prior position calling for global solutions.

This article aims to examine NCBMs in the light of the Strategic Restraint Regime (SSR) suggested by Pakistan and the Lahore Memorandum of Understanding signed between India and Pakistan. It will also examine the technological limitations of NCBMs, and consider the role the United States and the international community in managing proliferation in this region. The conclusion includes some suggestions and policy recommendations in view of the three points mentioned above.

Restraint Regime and Stability

Pakistan proposed what it calls the "Strategic Restraint Regime" (SRR) in October 1998, five months after the nuclear test explosions by India and Pakistan. It has since repeatedly presented this proposal to India at different regional and international fora. India has clearly and persistently declined the offer. For Pakistan, there may be little more to this suggestion than maintaining the high moral ground: repeating it over a prolonged period is not likely to get India to change its mind. India is looking at a much larger canvas as far as its defence requirements go. Pakistan, on the other hand, is vigilant in fulfilling its requirements and making advancements in military technology to match those made by India, to remove any gaps in what it terms the "equilibrium".

Pakistan also keeps India and the international community informed that it is mindful of these gaps (it "will retain the edge"– presumably a reference to Pakistan's nuclear deterrent) and that it does not appreciate India's creating imbalances through defence purchases.[3] What this amounts to if not an "arms race" is somewhat confusing since Pakistan maintains that "an arms race is not sustainable by Pakistan".[4] Finally, Pakistan has enunciated that its "nuclear deterrence level is not static", as the "deterrence level is linked to the Indian threat".[5] This is also symptomatic of Pakistan's disarmament policy rhetoric which might now be curtailed, after Pakistan Foreign Minister Khurshid Kasuri's call for a "rhetoric restraint regime" for both countries.

Pakistan's SRR proposal was based on three suggestions: (a) to prevent the accidental use of nuclear weapons; (b) to ensure the lowest possible quantity and quality of nuclear weapons; and (c) to prevent the spread of nuclear-weapons technology.

Some Indian analysts maintain that India needs ICBMs to potentially deter the United States, probably invoking India's sovereign right to make its security determinations. However, India has shown interest in the first suggestion in the SSR, putting the NCBMs talks on track. The second and third areas are of less significance to India. It has previously aspired to a level of deterrence commensurate with its global status, though it might now be open to further discussions on this issue, given Singh's statement, proposing a regional nuclear doctrine. On the other hand, proliferation of nuclear technology is something that India has claimed to have effectively controlled in the past and is doing a good job presently. Both of these, therefore, become issues that Pakistan has to contend with, with some possible assistance from India on the second point in, dealing with nuclear restraint.

In order to tackle the issue, Pakistan has suggested five measures within SRR. These are: a moratorium on testing; implementation of non-weaponisation and non-deployment; a moratorium on deployment; a moratorium on the deployment of Ballistic Missile Defence (BMD); and an implementation of risk-reduction measures. Some of these steps were embodied in the Lahore Memorandum of Understanding, signed between the Foreign Secretaries of India and Pakistan on February 21, 1999.

Lahore MoU and NCBMs

The Lahore MoU laid down a comprehensive set of eight CBMS, mostly nuclear, which have been largely neglected since the MoU was signed on February 21, 1999.

1. The Lahore MoU begins with a pledge for bilateral consultations on security concepts and "nuclear doctrines". After five years of the tests and four years after the MoU was

signed, Pakistan has no official "doctrine" which can be made the basis for official discussions. Some analysts have urged Pakistan to adopt a declaratory doctrine as "fudgy red lines can keep moving further back when it comes to the crunch and in Pakistan's situation, perhaps a clearly enunciated one-rung escalation ladder – given the prevailing asymmetries – may be more useful".[6] However, Pakistan's nuclear doctrine remains conjectural since it is the country's considered policy *not* to put forward a doctrine

On the other hand, Pakistan has already repeatedly conveyed its reservations about the robust Indian doctrine, which India converted from draft status to an official doctrine in January 2003.[7]

2. The second point deals with advance notification of ballistic missile tests. A strange record exists in this regard. The following is the Pakistani version since April 1999:

India: Three Agni tests were notified, one was not
Four Prithvi tests were notified, six were not
None of the seven Brahmos tests were notified.
Pakistan: Notification of all 13 Hatf, Shaheen and Ghauri tests.[8]

Pakistan accuses India of not abiding by the agreement of prior notification and also feels that India is sticking to the letter and not thc spirit of the MoU (since it is not notifying Brahmos tests at all because it is not a "ballistic" missile, but a cruise missile). It may be worth noting here that approximately 50 per cent of the total missile tests conducted by India and Pakistan have been in the last three years.[9]

3. The third point in the MoU deals with a commitment on the national level to undertake measures to reduce the risks of

accidental or unauthorised use of nuclear weapons under the respective control of both countries. Both India and Pakistan have in place formalised structures that deal with the command and control of nuclear weapons. Pakistan set up its National Command Authority (NCA) in February 2000 and India set up its NCA three years later, in January 2003.

4. Moratorium on conducting further test explosions: the moratorium on nuclear testing stands while India does not test. According to many analysts, this may also depend on whether America starts retesting and whether India considers its needs for testing fulfilled, both of which are tenuous assumptions.

5. Prevention of incidents at sea was a troublesome area as, occasionally, fishermen stray across assumed boundaries in search of catch and are apprehended and imprisoned for years. This is linked to the border dispute of the sixty-mile long estuary of Sir Creek in the marshes of the Rann of Kutch.

What could make the situation a little more complicated is the new Proliferation Security Initiative, instituted by the United States and other countries, which allows interdiction "to halt shipments of dangerous technologies to and from states and non-state actors of proliferation concern – at sea, in the air, and on land."[10] If there are to be joint Indo-US exercises, which, given the delicate nature of the peace process underway, are not desirable at present, a new situation will arise for Pakistan to worry about.

6. Neither side undertook periodical review of the implementation of existing CBMs.

7. Upgrading and improving communication links and

providing for fool-proof and secure communications: hotlines are considered limited in scope since they are voice communicators and can at times convey an unintended message; computer hotlines are being considered as apt replacements. Multiple channels would facilitate communication, though it should be mandatory to ensure some kind of centralization of the channels to eradicate confusion. Nuclear Risk Reduction Centres could prove helpful in this matter.

6. Bilateral consultations on security, disarmament, and non-proliferation issues for multilateral fora: positive diplomacy can yield dividends if both countries adopt stances favourable to each other and appreciate each other's point of view.

The NCBMs talks will most probably encourage this kind of communication; a further positive development for both countries would be to support each other, where possible, at international fora. A traditional Pakistani point of criticism against India has been that Indian nuclear ambitions are spreading "nuclear evil" in the region. Pakistan could instead turn its ire on the permanent members of the United Nations Security Council (P5) for being the perpetrators of this evil and not doing enough on the vertical proliferation front where the Nuclear Weapon States (NWS) that have signed the Non-Proliferation Treaty promised in good faith to move towards global nuclear disarmament. However, there are forums such as the Conference on Disarmament, where Pakistan would be unable to go along with the Indian position of not accounting for existing stocks in discussions on the fissile material treaty. It may now be possible to hope that both states will avoid sharp criticism of each other at international fora and devise some method of dealing with such issues at the bilateral level.

It needs to be noted here that, as opposed to the SRR which was a Pakistani suggestion spurned by India, the Lahore Memorandum of Understanding was signed by both India and Pakistan. This document merely contained the test moratorium element of the SRR, as India envisaged that it would place no immediate restraints on improving its nuclear arsenal. There is no mention in the Lahore MoU of non-weaponization, non-deployment, cessation of fissile material production, or any constraints to rein in the nuclear weapons programmes. India is willing to engage Pakistan, to a cautiously limited extent, to improve the nuclear environment. Nevertheless, we are still left with the question: how can India allay Pakistan's nuclear fears while continuing to fulfil its nuclear ambitions? In view of this question, we should keep in mind that, going by empirical evidence so far, there is no reason to assume that at any point in the future, the US may be able to exert any serious pressure on India, or for that matter even Pakistan, on non-proliferation.

Secondly, at this stage what seems even more significant is that there exists no common nuclear lexicon between India and Pakistan. For example, there seems to be no consensus on the term "deployment": what the Indians have termed as "forward storage" has been assumed by Pakistan to be "operational deployment".[11] However, the word "deploy" has been used by India with regard to its Agni missiles.[12]

Limitation of Technological NRRMs

Technological Nuclear Risk Reduction Measures (NRRMs) would certainly have a positive influence, facilitating further contact, generating an exchange of ideas and views, regardless of whether there is strict implementation of the measures themselves. However, we should also be clear that technological

CBMs or NRRMs also have a few special drawbacks. The simplest ones between India and Pakistan have a bad and, at best, a strange record of implementation, though this could change for the better in future with the improvement in relations. The second problem is that of verification and monitoring. And the last one pertains to the situational changes (before ideas can be materialised), since the nuclear situation is rather dynamic. For example, W. P. S. Sidhu, in an article on nuclear risk reduction measures, argued for a "third option under which the missiles are inducted, but not deployed..." suggesting that, "a series of innovative NRRMs are required".[13] We now know that the Prithvi missiles have been inducted and "deployed". It does seem that merely a series of NRRMs or NCBMs may not be enough without the bedrock of a progressive outlook, based on a long-term vision of nuclear weapons as mentioned earlier.

Let us examine the case of early warning systems which both states are endeavouring to obtain in order to further "stabilise" deterrence.

Early Warning Systems

An early warning system forewarns us of an external (nuclear) attack via missiles. This system, however, does not merely comprise a set of radar detectors and a platform. The system also includes an evaluation of the threat and formulation of a response strategy – and all this is to be done within the warning time provided by the system. The system could either be ground-based or via satellite. A recent study conducted at Princeton University, US, suggests that this warning time can be between four to seven minutes for both systems, and, if a capital city is being targeted, it would barely be enough for the warning to be communicated.[14] The study further envisages the three possible responses, all of which make this warning redundant. The three options include: feeding the warning signals into a missile defence system so that the interceptor can locate and destroy the incoming missile; the second option would be riding out a possible attack, that is, waiting to see if the attack is for real and then respond and the last possibility could be to retaliate immediately which would mean maintaining a launch-on-warning posture (which is fraught with numerous possibilities of technological mishaps and false warning actually bringing about a nuclear war). In all three cases, the early warning systems seem to be of no use. However, both India and Pakistan seem to be headed in that direction. India even has it in its doctrine to set up "early-warning capabilities … space-based and other assets …"[15]

Although these systems may, by and large, prove effective in this scenario, there are two major drawbacks. Firstly, there is considerable disparity between India and Pakistan in terms of technology for early warning; secondly, if such systems were to be in place, the next step, almost inevitably, for both countries would be to increase their arsenal. Increase of arsenals would in any case be underway, but the perspective and calculus would change with working EWS in place.

India's quest for the Green Pine and Phalcon radars from Israel, along with its capability to launch geo-synchronous satellites and its Tech Exp Satel with high-resolution camera, capable of "sensitive defence surveillance", are not only evidence of its resolve to pursue EWS in earnest but also of the fact that Pakistan lags behind in this sphere. Pakistani experts have already advised a high state of alert.[16] Pakistan's Ministry of Science and Technology hinted at matching Indian plans for EWS by launching a geo-stationary satellite to "meet its strategic and communication needs".

India might argue that its EWS has utility in its security calculus beyond Pakistan as well. Once the EWS are in place in both countries, the next step, a technological requirement, would be to have nuclear arsenals powerful enough to overcome the barriers posed by the EWS.

Role of the US and the International Community

Former Commisioner of the US Nuclear Regulatory Commission (NRC), Dr Victor Gilinsky, in his testimony on March 30, 2004, to the House Committee on International Relations on "The fuel cycle and the spread of the bomb" made two very pertinent points on non-proliferation. Firstly, he said that, "Nothing will be done to tighten the rules unless the United States takes the lead." In order to illustrate his point, he quoted former US President Ford who had said that, "We must be sure that all nations recognise that the US believes that non-proliferation objectives must take precedence over economic and energy benefits if a choice must be made." Secondly, he tried to emphasise that an approach was required that made non-proliferation a top priority in US foreign policy. However, empirical evidence shows us that the US has repeatedly and for an extended period of time, made choices in favour of politics and economics instead of non-proliferation in South Asia. This is what the US is doing currently and, in all likelihood, this is what it is going to do in future.

India, which supported the US when it decided to scrap the BMD, has found new moral force to go ahead with its own BMD plans, aggravating the nuclear situation between India and Pakistan. These are not the only US policies that have been detrimental for non-proliferation in South Asia. A certain amount of moral punch has been induced into the Indian actions and policies and statements as it saw the United States hounding the ghosts of 9/11 into far-flung lands, amidst calls for a "war on terror". It picked up the courage to say to the international community that, "We too should strike places that provide sanctuaries for our cross-border terrorists", meaning the alleged training camps in Pakistan. This created further tensions between the two countries. Thus, the new laws of pre-emption laid down by the sole superpower have not been without their fallout for South Asia, aggravating the nuclear situation in the subcontinent.

The US and the international community are in fact retaining and improving their nuclear arsenals, which puts India, an emerging global power, on firm ground to make provision for its own security needs. Instead of any earnestness to push for a re-think on Article 5, to come good on their promise of eventually getting rid of these weapons and cutting down on them, the P5 are generating a plethora of discussions on how to refurbish the NPT, so as to eliminate the problem of horizontal proliferation.

Fancy solutions have been put forward that speak of academic and innovative brilliance, without tackling the core issue. At the Moscow Carnegie International Conference 2003, American non-proliferation expert, George Perkovich, defended the NPT, saying that it was merely "a tool" that dealt with non-proliferation and that more tools needed to be produced in order to deal with states such as Iran. Victor Gilinsky, former US NRC Commissioner, and former head of Physical Sciences Department at the Rand corporation has presented a set of "do's and dont's" that he recommends be introduced into a new NPT, making it more difficult for states such as Iran to proliferate via the excuse of nuclear energy production.[17] And finally, Professor John Endicott from Atlanta suggests Nuclear-Free Zones and tackling proliferation on a regional basis and introducing that into the NPT.[18] A new report on Universal Compliance by five well-known non-proliferation experts in the US suggests that the strategic aim of the non-proliferation policy must now be to achieve universal compliance with the norms and terms of a deepened nuclear non-proliferation regime.[19] However, it is pertinent to mention here that South Asia is outside the US counter-proliferation policy, whose ambit only covers states like Iran, Iraq, and North Korea – the so-called "rogue" states.

It seems that the global ire expressed at the 2000 NPT conference and the hard time that the American delegation had in New York has been washed out of the US memory altogether. As long as the US and other P5 states think there is a way out of the proliferation problem by remaining outside the loop while trying to tighten the noose and rope others in, states like Israel, India, and Pakistan will continue to show the international community that they can defy all NPT norms, as they are NOT party to the treaty. Furthermore, they can get away with this stance, regardless of whether the US and the international community like it or not. Though there may be weaker states that the US can handle and console itself with the thought that the nuclear-weapons threat is controllable, challenges will arise regularly that will have to be dealt with on military rather than moral grounds. As far as South Asia is concerned, it is a region that is beyond this debate and the NPT anyway.

Military Détente with Pivotal Shifts and Concrete Steps

Strides towards relaxed military relations would be easier to seek once there is substantive progress in the resolution of disputes. However, if, in tandem with conflict-resolution, attention could be focused on the military aspect, room might be created for joint reflection by both India and Pakistan on where they want their nuclear capabilities to continue in the long term. In other words, a special emphasis must be placed by both parties on coming to a mutual understanding that the time is ripe for working out a "preamble" for NCBMs. This would surely go a long way in keeping it clear that the NCBMs are not an end in themselves, as they are not the vehicle to perfect our "deterrence". Deterrence in the South Asian case may never be perfected. At the same time, we should not be paranoid or naïve enough to subscribe to the alarmist view and believe that we are perilously close to a nuclear disaster and we need to abandon nuclear weapons immediately.[20]

In dealing with deterrence, first and foremost is the requirement for an admission by both countries that advancement of and addition to nuclear technology may be a limitless exercise, without a point which could be termed as the final point of security or of absolute, complete, and fully stable deterrence. Needless to say, "deterrence" is a word antithetical to the very process of peace and friendship that has begun here.

The psychological attitude towards nuclear weapons requires the pursuit of better technology as the ultimate solution. An exploration of the role of military and nuclear technology itself may be in order, to find out if under the tutelage of its military protectorate, not only in Pakistan but increasingly in India as well, it may have acquired a dynamics of its own.[21]

All such suggestions which can provide additional safety for the nuclear arsenals and facilities of India and Pakistan should be put on the table for brainstorming and mutual discussion. All "value-added" measures such as agreements ranging from notification of tests to a moratorium on testing to non-deployment agreements will be discussed in the coming months. The idea of risk reduction centres on either side would be a great leap forward and the foundation for further discussion on the technical side as well as providing a regular body for enhanced contact, regardless of the political temperatures. The maximum benefit is to be derived from measures that generate regular contact and encourage exchange of data and enhanced transparency – all of which are embodied in the risk reduction centre idea. [22]

As a central body, the NRRC could provide a structure dealing with unilateral measures as well as bilateral measures, which could include: improving domestic capabilities, such as threat analysis to all nuclear facilities; investing in indigenous physical security technology; performing system upgrades; and instituting more rigorous personnel reliability programmes. Though initially suggested as unilateral measures, these could be taken on to the bilateral level, once NCBMs between the two countries are well-established.[23]

Pakistan could take advantage of the turn in relations with India and shift the emphasis of its dissatisfaction with managing nuclear proliferation to the nuclear club members, without making India the prime target, even though it is the country of direct concern.[24] In fact, were it to form a partnership with India on matters of concern to both countries and forward a common cause at international fora, the international community might give South Asian concerns more recognition. For the people of the subcontinent, there are no indications that the world is moving towards nuclear disarmament, even though the weapons of mass destruction threat in Iraq may be taken care of, and Iran, North Korea, and other states may be brought in line. The case of vertical proliferation stands starkly neglected by the jury of nations that proactively seek to eliminate horizontal proliferation.

Endnotes

1. General (retd) Jehangir Karamat, Inaugural Address at IPRI seminar in Islamabad on "Arms Race and Nuclear Developments in South Asia", April 20-21, 2004.
2. Raja C. Mohan, statement made during a seminar on "Prospects of peace, stability and prosperity in South Asia" organized by the Institute for Regional Studies, June 8, 2004.
3. Statement by Pakistan's Foreign Office spokesperson, Masood Khan, "Indian arms shopping disturbing peace: FO", *News* (Rawalpindi), October 7, 2003,.
4. Statement by Pakistan's Foreign Secretary, Riaz Khokhar, "Arms race in South Asia termed economically unsustainable", *Dawn* (Islamabad), November 14, 2003.
5. Statement by Pakistan's Foreign Minister Khurshid Kasuri, "Pakistan N-Deterrence level not static: Kasuri London", *News* (Rawalpindi), November 5, 2003.
6. Shireen Mazari, "Pakistan's Nuclear Doctrine", paper presented at IPRI seminar.
7. "The Cabinet Committee on Security Reviews Operationalization of India's Nuclear Doctrine", Government of India Press Release, January 4, 2003.
8. Summary taken from tables included in Brigadier Naeem Salik's paper presented at IPRI seminar.
9. Rahul Roy Chaudry, paper presented at the IRS conference, June 7-9, 2004.

10. White House Press Release, Office of the Press Secretary, Washington, DC. *http://www.state.gov/t/np/rls/prsrl/23809.htm* (September 4, 2003.)

11. Interview with Brig. Naeem A. Salik, Director, Strategic Plans Division, Islamabad, April 21, 2004.

12. "India ready to deploy Agni", *Daily Times* (Lahore), October 6, 2003. Also see "India to produce 30 more Prithvi missiles; Agni deployment this year", *Nation* (Islamabad), September 8, 2003.

13. W. P. S Sidhu, "India's Security and Nuclear Risk Reduction Measures", Report No.26, , (Washington, DC: Henry L. Stimson Center, November 1998), p. 47.

14. M. V. Ramana, R. Rajaraman, Zia Mian, "Nuclear Early Warning in South Asia Problems and Issues", *Economic and Political Weekly*, EPW Special Articles, January 17, 2004. A lot of information from this article has been included in this section.

15. *Indian Nuclear Doctrine, available at: http://www. indianembassy. org/policy/ CTBT/nuclear_ doctrine_aug_17_1999.html*

16. Agha Shahi, Zulfiqar Ali Khan, and Abdul Sattar, "Securing Nuclear Peace", *News* (Rawalpindi), October 5, 1999.

17. Testimony of Victor Gilinsky, House Committee on International Relations hearing on "The Bush Administration and Nonproliferation", March 30, 2004.

18. John E. Endicott, paper presented at IPRI seminar.

19. George Perkovich, Joseph Cirincione, Rose Gottemoeller, Jon B. Wolfsthal, and Jessica Mathews, "Universal Compliance: A Strategy for Nuclear Security", June 18, 2004.

20. See Imtiaz H. Bokhari, "Adverse Partnership: A Paradigm for Indo-Pak Détente", *IPRI Journal*, (Islamabad), vol.3, no. 2 (Summer 2003), p.11, for a fine analysis on the requirements of deterrence and questionable assumptions that may have been made on Pakistan's part.

21. See M. V. Ramana, "Military Planning and Nuclear Weapons", *Daily Times*, January 16, 2003. According to his analysis, military control over nuclear weapons is likely to increase with time.

22. Farah Zahra, "Talking nuclear - with or without Agra", *News on Sunday* (Rawalpindi), July 22, 2001.

23. Arian L. Pregenzer, "Securing Nuclear Capabilities in India and Pakistan: Reducing the Terrorist and Proliferation Risks", *The Non Proliferation Review* (Monterey, California, USA, Spring 2003).

24. The Millennium Declaration as well as the NPT Review Conference 2000 pledged that Nuclear Weapons States would take their obligation towards nuclear arms control seriously.

The Role of Nuclear Weapons in Pakistan's Defence Strategy

Zafar Iqbal Cheema

A close reading of Pakistan's national security policy suggests that nuclear weapons have played an increasingly important role in its defence and deterrent strategy since the late 1980s. Addressing a conference in Islamabad, Pakistan's Foreign Minister in General Pervez Musharraf's government declared in November 1999: "Minimum nuclear deterrent will remain the guiding principle of our nuclear strategy."[1] He stated that, as India builds up its nuclear weapons arsenal: "Pakistan will have to maintain, preserve and upgrade its capability", in order to ensure the survivability and credibility of its nuclear deterrent.[2] Since then, this theme has been consistently reiterated at relevant occasions by General Pervez Musharraf and his top advisers.

This policy in fact was formulated before Musharraf's regime. Responding to the pronouncement of the draft Indian nuclear doctrine in August 1999 as offensive, and threatening regional and global stability, the Defence Committee of the Cabinet (DCC) under the former Prime Minister, Nawaz Sharif, stated that the future development of Pakistan's nuclear weapons programme would be determined solely by the requirement of our minimum deterrent capability, which is now an indispensable part of our security doctrine."[3] As former Chief of Army Staff, General (Retd) Mirza Aslam Beg, went a step further, stating that: as oxygen is basic to life and one does not debate its desirability, nuclear deterrence has assumed the life-saving property for Pakistan.[4] Since its development, nuclear weapons capability has not only been considered an integral component of Pakistan's defence strategy but is believed to have been actually invoked on a number of occasions in the past decade and a half, to ward off an all-out war with India in the three conflict situations the two countries faced. Although the precise details of what role nuclear weapons played, how they were invoked or their use threatened, has not been formally disclosed; however, some studies have appeared on the issue.[5]

This article attempts, firstly, to list Pakistan's threat perceptions; secondly, it expounds its nuclear policy; thirdly, it describes nuclear capabilities and delivery systems; fourthly, it analyses the nuclear doctrine and stability factor. Finally, it offers some suggestions and envisages likely future trends.

Pakistan's Threat Perceptions

Since its dismemberment in 1971, Pakistan's perception of threats from India has gradually been accentuated on account of various factors. First, the Indian conventional military superiority far exceeds Pakistan's conventional military capability in quantitative terms; the latter's ability to bridge that gap is increasingly being undermined due to a host of reasons. India's vast geographic base and consequent strategic depth, its large economy and industrial capacity not only allow it to maintain conventional military superiority but also to continue gradually increasing it. On the other hand, Pakistan's economic and industrial weaknesses undermine its military preparedness and logistical stamina. Since its development in the mid-1970s, a nuclear weapons capability is believed to compensate for the weaknesses in Pakistan's conventional military strength, notwithstanding the recently-bestowed status of a non-NATO ally by the United States, which might lead to a limited modernization of Pakistan's conventional military capability. US officials have, however, clarified that they will not disturb the current military equilibrium between India and Pakistan.

Second, Pakistan continues to perceive the possibility of limited or general war with India. This perception originates from the history of India Pakistan relations. Since independence, the two neighbours have fought three wars (1948, 1965, and 1970-71) and, most recently, a limited conflict in Kargil. All of these (except the 1970-71 war) were fought over the unresolved Kashmir dispute. Both countries are locked in an eyeball-to-eyeball confrontation on the Siachin glacier in the extreme north of Kashmir since India's occupation of the two-thirds of the glacier in 1983-84, in clear violation of the Simla Agreement of 1972. This agreement not only forbids the use of force to settle outstanding disputes, it also prohibits any unilateral changes in the Line of Control in Kashmir. In addition, both countries have faced many crisis-situations, such as the 1986-87 Brasstacks and the Kashmir crisis of spring 1990 which almost precipitated all-out war.

Given this pattern of hostility and armed conflict, Pakistan's perceptions of a threat of war with India are well-entrenched. Until recently, India and Pakistan co-existed in an emotionally charged strategic environment, which occasionally generated crisis-situations, with the potential for triggering armed conflicts. The recently adopted confidence-building measures (CBMs) and the thaw in mutual relations are unlikely to change the long-term strategic policies of either country, unless core issues like Kashmir are resolved. So, given the vast conventional military asymmetries and lack of strategic depth,

Pakistan's security policy is to use its nuclear weapons capability to deter India from starting another war, rather than fighting a war the outcome of which is likely to be unfavourable. The genesis of Pakistan's nuclear deterrent policy dates back to Z. A. Bhutto's rationale for the development of a nuclear capability for deterrence against the prospects of Indian aggression.[6] Giri Deshingkar suggests: if for any reason, India were to threaten the existence of Pakistan as a state as presently constituted, they are expected to use nuclear weapons against India first. With a doctrine of this kind, which can usefully be termed volatility, Pakistan would not be deterred by India's nuclear capability or even overt weaponization.[7]

Third, India's nuclear weapons capability, which has always been 15 to 20 years ahead of Pakistan and relatively much larger, is perceived as an instrument for nuclear blackmail and coercion in the absence of a nuclear counterweight. The first Indian nuclear test in 1974 served as a catalyst to the development of a nuclear weapons programme in Pakistan, although Z. A. Bhutto had expressed his individual motivation for the development of nuclear weapons by Pakistan before the first Indian nuclear test, there was no institutional support for that objective. Pakistan had not installed a single safeguards-free nuclear facility before 1974 and the first steps towards the establishment of the Uranium Enrichment Plant at Kahuta were taken in 1975, when Dr A.Q. Khan was approached to set up such a facility. From the proliferation perspective, a reputed specialist, James E. Dougherty, immediately anticipated Pakistan's response to the Indian nuclear test and its implications, and wrote: "Proliferation by reaction is a phenomena associated with pairs of conflict-parties or historic rivals rather than a chain-reaction involving an indefinitely long series of countries." [8]

Dougherty contended that, in reaction to the Indian nuclear test and weapons capability, Pakistan would be compelled to develop its own nuclear weapons capability because of its continued rivalry with India.[9] The Indian nuclear weapons capability is perceived as posing a serious threat to Pakistan. The Pakistani strategic community generally adheres to the common belief that there is no defence against nuclear weapons and the only response to the threat of use of nuclear weapons or blackmail is either to seek a nuclear umbrella or to develop nuclear weapons capability. Pakistan's non-acceptance of the Indian no-first use of nuclear weapons offer suggests that nuclear weapons are integral to its defence and deterrent doctrine.

Fourth, Pakistan also perceives its nuclear deterrent as a means to ward-off threats of pre-emption or of decapitation of its small nuclear force by India. Since 1982-83, India has planned to undertake pre-emptive air strikes against Pakistan's nuclear weapons facilities, especially in their embryonic phase. In 1982, the *Washington Post* reported Indian contingency plans to carry out pre-emptive strikes against Pakistani nuclear installations, especially the Kahuta Uranium Enrichment plant.[10] Press accounts again appeared about the pre-emptive strikes by the Indian Air Force against Kahuta in 1984 during a CIA briefing to US Senators.[11] India ultimately resisted execution of such plans fearing that it might not be able to totally destroy Pakistan's nuclear weapons capability and Pakistan might be left with some capability to retaliate against the Indian nuclear facilities.[12] The prospect of Pakistani air strikes with F-16s on the Indian nuclear facilities, especially at Mumbai, also created an atmosphere of fear.

Preceding the Pakistani nuclear tests on May 28 and 30, 1998, the Pakistani press carried reports about Indian pre-emptive air strikes, aimed at decapitation of Pakistan's nuclear facilities, thereby hinting at the prospects of its nuclear tests.[13] A Ministry of Foreign Affairs spokesman stated that he had convincing evidence of attack aircraft ready at the Indian airbase at Srinagar to undertake pre-emptive operations and eliminate Pakistan's nuclear weapons capability.[14] Pakistan threatened retaliation and deployed the Ghauri ballistic missiles at unidentified sites to lend credibility to the situation depicted.[15] One report suggested that some of the Ghauri missiles were equipped with nuclear warheads.[16] Pakistan's perception of Indian pre-emptive strikes against its nuclear facilities was reinforced by the provisions in the Indian nuclear doctrine to employ conventional military capability against the threats of use of nuclear weapons.[17] Such a scenario would compel Pakistan to continuously reject India's no first use posture and promote reliance upon nuclear weapons at the outset of a conflict-situation, rather than keeping them as weapons of last resort.

Fifth, India's declaration of a stockpile of chemical weapons introduces new uncertainties for nuclear stability with Pakistan.[18] In 1992, India and Pakistan signed a bilateral agreement not to use chemical weapons against each other on the understanding that both the countries were non-chemical weapon states. Both countries also signed the global Chemical Weapons Convention (CWC) as non-chemical weapons states; but afterwards, India declared a stockpile of chemical weapons before ratification in 1997, a stockpile which it is required to give up in ten years under the CWC provisions. The dramatic Indian disclosure of its possession of chemical weapons has not only added to the existing distrust between the two countries but generated apprehensions in Pakistan about the use of chemical weapons against its armed forces. Pakistan considers that the only available alternative to such a perceived threat of the use of chemical weapons is nuclear deterrence.

Pakistan's Nuclear Policy

Pakistan's policy on various elements of the non-proliferation regime has been closely linked with India's policy, more due to the Indo-centric nature of its decision-making process and less due to their intrinsic merits, as India is perceived as the principal threat to its security. Pakistan signed the Partial Test Ban Treaty (PTBT) in 1963 immediately after its conclusion, but withheld ratification until 1988 for reasons which have neither been made public nor fully investigated. [19] Perhaps it was due to India's keen interest and lead in underground nuclear explosive technology. Pakistan's approach to the Non-Proliferation Treaty (NPT) was different from India's. It took an active part in the NPT negotiations, hailed its conclusion, and expressed a hope that all non-nuclear weapon states would join it. [20] In an apparent response to the Indian objections to the NPT, Pakistan stated that it was "unrealistic to impose obligations on the nuclear powers similar in all respects to those which the treaty placed on the non-nuclear weapon states."[21] However, despite its general support for the NPT, Pakistan did not sign it due to India's refusal to do so. It explained its NPT policy in the following terms: in the final analysis, the position of Pakistan with regard to signing the treaty will turn on considerations of its enlightened national interest and security in the geopolitical context of the region in which Pakistan is situated. [22]

Simultaneous with its pursuit of nuclear weapons capability since the late 1970s, Pakistan had offered India a wide range of nuclear arms control proposals. These proposals are: i) creation of a nuclear weapons-free zone in South Asia; ii) simultaneous signatures to the NPT by India and Pakistan; iii) mutual acceptance of IAEA safeguards; iv) bilateral inspections of each others' nuclear facilities; v) joint declaration to renounce the development of nuclear weapons; and vi) signing of a regional test-ban treaty. [23] India rejected all these proposals on the plea that they failed to address the Indian perception of a Chinese nuclear threat and treated India and Pakistan as equals, elevating Pakistan's importance, despite India's far greater size, and economic and military power.[24] It also argued that all these proposals were part of an "insincere diplomatic offensive" by Pakistan to isolate India in the non-proliferation forums and, therefore, lacked credibility.[25]

During the Comprehensive Test Ban Treaty (CTBT) negotiations, Pakistan demanded that the treaty ought to be an instrument against both horizontal and vertical nuclear proliferation, and must effectively contribute towards nuclear disarmament.[26] Like the NPT, Pakistan has generally supported the CTBT, while strongly indicating that its policy was contingent upon the Indian position and behaviour, that is, that it would not sign the CTBT unless India did so. Pakistan's Ambassador to the Conference on Disarmament (CD), Munir Akram, reiterated former Prime Minister Benazir Bhutto's statement made during her visit to Japan: let (Indian) Prime Minister Rao join her anywhere in the world to ensure that what happened in Hiroshima and Nagasaki will never happen in Lahore and Delhi.[27] However, given its stand against the CTBT, India would have tested its nuclear weapons before

September 1999, no matter which government was in power.[28] It aspired to the status of a full-fledged *de facto*, if not *de jure*, nuclear weapon state, before the CTBT came into force. Politics, ideology, longstanding nuclear ambitions, and pursuit of strategic power played a decisive role. Analysing the Indian argument about the Chinese nuclear threat to its security, Eric Arnett observes: Their claim (India's) is not only cynical but inconsistent with the history of Indian defense planning.[29] "Fear of China, or later Pakistan's military power does not fully explain India's nuclear weapons program," observes George Perkovich.[30]

The Indian nuclear tests in May 1998 generated immense pressure on Pakistan to follow suit, due to their wide-ranging implications for its security and body-politic. Pakistan's nuclear tests were axiomatic after the India nuclear tests since it was under intense pressure to redress the resultant strategic imbalance and the adverse impact on national security, as well as to re-establish deterrent stability between the two adversaries. The dynamics of domestic politics also forced Pakistan to go for nuclear tests. According to Neil Joeck, the threat of being driven from office was patently clear to Prime Minister Sharif, which compelled his government to carry out the nuclear tests.[31] The Indian nuclear tests evoked a matching response from Pakistan on May 28 and 30, 1998. If the last fifteen years of Pakistan's nuclear policy were any index to the future, its leadership would not have carried out the nuclear weapon tests, had India not carried out its tests, even if the tests were deemed necessary by its atomic bureaucracy. The series of tests Pakistan carried out in May 1998 enabled it to produce first generation nuclear weapons, which are considered appropriate for a credible nuclear deterrence against India at this stage.

Pakistan's Nuclear Weapons Capability and Delivery Systems

Despite the high level of attention given to Pakistan's nuclear pursuits in the formative phase, Indian and Western strategic communities not only underestimated, but at times underplayed its propensity to rapidly acquire nuclear weapons capability.[32] Much before the series of nuclear tests in May 1998, Pakistan had acquired the capability to manufacture and assemble all the components of a nuclear device.[33] It claimed to have carried out five nuclear tests on May 28, and the sixth on May 30, 1998.[34] Broadly, these tests pertained to three main areas of weaponization: low-yield weapons, high-yield fission, and boosted-fission weapons.[35] According to Dr Khan, Pakistan used ready-to-fire nuclear warheads and not test bombs on May 28 and 30, 1998.[36] Before the May 1998 tests, India was perceived as maintaining an ambiguous nuclear posture and "non-weaponized" nuclear arsenal capability: it had produced fissile material and bomb components, but had not turned the components over to the military.[37] Late in the 1980s and 1990s, however, the Indian military did become much more involved in nuclear weapons matters, conducting studies of preventive attack options in developing counter-force capabilities, and producing missiles capable of delivering nuclear weapons. After May 1998, India claimed a 43 kiloton yield for the thermonuclear device and 12 kiloton for the fission device. International estimates suggested that the combined yields of the 11th May tests were between 10 to 15 kilotons.[38] The international community also questioned whether India had actually tested a thermonuclear device.[39]

The most preferred Pakistani aircraft for nuclear delivery

missions is likely to be the US-supplied F-16. It is a medium-range, multiple-role, high-performance aircraft that is considered especially suitable for nuclear delivery systems.[40] Pakistan procured 40 F-16 aircraft (the fighter-bomber version) in the early 1980s, under the terms of a limited force modernization programme, with US co-operation in the wake of the Soviet military intervention in Afghanistan.[41] The US took special care that no equipment was provided to Pakistan which could be used for or would assist in nuclear delivery missions.[42] It specially denied the electrical mechanisms necessary for safe maintenance, transportation, and delivery of nuclear weapons by F-16s.[43] However, various accounts have appeared since then, which suggest that Pakistan has carried out modifications to the F-16s for nuclear delivery missions. In 1989, *Foreign Report* suggested that Pakistan has formatted the bomb to be delivered from beneath the wings of an F-16 and indicated the possibility of flight training being carried out. [44] The bomb design had also gone through a series of wind-tunnel tests and programmed in-flight computer system to provide the correct flight path for a nuclear bomb run. [45] It is reported that the Indian Defence Research and Development Organization had been perfecting aerial bombing techniques, using the MIG-23 and MIG-27 aircraft. [46] If that were true, the Pakistani choice for an aircraft delivery system, that is, the F-16s, seems better than the Indian choice. However, India has a wider choice in the form of Jaguars, Mirage 2000, and MIG 29 aircraft.

Pakistan test-fired an intermediate range ballistic missile (MRBM) named Ghauri, on April 6, 1997. It is based upon a three-stage rocket with a 700 kg payload, has a range of 1500 km, and is capable of carrying nuclear warheads.[47] Equipped with the latest guidance technology, Ghauri (also called a Haft-

V) can engage targets throughout India, except in its extreme east. However, there are hardly any important strategic installations and bases in the extreme east at this stage, which can operate against Pakistan. Most of such targets are located in central, southern, and western India, and are within Ghauri's range. It can also engage India's naval deployments and bases within a range of 1,100 to 1,500 km, if deployed near Karachi. Its range can also be further extended to engage targets throughout India. In April 1999, Pakistan test-fired a short-range ballistic missile, Shaheen-I, with a range of 1000-1100 km, terminal guidance, and solid-fuel system, which provides it with rapid reaction capability. It has significantly enhanced Pakistan's strategic and political position vis-à-vis India.

Pakistan test-fired its longest-range nuclear-capable ballistic missile, Shaheen-II, on March 9, 2004, which can hit targets up to 2,000 km.[48] The missile's actual range is up to 2,500 km, but was restricted to 2,000 km so as not to cross Pakistan's declared territorial sea limit. The Shaheen-II is a solid-fuel and nuclear-capable ballistic missile, which gives Pakistan a ready-response capability. "It reflects Pakistan's resolve to maintain minimum credible deterrence as the cornerstone of its security policy," an ISPR statement said.[49] Pakistan had notified India as required under the mutually signed MoU on the advance notification of ballistic missiles tests and as a CBM in the prevailing environment to normalize relations.

Pakistan's choice of medium and intermediate range missiles (for example, Hatf-3, Ghauri, and Shaheen), provides it with a diversity of nuclear force deployment options. The upgraded versions of Ghauri and Shaheen (Ghauri-II and Shaheen-II), with a range up to 2,000 to 2,500 km, would enable

Pakistan to cover the entire Indian territories in its missile-targeting options. Pakistan has acquired the technology to miniaturize nuclear warheads for missile-based delivery systems and to develop boosted weapons.[50] Testing was necessary before it could undertake to deploy these missiles.[51] Some observers suggest that Pakistan could have already produced warheads compact enough to be carried by missiles.[52]

India-Pakistan Nuclear Doctrines

India's draft nuclear doctrine, announced on August 17, 1999 by its National Security Advisory Board constituted by the BJP government, is perceived in Pakistan as an aggressive and provocative strategy, which would not only fuel a nuclear arms race but enhance strategic instability between India and Pakistan.[53] Although the draft doctrine has yet to be formally approved by the Indian government, it is believed axiomatic in Pakistan that the Indian government would, by and large, embrace it.[54] The doctrine proclaims the development and maintenance of credible minimum deterrence, based upon a strategic triad of nuclear forces (land-based, air-based, and sea-based), second-strike capability, and punitive retaliation with nuclear weapons if deterrence were to fail.[55] It proclaims: the fundamental purpose of Indian nuclear weapons is to deter the use and threat of use of nuclear weapons by any state or entity against India and its forces. India will not be the first to initiate a nuclear strike, but will respond with punitive retaliation should deterrence fail.[56]

It declares that credible deterrence requires: sufficient, survivable, and operationally deployable nuclear forces, with robust command and control, and efficient intelligence and early warning systems.[57] The nuclear forces are to be under exclusive civilian command and control, with final authority to launch nuclear weapons resting with the Indian prime minister. [58]

The danger of the proposed doctrine is that it relies upon the maintenance of highly effective conventional capabilities, not just to raise the threshold of conventional military conflict, but to deal with the threat of use of nuclear weapons by an adversary. By pronouncing such a nuclear war-fighting strategy, the doctrine is a recipe for a nuclear disaster, since any conventional pre-emptive strikes against an adversary's nuclear weapons to ward off threats of their use might automatically lead to a nuclear exchange. According to Rodney W. Jones, the Indian nuclear doctrine is based upon an expansive war-fighting force structure, without specifying adversaries, or an actual threat, language of which alludes provocatively to using conventional pre-emptive capabilities offensively against any party that might threaten to use nuclear weapons against India.[59] He opines : By calling this strategy document a draft, the authors may hope to draw Pakistan reactively into public declarations of its own nuclear policy." [60] The proposed Indian nuclear doctrine is also an almost verbatim version of the Western strategic models on nuclear deterrence, and lacks ingenuity, except in its no-first-use offer, which is modelled on the former Soviet and Chinese proclamations.

On January 4, 2003, the Indian Cabinet Committee on Security reviewed the operationalization of India's Nuclear Doctrine and summarized a version, which, in some ways, significantly departs from the August 1999 draft document.[61] It omits the development of a triad of strategic nuclear forces (land-based, air-based, and sea-based), which in any case was beyond India's short-term capacity to develop. [62] The no-first-use posture has been modified in two ways. First, the word "anywhere" has been added to the provision to the no-first-use clause: nuclear weapons will only be used in retaliation against a nuclear attack on Indian territory or on Indian forces anywhere." This implies that India may use nuclear weapons, even if the Indian forces happen to be in another state's territory, thus not ruling out an aggressive mode or occupation.[63] Article VI of the operationalised nuclear doctrine renders the no-first-use declaration invalid by stating: "However, in the event of a major attack against India, or Indian forces anywhere, by biological or chemical weapons, India will retain the option of retaliating with nuclear weapons."[64]

Pakistan has not issued a document which can be termed a nuclear doctrine, perhaps deliberately so, to maintain flexibility. However, its policy of maintaining a minimum and credible small nuclear force, and addressing asymmetric strategic equilibrium with India by invoking nuclear weapons suggest the outlines of a nuclear doctrine. As indicated above, Pakistan has often declared that minimum nuclear deterrent will remain the guiding principle of its nuclear strategy.[65] "The minimum nuclear deterrence can and will never be compromised," General Musharraf reiterated, while inaugurating the 26th International Nathiagali Summer College on Physics in 2001.[66] He further stated: "Pakistan believes in maintaining a minimum credible deterrence and does not want to direct its available resources towards the race of weapons of mass destruction."[67] This statement has been reiterated many times, as recently as during the latest visit to Islamabad by the US Depuy Secretary of State, Richard Armitage. Since the late 1980s, Pakistan has pursued a doctrine of minimum nuclear deterrence and adequate conventional defence to balance India's nuclear and conventional forces. As a note of caution, declarations about the doctrine need to be differentiated from its operational and functional dimensions. Pakistan's rejection of India's "no-nuclear-first-use" pledge also suggests that nuclear weapons are integral to its defence and deterrent doctrine. Pakistani leaders consider India's no-first-use offer as declaratory posturing, rather than an actual policy. Second, it would undermine the credibility of Pakistan's deterrence against an Indian attack or coercion. Pakistan's nuclear strategy aims to prevent an all-out war with India. The policy to downgrade Pakistan's conventional military capability unwittingly lowers its threshold to invoke the threat of use of nuclear weapons. It feels compelled to threaten the use of nuclear weapons at an early stage if a war looms on the horizon.

Pakistani officials have described general contingencies, which would warrant the threat or use of nuclear weapons. For example, an Italian report, based upon interview of Liuetenant-General Khalid Kidwai, Director-General of the Strategic Plans Division (SDP) by a team of Italian researchers, describes some scenarios for Pakistan's employment of nuclear weapons.[68] The interview-based report offers an analysis of Pakistan's nuclear posture and outlines contingencies under which Pakistan might resort to the threat or use of nuclear weapons. It states that Pakistan would resort to nuclear weapons' employment in the following eventualities:[69]

i) India attacks Pakistan and conquers a large part of its territory.

ii) India destroys a large part either of its land or air forces.

iii) India proceeds to the economic strangulation of Pakistan.

iv) India pushes Pakistan into political destabilization or creates large-scale internal subversion.[70]

Pakistan's foreign and defence policies set the general terms under which the doctrinal foundations of its nuclear policy are based. An analysis of its overall decision-making process suggests that Pakistan's nuclear doctrine has evolved, rather than having been formulated at a given point in its nuclear history. Its fundamental objective is deterring rather than fighting a war with India. Other objectives of the Pakistani nuclear doctrine in dealing with the perceived threat from India are to maintain an overall strategic equilibrium, to neutralize conventional military asymmetries against India, and to maintain its territorial integrity and political sovereignty. Conventional military disparities vis-à-vis India and lack of strategic depth compel Pakistani military leaders to threaten the use of nuclear weapons as a deterrent against a large-scale Indian invasion that threatens its territorial integrity.

There is general recognition in Pakistan that nuclear weapons played a role in diffusing various conflict-situations between India and Pakistan in the past decade and a half. It is believed that to defuse the 1986-87 Brasstacks crisis, Pakistan invoked its nuclear weapons capability through the good offices of Dr A. Q. Khan, who communicated a veiled nuclear threat to India about Pakistan's possession of the nuclear bomb and the likelihood of its use, should Pakistan's territorial integrity be at stake.[71] Khan's statement was followed by an interview of General Zia-ul-Haq in the *Time* magazine, in which he confirmed Pakistan's acquisition of nuclear weapons capability, although the Brasstacks crisis had passed its peak by then.[72] Some experts believed that the interview was prompted by India's threatening military manoeuvres against Pakistan's relatively vulnerable southern sector around Rajasthan in Sindh province. [73]

Pakistan once again considered invoking its nuclear weapons capability to avert the fear of a war with India during the spring 1990 Kashmir crisis. This crisis precipitated due to an unprecedented and largely indigenous Kashmiri struggle for independence from India from 1989 onwards. India perceived Pakistan as abetting and aiding the Kashmiri struggle and consequently deployed its troops along Pakistan's border. The Indian leaders threatened that Pakistan could not gain Kashmir without a war. [74] While rapidly deploying its conventional armed forces, Pakistan signalled the threat of the use of nuclear weapons by pre-positioning its F-16s, equipped with nuclear weapons, on full alert. [75] Due to the high risk of a nuclear war between India and Pakistan, the United States mediated to defuse the crisis. However, a study sponsored by the US Energy Department discounts the possibility of the use or threat of use of nuclear weapons. [76]

K. Subrahmanyam assesses the role of nuclear weapons in the 1990 crisis as follows: "In 1965 after Pakistan's 'Operation Gibraltar', the war of 1965 happened. India didn't resort to a similar course of action in 1990." [77] The restraint imposed by the nuclear factor on the conventional military confrontation between India and Pakistan was all too obvious. Whether or not nuclear-weapons capabilities played a decisive role in averting the 1986-87 and 1990 crises, there is a widespread perception of the influence of nuclear weapons on strategic decision-making and of restraint imposed on the usually belligerent behaviour of the two long-standing adversaries.

The Kargil crisis in May 1999 was yet another stark reminder of the potential for an India-Pakistan conflict over the Kashmir dispute which could lead to a nuclear exchange. India internationalized the conflict, resulting in explicit demands from the international community, especially the great powers, for Pakistan to withdraw its forces as well as the Kashmiri militants from the Kargil sector to avert the possibility of an all-out war with India, which might well have escalated into a nuclear clash between the two South Asian neighbours.[78] Hoyt cites a source which states that, Indian and Pakistani officials and leaders exchanged direct or indirect nuclear threats no fewer than 13 times between May 26 and June 30.[79] According to an Indian study, nuclear warheads were readied, and delivery systems, including Mirage 200 aircraft, short-ranged Prithvi missiles, and medium-ranged Agni missiles, were prepared for possible use.[80]

Deterrent Stability in South Asia

There is a voluminous body of literature, variously favouring and opposing the prospects of deterrent stability between India and Pakistan. The lines of divisions between the proponents of nuclear deterrence and its opponents are drawn along culturally-ingrained orientations and preferences, which often colour so-called rational analyses and conclusions. Many South Asian experts generally agree that a state of mutual deterrence has been established between India and Pakistan, though the various descriptions of this deterrence differ. The deterrence relationship between India and Pakistan in the pre-tests (nuclear) scenario has not been explained by any known models of the Cold-war era; instead, some new terms have been coined such as non-weaponized deterrence, recessed deterrence, and existential deterrence. The concept of non-weaponized deterrence was proposed by George Perkovich, recognizing that India and Pakistan could retain nuclear weapons capabilities and fissile material, but remain short of manufacturing nuclear warheads. [81] For a stable non-weaponized deterrent regime, India and Pakistan would undertake not to assemble or deploy nuclear weapons and nuclear-capable ballistic missiles. [82] A non-weaponized deterrence posture had an inherent time-lag built into the system, which provided sufficient time for crisis management or decisions to employ nuclear weapons. Non-weaponized deterrence also visualized complementary CBMs in the nuclear and related non-nuclear fields.

Recessed deterrence, a term attributed to Jasjit Singh, favours the development of nuclear weapons components and fabrication of warheads, but also requires them to be maintained in unassembled modes.[83] Former Army Cheif General Sundarji added to the concept of recessed deterrence by suggesting that India and Pakistan need not place their nuclear weapons components under military control, but instead could store components, fissile materials, and triggering devices at civilian laboratories in unassembled form and separate from delivery systems.[84] Recessed deterrence envisioned centralized negative controls and the weapons components to be so located that they could be air-transported to a central location, assembled and mounted on delivery systems in approximately six to twelve hours, to enable the launch of a retaliatory strike after riding out the adversary's first strike.[85] Both these concepts were based upon the traditional postulation that nuclear weapons – being weapons of mass destruction – have no tactical value or any significant ancillary role except to deter a nuclear attack or be used in a retaliatory second-strike mode. They are, therefore, essentially considered weapons of deterrence. The inherent problems in a non-weaponized deterrence regime were that unassembled arsenals diminished the possibility that nuclear weapons would always be available when needed and were more vulnerable to decapitation. However, the non-weaponized deterrence regime entailed an element of ambiguity that lacked transparency about the nuclear weapons capabilities of India and Pakistan and adversely affected deterrent stability.

The weaponization policies that India and Pakistan announced after their nuclear tests in May 1999 and the attendant doctrinal development should add transparency and may enhance stability, although at a higher threshold, and provided other essential pre-requisites of nuclear deterrence are fulfilled. These may include early warning systems, C^3I networks, survivable weapons capabilities, including second-strike capabilities, and credible delivery systems. The non-weaponized deterrence regime between India and Pakistan has been transformed into a weaponized regime after their nuclear tests. Both India and Pakistan are now *de facto* nuclear weapon states, if not *de jure*.

Scott Sagan renouned professor of political science maintains that within the rationalist deterrent theory, three major elements for stable nuclear deterrence are pre-requisites: i) the absence of preventive war during the transition period, when one state has developed a nuclear weapons capability and the other has not; ii) both states must develop not only the ability to inflict unacceptable damage on the other, but also a reliable second-strike capability; iii) their nuclear arsenals must not be prone to accidental or unauthorized use. [86] In view of these requirements, Sagan believes that, from the organizational theory perspective, it is a formidable task for the new nuclear states.[87] India and Pakistan seem capable of inflicting unacceptable damage upon each on the basis of their existing nuclear weapons capabilities. In addition, they are in the process of building second-strike capabilities, for example, the development and deployment of various categories of nuclear-capable ballistic missile systems. Moreover, there would be no guarantee to completely rule out accidental or unauthorized use of nuclear weapons with any degree of definiteness. India and Pakistan are passing through the formative phase of such processes about the safety of their nuclear arsenals. They may acquire technologies to install PAL and EMP devices, and institute processes to forestall accidental and unauthorized uses of nuclear weapons in the long-term perspective.

Neil Joeck, a fellow at University of Berkeley, believes that India and Pakistan's nuclear capabilities do not reduce or eliminate factors that contributed to past conflicts, and therefore, neither explain the absence of war over the past decade nor why war is currently unlikely."[88] He maintains that limited nuclear capabilities increase the potential costs of conflict, but do little to reduce the risk of its breaking out. However, without admitting the stabilizing effect of nuclear weapons capabilities, he recognizes that the development of command and control mechanisms would enhance stability in a crisis, and improve the ability to avoid nuclear use in the event of war. [89] Joeck suggests that operational considerations, for example, nuclear doctrine, weapons safety, alternative response options, intelligence and early warnings would help to reinforce deterrence at ground level, and ensure that both sides have a choice, other than suicide or surrender.

Kenneth Waltz, a prominent scholar of international relations, takes an optimistic view of deterrent stability among new nuclear nations, their weapons capabilities, and C^2 problems, and opines that over a period of time they would be able to resolve these problems, as did the existing nuclear weapon states.[90] Waltz further maintains that lesser (nuclear) states would not be able to disrupt nuclear equilibrium, as nuclear weapons make miscalculation difficult, they can be used both for defence and deterrence, and, if employed responsibly, nuclear weapons make wars hard to start. [91]

Analysing the logic and prospect of deterrent stability in South Asia, Ashley Tellis opines: The Indian subcontinent is likely to enjoy an extended period of ugly stability that will probably last for at least a decade and possibly longer at the strategic level, simultaneously generating instability at the lower end of the conflict spectrum."[92] However, he points out: the small number of nuclear weapons, the relatively provocative character of some of the delivery systems, the questionable command and control arrangements, the severely limited intelligence and warning systems, the casual attitudes towards nuclear deterrence, the lack of a clear and articulated deterrence doctrine, and the presence of few confidence-building measures, all combine to make successful deterrence stability a less-than-automatic outcome. [93]

It is claimed that an elementary form of nuclear deterrence between India and Pakistan has been operative since 1988. Indicating the existence of nuclear deterrence between India and Pakistan in the pre-nuclear tests scenario (May 1998), General Beg stated as Chief of Army Staff in 1989: "Whether we have a nuclear device or not is a different matter, but the very fact that people believe we have the nuclear capability is in itself a meaningful deterrent." [94] "The influence of nuclear weapons on the use of military force is widely recognized by influential opinions in India and that nuclear deterrence has kept wars in South Asia at bay."[95] Answering the question whether India and Pakistan would have refrained from the three wars they fought in 1948, 1965, and 1971, had both of them possessed minimal nuclear deterrents, a former Chief of the Indian Army and a respected analyst of strategic issues has expressed his views thus: "These wars would not have occurred."[96] Pakistani professionals agree with the assessment that, had Pakistan possessed a nuclear deterrent in 1971, the dismemberment of Pakistan could have been averted.[97] Commenting on the prospects for the future, a former Chief of the Indian Naval Staff has observed that, with nuclear capability, "Pakistan would be able to establish a deterrent nuclear posture against India, rendering in the process its conventional forces considerably less significant than it is today." [98] Another senior Indian general has remarked: "What the nuclear capability does is to make sure that the old scenarios of Indian armor crossing the Sukhur barrage over the Indus and slicing Pakistan into two are a thing of the past." [99]

Nuclear weapons generally erode conventional disparities. According to an opinion in the *Times of India*, perhaps India could flatten Islamabad twenty times over instead of Pakistan flattening India five times, but overkill is an illusive strategy. [100] It continues: "Twenty bombs against 40 bombs, though less in number, still constitute unacceptable damage."[101] Nuclear weapons are believed to have a great equalizing effect. Unlike conventional weapons, nuclear weapons are not militarily usable, but are in fact political and psychological weapons and, therefore, meant to deter aggression and war. Qualitative asymmetries in nuclear weapons, like the one side having tested and the other untested ones, generate a serious power vacuum and strategic imbalance, which is prejudicial to the vital national security interests of the country that has not conducted tests. Although Pakistan had carried out cold tests of its nuclear devices as far back as 1987, through computer simulation techniques, a detonation was considered the litmus test to ensure that nuclear weapons will work reliably and enhance deterrent stability. The general perception in Pakistan is that its nuclear tests redressed the asymmetries in the strategic equilibrium and restored the power balance.

The Indian and Pakistani nuclear deterrents dissuade both countries from embarking upon a course of action perceived prejudicial to their vital national security interests. It is a policy as well as a condition for establishing a new psychological relationship between the two antagonists. Both the adversaries would be dissuaded from undertaking a course of action injurious to the other's vital interests, due to the fear of infliction of unacceptable damage which would far outweigh the perceived advantages. Each adversary's dissuasion is, therefore, based upon a rational calculus of costs and benefits. India and Pakistan do not possess formidable weapons capabilities compared to the superpowers; yet those they do possess are sufficient to cause unacceptable damage in case of counter-value targets in both countries. Nuclear deterrence, unlike conventional deterrence, is not decisively degraded by quantitative or qualitative disparity. So long as a state's strategic arsenal is sufficient to survive the first strike and still inflict unacceptable damage, it does not have to match the adversary's arsenal in numbers. [102] Credible deterrence can be achieved with a small nuclear force.[103] One analyst has concluded that five or six nuclear warheads should be sufficient; even fewer should suffice to deter, provided they can be delivered on targets of high values. [104] Nuclear weapons "make the cost of war seem frighteningly high and thus discourage states from starting any wars that might lead to the use of such weapons."[105]

As the nuclear capabilities of India and Pakistan mutually hold their cities hostage, any thought of the annihilation of tens of thousands of civilians does amount to unacceptable damage. The excruciating damages of a possible nuclear exchange between India and Pakistan would be unpalatable for both countries, militarily, politically, socially, and economically. And this is what makes their counter-value deterrence stable. According to Haggerty: If history discloses an unblemished record of political leaders resisting the temptation to decapitate their enemies' nuclear forces, opacity enhances their extreme caution. After all, opaque nuclear forces are even less attractive targets for first strike than transparent ones, because they are even more shrouded in ambiguity and secrecy. [106]

That scenario has, however, changed in South Asia after India and Pakistan conducted nuclear tests in May 1998. The proponents of nuclear deterrence suggest that their argument is also upheld by empirical evidence. Nuclear weapons have helped to maintain peace and prevented military adventures in the past, and there is no reason to believe that they will not do so in the future. Even a powerful state is unlikely to commit aggression if it concludes that the potential gains are not worth the losses it has to risk. It is not necessary to conjure up doomsday scenarios of annihilation that entail an "unmitigated disaster."[107] There is almost complete consensus in Pakistan's strategic, scientific, and bureaucratic community that a nuclear deterrent capability is the best guarantee–if there can be one–

to ensure peace, stability, and the absence of all out war with India. Ashley Tellis, in his post-1998 voluminous study of the Indian force posture, suggests: "The prospects of deterrent stability are therefore high because no South Asian state is currently committed to securing any political objectives through the medium of major conventional and, by implication, nuclear war."[108]

Kamal Matinuddin provides a lengthy narrative on the existing theories of deterrence and briefly mentions opposing sides in the case of India and Pakistan, but is personally evasive on the subject of deterrent stability versus instability in South Asia. [109]

Conclusion

The present state of strategic stability between India and Pakistan is a precarious one, which needs more constant monitoring and vigil than the former Cold-War models. The geographical proximity of India and Pakistan does not permit enough early warning information and time: the three to five minutes time-lag at present is inadequate for a rational and calculated response. This might prompt launch-on-warning responses, enhancing the chances of miscalculation. The relatively less sophisticated command and control systems may cause difficulties in dealing with problems of accidental and unauthorized launch of nuclear weapons. The increase in mistrust and hostility between India and Pakistan in the wake of the Kargil crisis and the unresolved Kashmir dispute compounds the problems of nuclear arms' competition, missile proliferation, and deployment, and adds to divergent perceptions about strategic stability and regional security in South Asia.

Pakistan has to be mindful that it does not engage in an open-ended nuclear arms race with India, since the latter's larger economy enables it to allocate stupendous resources for nuclear military development, which the former simply cannot afford. It needs to dispassionately work out the essential requirements of a sufficient and stable deterrence against India and then guard against unnecessary escalation. An over-kill capability would be superfluous. The announcement of a Pakistani nuclear doctrine, not in rapid response to the draft Indian nuclear doctrine, but based upon its own merits of credible minimum deterrence, would mitigate the chances of misperception and provocation by India.

Both India and Pakistan should not ignore the global trends in favour of restraint on their nuclear capabilities. The present nuclear capabilities of India and Pakistan, based upon the demonstration of the recent nuclear tests, could help to promote stability and prevent the outbreak of war, provided disputes like Kashmir are immediately addressed. Limitation of their nuclear capabilities could be gradual, through the strengthening of mutual security. India and Pakistan should agree to contain their nuclear weapons capabilities within safe and manageable limits, mutually agreed upon by both countries. They must be willing to address the horrific consequences of a nuclear war, if deterrence were to fail.

The current CBMs have helped to normalize the political relationship among the two states. It is hoped the atmosphere will further improve after peace and security negotiations scheduled in June 2004, which might result in instituting nuclear-related CBMs. Through confidence and security-building negotiations, India and Pakistan can obviate the requirements for hardened silos, nuclear submarines, and even a search for the improvement of second-strike capabilities, which are at present considered essential for stable deterrence. Only then can a mutually beneficial and long-lasting peaceful atmosphere be created in the subcontinent. The long-term maintenance of a nuclear deterrent relationship by itself is a complex strategic issue, which, in the case of India and Pakistan, will be a much more demanding task. A resolution of the Kashmir dispute will eliminate the *raison d' être* of hostility between India and Pakistan.

* (Re-printed with permission from Islamabad Policy Research Institute Journal, Pakistan, Summer 2004)

Endnotes

1. "Pakistan to upgrade nuclear deterrent", *Dawn* (Karachi), November 25, 1999.
2. Ibid.
3. "Pakistan says Indian nuclear plan threaten global stability", *News* (Rawalpindi), August 26, 1999.
4. General (retd.) Mirza Aslam Beg, *Development and Security: Thoughts and Reflections* (Rawalpindi: FRIENDS, 1994), pp. 168-79.
5. For the 1986-87 Brasstacks crisis, see *Brasstacks and Beyond: Perception and Management of Crisis in South Asia,* ACDIS Research Report, (Urbana-Illinois, Program in Arms Control, Disarmament, and International Security, University of Illinois at Urbana-Champaign, 1995); for the spring 1990 crisis, see Stephen P. Cohen, P. R. Chari and Pervaiz Iqbal Cheema, *The Compound Crisis of 1990: Perception, Politics and Security*, ACDIS Research Report (Urbana-Champaign, University of Illinois, 2000); and Seymour M. Hersh, "On the Nuclear Edge", *New Yorker*, 29 March 1993, pp. 68-73. No study on the 1999 Kargil conflict has yet appeared from this perspective.
6. Z. A. Bhutto, *The Myth of Independence* (Karachi: Oxford University Press, 1969), see chapter on "Deterrent against Aggression."

7. Giri Deshingkar, "Indian politics and arms control: recent reversals and new reasons for optimism", in Eric Arnett, *Nuclear Weapons and Arms Control in South Asia after the Test Ban* (Oxford: Oxford University Press, SIPRI, 1998), p. 32.

8. James E. Dougherty, "Proliferation in Asia", *Orbis* (Fall 1975), Special Issue, p. 926

9. Ibid.

10. Milton R. Benjamin, "India said to Eye-Raid Pakistani A-Plants", *Washington Post*, December 20, 1982.

11. *Nucleonics Week*, vol. 25, no. 38 (September 1984), p. 4.

12. W. P. S. Sidhu, "Indian Nuclear Doctrine", in James Wirtz, Peter Lavoy and Scott Sagan, eds., *Planning the Unthinkable: How New Nuclear Powers will Use Nuclear, Biological and Chemical Weapons* (Ithaca and London: Cornell University Press, 2000), pp. 125-157.

13. *Nation* (Islamabad), May 28, 1998, p.1.

14. Ibid.

15. Ibid.

16. "Redefining Nuclear Order", *Nation* (Islamabad), 9 September 1998, special report, p. 5.

17. Please see section above on the Indian nuclear doctrine.

18. Pakistan accused India of using chemical weapons during the fighting at Kargil. "World: South Asia–India 'using chemical weapons' in Kashmir", *BBC News South Asia* (14 June 1999) http://news.bbc.co.uk/hi/english/world/south_asia/newsid_36700/367930.stm; "Pakistan accuses India of lobbing chemical shells into Kashmir", *CNN.com* (13 June 1999) http://www.cnn.com/WORLD/asiapcf/9906/13/india.pakistan.02/index.html.

19. United Nations, *Disarmament Newsletter*, 7(5), October 1989, p. 8.

20. *Documents on Disarmament: 1968* (Washington DC: ACDA, 1968), p. 317.

21. Ibid.

22. SIPRI, *The Near-Nuclear Countries and the NPT* (Stockholm: SIPRI, 1972), p. 26

23. *US Congressional Records*, August 5, 1988, p. S11005.

24. "India not in favor of regional disarmament", *News India*, November 14, 1987.

25. Ibid.

26. Text of the statement at the Conference on Disarmament by Ambassador Munir Akram, Pakistan's Permanent Representative to the United Nations Office, Geneva, on January 24, 1996.

27. Ibid.

28. For India's CTBT policy, see Zafar Iqbal Cheema, "Background Factors Relating to Nuclear Disarmament Issues, Including NPT, CTBT and Likely Future Developments", in Fasahat H. Syed (ed.), *Nuclear Disarmament and Conventional Arms Control Including Light Weapons* (Rawalpindi: FRIENDS, 1997), pp. 67-96.

29. Arnett, *Nuclear Weapons*, pp. 1-18.

30. George Perkovich, *India's Nuclear Bomb: Impact on Global Proliferation* (Berkeley and Los Angeles: University of California Press, 1999), p. 12.

31. Neil Joeck, "Nuclear Developments in India and Pakistan", *Access Asia Review*, vol. 2, no. 2 (July 1999), pp. 29-30.

32. Dr Homi Sethna, Chairman of the Indian Atomic Energy Commission, contemptuously dismissed the possibility of a Pakistani nuclear response after India's 1974 nuclear test by saying that Pakistan neither had the technology nor the capable men to produce nuclear weapons. Full details of Dr Sethna's observation are available in Dr A. Khan's interview in *The Muslim* (Islamabad), March 1, 1987; and Kuldip Nayyar, "Pakistan can make an A-Bomb: Says Pakistan's Dr Strange Love", *Observer* (London), March 1, 1987. A US Congressional study in 1982 suggested a considerable underestimation of Pakistan's development of nuclear weapons capability when it had virtually acquired most of the equipment for the Kahuta Uranium Enrichment Plant. *Analysis of Six Issues About Nuclear Capabilities of India, Iraq, Libya and Pakistan*, prepared by the Natural Resources Policy Division for the Subcommittee on Arms Control, Oceans, International Operations and Environment, Committee on Foreign Relations, United States Senate, January 1982 (Washington DC: US GPO, 1982),

p. 18. In another context, US officials underplayed the initial reports of Richard Barlow, a CIA officer monitoring Pakistan's nuclear pursuits in the 1980s. For further details, see, Hersh, "Nuclear Edge", pp. 68-73.

33. Aslam Beg, pp. 176-7.

34. *News* (Rawalpindi), 29 and 31 May 1998, p, 1; *Nation* (Islamabad), May 29 and 31, 1998, p. 1.

35. Ibid.

36. "Ready-to-Fire N-Warheads Used", *Nation* (Islamabad), May 29, 1998, p. 1.

37. Eric Arnett, "Nuclear Stability and Arms Sale to India: Implications for US Policy", in *Arms Control Today*, vol. 27, no. 5 (August 1997), pp. 7-11.

38. Perkovich, *India's Nuclear Bomb*, p. 426.

39. Ibid., p. 427.

40. *Aid and the Proposed Arms Sale of F-16 to Pakistan*, Hearing before the Committee on Foreign Relations, United States Senate, 97th Congress, 1st Session, November 12-17, 1981 (Washington DC: USGPO, 1981), p. 13.

41. Ibid.

42. *Weapons Proliferation in the New World Order*, Hearing before the Committee on Government Affairs, United States Senate, 102nd Congress, 2nd Session, January 15, 1992, pp. 20-5

43. Ibid.

44. "Pakistan's Atomic Bomb", *Foreign Report* (January 12, 1989), p. 1. However, *Foreign Report* is not generally regarded as a very reliable source.

45. Ibid.

46. David Cortright and Amitabh Mattoo, eds., *India and the Bomb: Public Opinion and Nuclear Options* (Notre Dame, Indiana: University of Notre Dame Press, 1996), p. 8.

47. *News* (Rawalpindi), April 7, 1998.

48. "Pakistan tests its longest-range missile", *Dawn* (Internet Edition), March 10, 2004.

49. Ibid.

50. "Pakistan Working on Miniaturized N-Warhead", *Nation* (Islamabad), April 16, 1998, p. 9.

51. Ibid.

52. Hersh, "Nuclear Edge", pp. 55-73.

53. "Pakistan says Indian nuclear plan threatens global stability", *The News International*, August 26, 1999.

54. Ibid.

55. Draft Report of the National Security Advisory Board on Indian Nuclear Doctrine (New Delhi: Government of India, August 17, 1999).

56. Ibid.

57. Ibid.

58. Ibid.

59. Rodney W. Jones, "Pakistan's Nuclear Posture", *Dawn* (Karachi), September 14, 1999.

60. Ibid.

61. The Cabinet Committee on Security Reviews Operationalization of India's Nuclear Doctrines (New Delhi: Government of India Press Release, January 4, 2003).

62. Ibid., p. 1.

63. Ibid., article ii.

64. Ibid, article vi.

65. "Pakistan says Indian nuclear plan threatens global stability", *The News International*, 26 August, 1999.

66. Faraz Hashmi, "Nuclear Deterrence Vital to Security: Musharraf Rules out Compromise", *Dawn* (Internet Edition), June 26, 2001.

67. Ibid.

68. Paolo Cotta-Ramusino and Maurizio Martellini, *Nuclear Safety, Nuclear*

Stability and Nuclear Strategy in Pakistan (Como: Landau Network, January 2002).

69. General Kidwai later denied the use of the wording of the contingencies.

70. The wording of these thresholds is that of the Italian interviewers, Paolo Cotta-Ramusino and Maurizio Martellini, see note above, p. 5.

71. Nayyar, "Pakistan can make an A-Bomb", *Brasstacks*, p. 30.

72. "Knocking at the Nuclear Door", *Time* magazine, April 30, 1987.

73. Ibid.

74. Hersh, "Nuclear Edge", p. 64.

75. Ibid.

76. Cohen, et. al., *Compound Crisis*, pp. 98-102.

77. Quoted in Devin Haggerty, "Nuclear Deterrence in South Asia: the 1990 Indo-Pakistan Crisis", *International Security*, vol. 20, no.3 (Winter 1995-96).

78. According to Timothy Hoyt, "Nuclear threats, usually veiled, were part and parcel of the crisis." Timothy Hoyt, "Kargil: the Nuclear Dimension", a chapter in a forthcoming book on Kargil by the Naval Postgraduate School, Monterey, California, pp. 12-13. Hoyt cites a source which states that, "Indian and Pakistani officials and leaders exchanged direct or indirect nuclear threats no fewer than 13 times between May 26 and June 30."

79. "India-Pakistan: Kargil Raises Risk of Nuclear War", commentary by Praful Bidwai, *Inter Press Service* (New Delhi), 27 July 1999.

80. Raj Chengappa, *Weapons of Peace* (New Delhi: HarperCollins Publishers India Pvt Ltd, 2000), p. 437. Nuclear weapons, according to this report, were placed at "Readiness State 3" –ready to be mated with delivery systems at short notice. Presumably, this means that they were assembled or virtually assembled.

81. George Perkovich, "Non-Weaponized Deterrence: The Case for Pakistan," *Strategic Studies* (Islamabad), vol. XVII (Autumn-Winter 1994), pp. 142-6.

82. Ibid.

83. Air Commodore (retd.) Jasjit Singh is the Director of IDSA, New Delhi. For his views, see Naeem A. Salik, "A Minimum Deterrent Regime in South Asia" (under publication), pp. 3-4.

84. Ibid.

85. Ibid.

86. Scott Sagan, "The Perils of Proliferation", *International Security*, vol. 18, no. 4 (1994), p. 71

87. Ibid., pp. 71-102.

88. Neil Joeck, *Maintaining Nuclear Stability In South Asia*: Adelphi Paper No: 312 (London: IISS, 1997), pp. 12, 36-48. It needs to be mentioned that this paper was written before the May 1998 nuclear tests.

89. Ibid., p. 13.

90. Kenneth Waltz, *The Spread of Nuclear Weapons: More May Be Better* (London: IISS, 1981), pp. 20-4.

91. Ibid, p. 30.

92. Ashley J. Tellis, *Stability in South Asia* (Santa Monica: Rand Documented Briefing, 1997), p. viii.

93. Tellis, p. 52. It is noteworthy that Tellis' monograph was written before the 1998 nuclear tests.

94. See in Munir Ahmad Khan, "Understanding Pakistan's Nuclear Plans", *News* (Islamabad), March 8, 1995, p. 6.

95. *The US and India*, A Report (Washington DC: Washington Council on Non-Proliferation, 1993), p. 24.

96. Ibid., pp. 24-6.

97. Ibid. p. 26.

98. These views are cited in Mahbubul Haq, "Internal Nuclear Threat to South Asia", *Regional Studies*, vol. xiv, no. (1996), p. 27.

99. Ibid.

100. Op-ed article, "India can no longer beat Pakistan in war", *Nation* (Islamabad) June 4, 1998.

101. Ibid.

102. Mitchell Reiss, *Without the Bomb: Politics of Nuclear Non-Proliferation* (New York: Columbia University Press, 1988), p. 28.

103. Waltz, *More may be better*, pp. 16-17.

104. Andre Beaufre, *Deterrence and Strategy* (London: Faber and Faber, 1995), p. 66.

105. Ibid., p. 26

106. Haggerty, "Nuclear Deterrence", pp. 67-8.

107. Ibid., p. 68.

108. Ashley Tellis, *India's Emerging Nuclear Posture: Between Recess Deterrent and Ready Arsenal* (Santa Monica: RAND, 2001) p. 742.

109. Kamal Matinuddin, *The Nuclearization of South Asia* (Karachi: Oxford University Press, 2002), pp. 171.

Nuclear-capable Navies of India and Pakistan: Impact on the Strategic Environment of Indian Ocean Region

Zafar Nawaz Jaspal

The era in which we are living has challenges of its own. Economic growth has made all of us dependent on access to international markets and resources. Fusion between expanding international commerce and peace is inevitable for the prosperity of mankind. In such a scenario, the peace and free flow of trade through Indian Ocean is not only in the interest of its littoral and hinterland states, but also in the entire world. Unfortunately, the concept from "Indian Ocean as a Zone of Peace" has failed to materialize. Moreover, the May 1998 nuclear tests of India and Pakistan and subsequent developments appear to have a destabilizing effect on the Indian Ocean's strategic environment. In addition, since the last decade India's blue water navy has been on the rise and will have a major influence on the Indian Ocean region's political, strategic and economic environments.

India has been developing its sea-based nuclear assets. Pakistan's force inventories and weapons acquisition policies indicate that its Navy does not possess nuclear capability at present. But one cannot rule out the possibility that in the future Pakistan would equip its Navy with nuclear weapons. This policy shift would be because of Pakistan's primary concern with India's improved nuclear arsenal and Pakistan's deterrence need to reciprocate by reducing asymmetry. Like Indians, Pakistanis are well aware that the nuclear powered, missile-carrying submarines provide assured second-strike capability in the nuclear age. To be precise, a nuclear accident or nuclear battle in the Indian Ocean region is not beyond the realm of possibility. The nuclear accident or war would have perilous repercussions for the international community in general and Indian Ocean littoral and hinterland states in particular. It is because the Indian Ocean provides major sea routes connecting the Middle East, Africa, and East Asia with Europe and the Americas. It carries heavy traffic of petroleum and petroleum products from the oilfields of the Persian Gulf and Indonesia.

Realist international relations theories have been dominating policy-makers mindset in New Delhi and Islamabad. Like Cold-War era realists, they derive their national interest from the international balance of power, and assess the utility of both military and economic instruments of statecraft. Nevertheless, in real terms, India and Pakistan discount the concept of regional unification and overlook the deeper set of connections between economic prosperity and mutual cooperation within the South Asian regional context. In simple words, both India and Pakistan define their respective security in military terms. What are the repercussions of defining security in military terms? How does the nuclear weaponization of the subcontinent affect Indian Ocean region's strategic environment? What could be the processes by which we could cope with the evolving challenges?

The article seeks to examine the anticipated impacts of India-Pakistan's nuclear strategies on the geo-political and geo-economic environment of the Indian Ocean. The repercussions of South Asian nuclearization sound straightforward, yet it is a very complex issue. Therefore, the following discussion begins with a brief overview of the strategic positioning and strategic environment of the Indian Ocean. Subsequently, followed by the discussion about nuclear dimension of India and Pakistan's maritime strategies, this discussion takes into consideration both the theoretical assertions and practical developments which would adversely affect the security environment of the Indian Ocean region. This is followed by the anticipated repercussions of the nuclear weaponization of the subcontinent and recommendations for tackling and decreasing the evolving danger to the regional security arrangements.

Geo-strategic positioning of the Indian Ocean Region

The Indian Ocean is the third largest of the world's five oceans (after the Pacific Ocean and Atlantic Ocean, but larger than the Southern Ocean and Arctic Ocean). Unlike the Atlantic or the Pacific, however, four continents Africa, Asia, Australia, and the frozen Antarctica surround it. Four critically important access waterways or choke points of the Ocean are the Suez Canal (Egypt), Bab-el-Mandeb (Djibouti-Yemen), Strait of Hormuz (Iran-Oman), and Strait of Malacca (Indonesia-Malaysia). Moreover it includes Andaman Sea, Arabian Sea, Bay of Bengal, Great Australian Bight, Gulf of Aden, Gulf of Oman, Mozambique Channel, Persian Gulf, Red Sea, Strait of Malacca, and other tributary water bodies.

The Indian Ocean includes 44 littoral states and eleven hinterland states. The United States, United Kingdom, China, Japan, France and New Zealand are the user countries of the Indian Ocean.[1] For an analysis the Ocean can be divided into six distinct areas of study South Africa, the Red Sea region, the Persian Gulf, South Asia, South East Asia and Australia. Notably, these divisions of the region around the periphery of the Indian Ocean should not be viewed as watertight compartments.

Strategic Environment of the Indian Ocean Region

The British withdrawal from Diego Garcia and subsequent sale of the island to the United States, in the heart of the Indian Ocean in 1968, brought a fundamental shift in the strategic environment of the Ocean.[2] The deep involvement of the super powers as a consequence of cold-war rivalry and instability in the region because of local disputes and regional conflicts between the littoral states resulted in the militarization of the ocean. The non-regional powers justify their military involvement by asserting that the littoral states were unable to ensure the safety of the sea-lanes of communication. Michael Klare opined, "... An interruption in the supply of natural resources would portend severe economic consequences, the major importing countries now consider the protection of this flow a significant national concern... Large energy importers, such as China, Japan, and the major European powers, have made ensuring the stability of their supplies a top priority."[3] Significantly, the Western states are dependent on the import of 50 different strategic materials such as manganese, cobalt, titanium, chromium, platinum, tin, nickel, iron, lead, copper from the Indian Ocean region. European, Japanese, and the United States economies import 70 per cent, 76 per cent, 25 per cent of their crude oil requirements, respectively, from the Indian Ocean. Beside crude oil, the West imports agricultural produce such as tea, coffee, rubber, and sesame in large quantities from littoral states of the Indian Ocean.[4] To be precise, this dependency element has necessitated the emergence of a new Europe-United States-Japan centric alliance or consensus of approach about controlling and managing the natural resources of the Indian Ocean.

The fear among the smaller regional states of the enduring dominance over them by the big local/neighbouring power(s) has often been the cause of inviting non-regional powers into Indian Ocean affairs; for example, the concerns of smaller South Asian states about India, Singapore about Indonesia and Israel about its Arab neighbours. J. N. Dixit, stated that "the tensions of the region are resulting in the presence of foreign military forces of every category in the region, either under the UN umbrella, or under direct bilateral arrangements." [5] Parallel to it, Australia's best defense strategy is taking shelter under the United States military umbrella and India is seeking strategic partnership with the United States. India and Australia are regional powers, but they want to enhance their political and strategic significance by such arrangements with the sole super power.

The military presence of the super powers in the ocean brought a sense of insecurity among the littoral states. The military presence of the non-regional powers and the local disputes led the littoral states to address their insecurity by strengthening their individual military muscles as well as seeking support of the major powers through alliance arrangements. Consequently, the United States and France had openly established military pacts and bases, whereas, the former Soviet Union had denied setting up bases, but found it necessary to maintain a permanent naval presence in the Ocean.[6] This further generated suspicion and mistrust among the littoral states and unleashed an unending arms race among them. Consequently, the region has seen considerable militarization, including the introduction of latest weaponry in the last two decades. Almost every littoral state has missile firing ships and craft. Despite the end of the cold war, the littoral states have failed to address their security dilemma. For instance, none of the seven Gulf Emirates have been able to settle their maritime boundaries.

Importantly, during the Cold War and in the aftermath of it, the overwhelming majority of the littoral states of the Indian Ocean advocated Indian Ocean as a zone of peace, free from intrusion of foreign navies and a Nuclear Weapons Free Zone. These cherished objectives, however, have not been realized due to the multiple interests of the non-regional powers,[7] and the divergent regional political aspirations. The United States war against terrorism and National Strategy to Combat Weapons of Mass Destruction ushered a new era of non-regional interference and military presence in the Indian Ocean. The USA is continuously enhancing military presence in the region by renewed security links with Pakistan, and through its growing relationship with India. Consequently, the Indian Ocean remains strategically an area of multi-polarization, multi-rivalry and volatility.

The security dilemma is more acute in South Asia. The situation remains complex because of demographic, geographical and economic disequilibrium between India and its South Asian neighbours. Perhaps the biggest obstacle to peaceful coexistence in South Asia has been the ongoing tension between India and Pakistan, especially over Kashmir. This tension between India and Pakistan continues to pose the most likely risk of a nuclear exchange. For instance, India mobilized from December 2001 to October 2002 over 700,000 troops on its Western border to dissuade Pakistan from its stance on Kashmir. In summer 1999, India and Pakistan fought a limited war in Kargil along the Line of Control in Kashmir.

It is generally viewed that an escalation from the freedom movement in Indian held Kashmir to conventional war and to nuclear exchanges is a possibility as Kashmir is recognized internationally as a flashpoint between two nuclear neighbours in South Asia. Chris Gange argues that "the risk of an accident leading to nuclear war would be particularly great in South Asia, where there would be almost no time to distinguish between a deliberate launch, an accident, or a false alarm". [8] In addition the spectre of nuke of fissile materials falling into the hands of non-state actors or an odd problem in command & control system remain a security concern.

The possession of nuclear weapons might have prevented escalation of limited border war into total war, but it has not brought any significant change in the military postures of India and Pakistan. Both states have continued a military build-up. They not only have tested nuclear capable short and medium range missiles, but also handed these over to their armed forces. The surface to surface Ghauri-I medium range and Shaheen-I short-range ballistic missiles were handed over to Pakistan Army's Strategic Force Command for induction on January 8, 2003 and March 6, 2003, respectively. [9] India had already handed over her surface to surface Prithvi-I, nuclear-capable short-range ballistic missiles to its army in May/June 1997, [10] which deployed them at some distance from the Pakistan border. Furthermore, India is expected to deploy Agni-I within a year. [11] These developments indicate a drift towards launch-on-warning posture between India and Pakistan.

Sri Lanka is a strategically located island state, that is, neither militarily powerful nor economically strong. Its Armed Forces are designed primarily for internal security and coastal defence. Britain maintained a large naval base at Trincomalee harbour on the East Coast, which lost its military character since the British withdrawal from the Indian Ocean. Recently, India has acquired some rights for the use of Trincomalee on lease from Sri Lanka. This lease will have strategic repercussions for the Indian Ocean region once the Indian plans are fully operational.

A number of littoral states are in the process of developing their sea power and have attained varying degrees of achievement. Geoffrey Till states that "many Indian Ocean states are steadily developing their amphibious forces too. Although this is part of a global trend, such forces seem likely to be of particular utility in South Asia because of the variety of their possible use."[12] Admittedly, the general trend among a majority of the states is one of concern for their self-defence and safeguarding their maritime interests.

India-Pakistan Blue Water Navies: Role of Nuclear Weapons

A nation that has any sort of link with the sea can be termed as a maritime nation. Significantly, any strategic assessment independent of maritime security for a maritime state contradicts the very concept of national security.[13] In the following discussion, however, the term maritime strategy would not be aimed at maritime security, but exclusively associated with naval strategy and war at sea. Ashley J. Tellis states: "All observations pertaining to any tactical balance must be situated within the relevant nation's grand strategy, and in the Indo-Pakistani case in particular, it is geography that plays a pivotal role in determining strategic postures and, inturn, forces inventories and weapons acquisition policies."[14] India and Pakistan have been building up their maritime strike capabilities in the Indian Ocean. It is in this context that the inquiry becomes relevant about India and Pakistan maritime strategies in general and naval strategies in particular.

India and Pakistan's official statements increasingly envisage that both belligerent neighbours would establish a triad based nuclear deterrence. Honore M. Catudal stated: "In fact, there is a growing body of evidence that would indicate that the doctrine of nuclear deterrence serves as a convenient rationalization for the development and deployment of the weapons made available by military technology."[15]

Many Indian and Pakistani strategic analysts argue that sea-based nuclear assets are very important for their credible nuclear deterrence. J. N. Dixit, former Indian Foreign Secretary argued: "The Navy is conceived of as not just, but perhaps the most effective triad of platforms on which nuclear weapons are/can be deployed. Both surface and submarine deployments of nuclear warheads endow a nuclear defense posture, with the virtue of surprise of mobility and survival in case of a first strike by an opponent."[16] In fact, they believe that the submarine's mobility and its invisibility under water not only protect it from a first strike, but also from theft. In the case of a physical accident (as happened to a Soviet ballistic missile submarines), the vessel simply sinks into deep water, with minimal environmental effects.

India

India has maritime boundaries with as many as seven countries. India's interests are inextricably linked with the Indian Ocean. Therefore, it has deep and enduring interests in the strategic environment of the Ocean. In the post cold war international order, New Delhi seems comfortable with the emergence of the United States as the sole super power and a dominating Indian Ocean player. P. S. Das, the former Indian Commander-in-Chief, Eastern Naval Command stated: "However, there is no basic conflict between core American interests and Indian concerns, and in fact there are several areas of convergence. It is, therefore, possible to evolve strategies, which further our interests in the new global environment."[17] At the same time, the Indians consider another non-littoral Indian Ocean user state, China, a potential adversary. China's relations with Myanmar and Pakistan[18], its facilities in the Coco Islands off the Andaman and its ability to influence political postures in many Indian Ocean littoral states figure prominently in India's security calculus. In the evolution of India's nuclear policy, which Prime Minister A. B. Vajpayee submitted to the Indian Parliament on May 27, 1998, he stated that "the decades of the 80s and 90s witnessed the gradual deterioration of our security environment as a result of nuclear and missile proliferation. In our neighborhood, nuclear weapons increased and more sophisticated delivery systems were inducted. It is a Pakistan specific allegation and can be deleted. [19]

Many Indian analysts believe that build up of India's own navy would ultimately neutralize the naval power of foreigners in the Indian Ocean region and ensure its own impressive status. The motto of the Indian Navy is "Sanho-Varunah," which means let the Lord of the Seas Neptune be our companion, our protector. Implicit in the motto is the concept that the navy is a major factor in the sustenance of Indian security, as are the navies of other countries in relation to their security.[20] This professed concern for security in the Indian Ocean region is not a recent development. The late Prime Minister Jawaharlal Nehru summed up India's concerns regarding the Indian Ocean region in 1958 when he stated. "History has shown that whatever power controls the Indian Ocean has, in the first instance, India's sea-borne trade at her mercy, and in the second India's very independence itself." [21]

Though the Indian Navy remains the most powerful in

the Central and South Asian region, the Indian Naval Doctrine 2000 stressed the need to have a fleet capable of operating in both Eastern and Western Indian Ocean by having two operational aircraft carriers and highly capable submarines.[22] On August 17, 1999, an officially constituted advisory panel to the Indian National Security Council released the draft of its nuclear doctrine which awaits a formal approval of the Indian parliament. Nevertheless the Draft of Nuclear Doctrine is an important document, which discloses India's nuclear policy. According to it, India's nuclear policy appears to be too ambitious in the sense that an upper limit of nuclear capability is not clearly delineated. According to Bharat Karnad, "the deterrent in the Indian definition is, therefore, minimum, relative only to the existing American and Russian inventories, each numbering in tens of thousands of nuclear armaments."[23]

Moreover, a reference to a nuclear triad of aircraft, mobile land-based missiles and sea-based assets was made in the draft. The notable point here is that the Indian government and the strategic community have always made a pretext of threat of China for India's nuclear weapons program. But its maritime strategy reveals its ambitious agenda, which it desires to accomplish by its overt nuclearization, that is to deny Chinese and the United States presence in the Indian Ocean. In December 1998, the Standing Committee on Defense in the Lok Sabha recommended that the government "review and accelerate its nuclear policy for fabricating or acquiring nuclear submarines to add to the deterrent potential of the Indian Navy in the face of the presence of the subsurface nuclear submarines and subsurface ballistic nuclear submarines of China and the United States in the Indian Ocean."[24]

In 1998, India set out to introduce nuclear reactor technologies by acquiring on lease a Charlie-1class nuclear powered cruise missile submarine from the Russian Federation. It is estimated that the construction of a prototype will be completed around 2006 and the vessel will be ready for missile loading in 2010.[25] Raja Menon argues that a nuclear submarine is undetectable "... An Indian nuclear submarine could possibly be on either side of the peninsula without anyone knowing about it. Its undetectability makes the command system confident that retribution can be made unhurriedly after careful evaluation, and that the effect on the enemy would be catastrophic."[26]

India is placing extensive resources towards the development of submarine-launched cruise missiles (SLCM). An India SLCM Sagarika is likely to be nuclear capable and would be carried by a Russian kilo-class submarine. In April 2000 India had tested Dhanush, a naval version of its short range Prithvi SSM, from a launch pad in the Bay of Bengal.[27] It was reported in the *Indian Defence Yearbook 2002* that Dhanush will soon be integrated into the Indian Navy.[28] It was also reported that India has a plan to equip some of its principle surface combatants with the Brahmos supersonic nuclear capable missiles. The decks have been cleared for the induction of French made Scorpene submarines in the Indian Navy.[29] Significantly, there is a strong pro-nuclear submarine lobby in India. Matin Zuberi, former member, National Security Advisory Board, argued: "The nuclear-powered, missile-carrying submarines, protected by mobility and by the shroud of concealment provided by the waters surrounding it, will continue to ensure second strike survivability in the nuclear age."[30]

Pakistan

Despite the recent thaw, Islamabad does not expect a major strategic change in India's hostile posturing in a long term perspective. In the aftermath of nuclear weaponization of subcontinent, in pure military terms, most of Pakistani analysts believe that India cannot impose total war against Pakistan. They argue that any such military misadventure would lead to its own detriment including a possible nuclear armageddon. The conclusion, however, is inescapable that New Delhi has a grand design for political, military and economic dominance over peoples and territories extending from South Asia to the littoral states of the Indian Ocean. To be precise, a massive, and sudden Indian attack on the LoC and a subsequent total war is the threat that has driven Pakistani strategic planning since Independence, may have lessened due to nuclear weapons but has not ceased to exit.

The strategic mindset in Pakistan has heretofore perceived the balance of power between India and Pakistan mainly as strenuous interactions between land and air force. The clearest evidence of this pervasive land-oriented mindset is the defensive strategies developed since 1947 by Pakistan. Though the continental concept of strategy has been a determining factor in the making of Pakistan's defense strategy, the situation is bound to change in the post-May 1998 strategic environment, particularly since 2002 eyeball to eyeball confrontation and realization that the United States has been taking a more pro-India policy.[31] In fact, during April-May 2002, the Indian Navy was reportedly ready to impose a naval blockade against Karachi, having transferred five principal surface combatants from the Eastern to the Western Indian Ocean for this purpose.[32]

Importantly, the bulk of Pakistan's foreign trade moves by sea. Unlike India's grand strategic designs, Pakistan has set a very modest role for its naval forces. The first and foremost responsibility of the Pakistan Navy is defence of the 830-kilometre coastline. This includes securing Karachi harbour and the smaller ports of Gwader, Jiwani, Rasormarah, and Pasni.[33] The Indian naval build-up fuels suspicions, fears and causes apprehensions in Pakistan because of historical antagonism and proximity. Therefore, majority of analysts believes that for the credibility of its sea denial strategy, Pakistan must start strengthening its navy now. Otherwise, it is likely to face block obsolescence in times to come.

Notwithstanding various constraints, Pakistan has not only continued to induct modern weapons like the modified Agosta-class submarines, it has also initiated a modest ship-building project. Admittedly, Pakistan's nuclear weapons force posture indicates that it lacks sea-based nuclear assets. It has nuclear capable aircraft and mobile land-based missiles. Nevertheless, the Pakistani Navy is seen as becoming nuclear capable in the near future. This assertion is based on the following facts:

- Pakistan lacks strategic depth, which means that the core of its striking air and armored forces are within easy reach of the international border. Thus, geography dictates that a nuclear capable navy is the best form of deterrence, which in practical terms means to enhance survivability of retaliatory forces. Submarines, loaded with nuclear capable submarine launched missiles, cruising in Ocean waters can easily save themselves from the adversary's preemptive strikes.

- Interstate violence becomes more frequent when vast asymmetries develop in weapons capabilities of nations and there is no balance of power. Therefore, Pakistan cannot separate the implications of nuclearization of Indian Navy from its overall military capability. In both war and peace, India would mobilize its combined military power to achieve its political and strategic objectives. Hence, Pakistan is forced to revise its maritime strategy.[34] In brief, the nuclear capable Pakistan Navy would ensure that there is no gross asymmetry in weapons capabilities between India and Pakistan.

Impact on Strategic Environment of Indian Ocean

Though it is always difficult to predict the course of world events, there is no doubt that India and Pakistan's nuclear weaponization would increase the security dilemma of the Indian Ocean's littoral states, especially in a situation when the peace zone concept is a matter of speculation.[35] India's nuclear strategy has also discarded the concept of making Indian Ocean a nuclear weapons free zone. Each littoral or hinterland or user state interprets India and Pakistan's nuclear weaponization according to its own strategic environment and its relations with them.

It is unfair to blame India and Pakistan alone for nuclearizing the Indian Ocean. The Indian Ocean has already been converted into a launching base, as well as a target base for nuclear weapons since the British withdrawal from Diego Garcia and subsequent sale of the island to the United States in 1968. Donald L. Berlin observes that "Diego Garcia has been developed from a small communications station to track submarines to a multipurpose base. The development of Diego

Garcia is continuing."[36] The development and maintenance of the American Naval base at Diego Garcia indicated that during the cold war they were not ignoring the increasing influence of the former Soviet Union in the region.

It is not a misleading assessment that the United States and the former Soviet Union's competition for military superiority in the Indian Ocean served as a catalyst for India to develop nuclear weapons. Notably, the United States Navy maintained the policy of neither confirming nor denying the presence or absence of nuclear weapons on its vessels. In 1974, retired Vice Admiral Gene R. La Rocque stated: "My experience has been that any ship that is capable of carrying nuclear weapons, carries nuclear weapons. They do not off-load them when they go into foreign ports such as Japan or other countries."[37] On March 23, 1963, Ram Chandra Bade, Jan Sangh Parliamentarian, said in the Lok Sabha (Indian Lower House of the Parliament), "only those who wish to see Russians or Chinese ruling India will oppose the development of nuclear weapons".[38] K. Subrahmanyam stated: "The ability of three nuclear weapons states, the United States, Britain, and France to devastate a non-nuclear weapon state, Yugoslavia, while the other two nuclear weapons states, Russia and China, could do nothing to stop it, reinforces the Indian case for pushing a credible minimum nuclear deterrent."[39] Similarly, the objective of Pakistan's pursuit of nuclear weapons was to neutralize both India's conventional superiority and nuclear capability.

The perilous nuclear arms race between India and Pakistan has been undermining regional security. It is increasing the likelihood of a nuclear showdown both by accident or by design. India and Pakistan's nuclear strategies suggest that they may wage nuclear war not solely along their continental frontier. Their naval forces may also conduct nuclear related offensive and defensive operations, in a future total war. Any war between these belligerent neighbours would be extremely destructive for them, but one in which the Indian Ocean is a theatre of the war could be equally destructive for the littoral states. The increasing emphasis on nuclear weapons, is a reflection of what has been called the "deadly trinity" in which weapons are gaining in range, becoming more precise and more deadly.

The following are some of the important areas of impact:

Regional Hegemony

Naval forces can be used to compel an adversary to do something he does not want to do, or to deter him from doing something he wants to. The recent Gulf war illustrates the various ways in which naval forces can be used. The Coalition naval forces also played an important role in military victory in Iraq. A strong blue water navy of India increases the security dilemma of the neighbouring littoral states. Geoffrey Till argues: "In the Indian Ocean area the inevitable disparity between the maritime forces of India and everyone else naturally raises concerns and tensions (especially when there are other things in dispute as well)."[40]

India has maritime boundaries with seven countries. In addition, more than a thousand miles from the Indian mainland, the Andaman and Nicobar Islands lie at the mouth of the Malacca Strait, the second busiest sea-lane in the world. Vice Admiral Arun Prakash stated: "They (Andaman and Nicobar) could be lucrative objects of desire for any country, which may harbour ambitions of dominating the Bay of Bengal and holding to ransom, vital sea-lanes of communications. At the same time, they form a springboard from where India can reach out and project power, exert influence or strike bonds of friendship in with our eastern neighbours."[41] In brief, nuclear weaponization of the Indian Navy ensures India's emergence as a dominating power in the Indian Ocean region at the cost of endangering the security of other states. Consequently, in times of crisis, the Indian Navy could opt for a blockade strategy for dictating its own terms and conditions.

A militarily strong Pakistan can counter any outside threat to the continuous flow of oil and gas supplies from the Gulf. Pakistan sits astride the sea-lanes out of the Persian Gulf and that fact of geography allows it adequate opportunity to neutralise any attempt at naval blockade of the oil tanker sea lanes from the Gulf easily from its bases on the Makran Coast. However, Pakistan has no designs for domination, nor should its neighbours feel uncomfortable with its nuclear capable navy, which has purely defensive portents. Yet India also showed its uneasiness over Pakistan's efforts for correcting the naval balance of power between the two countries. While commenting on India about a stronger Pakistan Mohan Malik wrote: "India also worries that a stronger Pakistan, aided by the United States, Europe, Japan, and international financial institutions, would not only be better able to contain India, but also continue its hostile policies."[42]

Freedom of Navigation

The safety and security of Indian Ocean shipping is a vital concern of many countries around the world. The major east-west sea-lanes, from the Indian Ocean pass through two choke points, the Straits of Malacca in the east and the Gulf of Aden and Suez Canal in the west. More than half of the oil exported through the Gulf of Hormuz, passes through the Straits of Malacca. Kenneth M. Pollack argues: "America's primary interest in the Persian Gulf lies in ensuring the free and stable flow of oil from the region to the world at large."[43]

It seems possible for a power exercising control of these choke points to seriously interfere with the interests of others.[44] India's feverish arms build-up and its hegemonic ambitions may disrupt the freedom of navigation in the Indian Ocean. In fact, India lies within striking distance of these choke points. Any future conflict between India and Pakistan could threaten the Indian Ocean's freedom of navigation because they would use their naval power for their military objectives and the seabed for their nuclear submarine's strategic manoeuvres. In addition, here one cannot ignore India's desire to free the Indian Ocean from Western colonialism and dominate it by itself. The pursuit of this objective would have serious repercussions for the navigating states of the Indian Ocean.

Horizontal Proliferation of Nuclear Weapons

Proliferation begets proliferation. This is understandable, because any new political entity endowed with additional military capacities disturbs the security and strategic status quo. The point to remember, however, is that several Indian Ocean rim states such as Israel, South Africa[45] and Iran have harboured a desire to develop nuclear weapons. At the same time the potentialities of Japan could not be underestimated.[46] The May 1998 nuclear explosions by India and Pakistan and their intention to disburse their nuclear deterrence among the three military forces have a nuclear weapons' proliferating impact on the strategic policies of these states. Thus, there are ample chances that in the near future they would employ the Indian

Ocean as a patrol zone for submarine or surface warships equipped with nuclear-armed missiles.

Nuclear Weapon States' Competition

The United States, Russian Federation, European countries, Japan and China have vital interests in the Indian Ocean region. The proliferation of nuclear weapons and expansion of Indian naval strength would worry these user states. While analyzing India's nuclear deterrence objectives Raju G. C. Thomas states: "These ballistic missile and space rocket programs suggest the intention to create a global nuclear deterrent that goes beyond India's regional rivals, China and Pakistan, to the other major nuclear powers."[47] The nuclear weapons, certainly, enhance the military potential and political influence of India and Pakistan. Being adjacent to choke points India more than Pakistan could impose stricter regulations on passing ships and oil tankers than those generally accepted by the international maritime community for the sake of political, strategic and economic benefits. While examining the salience of the Indian Ocean, Donald Berlin wrote, ".... New Delhi's interest in the affairs of this Ocean will grow, and this will be accompanied by a growing interest of others-especially major states-in these waters, either to check India or to ally with it."[48]

There is, at present, nuclear naval presence of the United States and China in the Indian Ocean. Though it is not quite clear about similar Russian Federation naval presence, its possibility cannot be denied. The United States and China would further strengthen their naval presence in the Ocean with all types of weapons in order to meet challenges posed by the newly emergent nuclear weapon states of South Asia. The United States strategic partnership with India indicates that

Western states and Japan would protect their interest in Indian Ocean by allying with India, instead of checking it. Beijing's course of action, however, would be strengthening its strategic posture in the area. China has been enhancing its strategic relations with its Indian Ocean littoral allies-Pakistan and Burma-by developing the port at Gwadar in Pakistan and building a naval base near Kyaukpyu and naval and air base near Kawthaung off the Tenasserim Coast, in Burma.[49]

The naval build-up of China would instigate the United States to increase its naval forces in the Indian Ocean region. In fact, the primary strategic objective of the United States in the post cold war era is to prevent the reemergence of a new rival similar to its cold war competitor the former Soviet Union.[50] Joseph S. Nye Jr. opined that "George W. Bush entered office committed to a realist foreign policy that would focus on great powers such as China and Russia…China was to be a strategic competitor not the strategic partner of Bill Clinton's era, and the United States was to take a tougher stance with Russia."[51] The strategic competition between India and China, and China and the United States would produce a new geography of conflict in the Indian Ocean, that would negatively influence the peace and prosperity of the Indian Ocean littoral and hinterland states.

Ecological Impact

India and Pakistan's nuclear programes have serious ecological implications for the Indian Ocean region. Nuclear waste dumping in the Indian ocean pollutes the ocean. In addition, both India and Pakistan's offensive and defensive strategies indicate that they would operationalize their sea-based arms of their nuclear triad during the war. Any nuclear related mishap at sea or authorized or unauthorized use of nuclear weapons would not only harm the maritime life at the ocean, it would also have long-term backlash for maritime states.

The ocean environment governs climate conditions. Geoffrey Till writes: "Even more fundamentally, and although we do not fully understand the way it works, the ocean is not just a barometer but also a regulator of the world climate to the extent that the physical health of the planet may depend on that of the ocean."[52] In brief, a nuclear accident would negatively affect the fisheries industry, which is already facing catastrophic depletion in many areas.

Recommendations

That India and Pakistan are nuclear-weapon states is a reality people cannot just ignore. Therefore, the nuclearization of their navies would be a matter of vital and continuing concern. The Indian Ocean's security and peace requires the promotion of existing peace initiatives coupled with innovative approaches to reduce and finally exclude the prospects of micro-level and macro-level conflicts and destructive competition between India and Pakistan, so that the Indian Ocean littoral states exploit the Ocean's economic resources for their economic prosperity. Following are a few recommendations for achieving such objectives:

- Despite the end of the Cold War, the creation of the Indian Ocean as a Zone of Peace is not an exercise in futility, as the western nations concluded in 1989. All the states of the Indian Ocean would support the concept of a zone of peace. It would not only serve as a bulwark against non-regional intruders, it would also reduce the arms race among the Indian Ocean's littoral states.

- India and Pakistan must define their security paradigms in economic, not just military, terms. They should opt for a way to alter their military competition into economic competition by institutionalizing bilateral, regional, and international economic cooperation. The two sides should conclude an agreement on prevention of incidents at sea in order to ensure safety of navigation by naval vessels, and aircrafts belonging to the two sides.

- The proper approach to tackle nuclear dangers in the Indian Ocean is to seek to create an equitable global regime that actively devalues nuclear weapons and creates conditions for their eventual elimination. The first step in this regard could be the creation of the Indian Ocean as a nuclear weapon free zone and the implementation of the February 1999 Lahore summit's Memorandum of Understanding between India and Pakistan.

- India and Pakistan should exercise restraint in using their naval power lest they prove counter-productive. Their non-provocative attitude and positive interaction could make a constructive contribution to arms control, reduction of arms and defense expenditure, and perhaps ultimately, to the process of genuine disarmament in the region.

- Pakistan and India must exploit the commonality of interests within the region, which includes oil/gas pipelines laid from Iran, Persian Gulf and Central Asia to India across Pakistan. Jasjit Singh opines that "the best techno-economic method of supply of natural gas from the huge reserves of these areas is by an overland pipeline. The other options, of offshore transportation of natural gas, whether by surface ships, by sub-surface pipeline in shallow waters or those laid in deep sea, would be costlier to build by 30 per cent or more, and to maintain and repair."[53] These pipelines could also be outlets for Japan, to be picked up from the Indian ports. Such an arrangement could not only facilitate the supply, but also build confidence and trust among the conflicting parties resulting in conflict reduction.

Conclusion

India and Pakistan's preoccupation with the military dimension of statecraft and the deadly rivalry between them has not only endangered their own strategic environment, but also jeopardized that of the Indian Ocean region. India is determined to strengthen and equip its blue-water navy with nuclear weapons. Moreover, the end of the cold war terminated super power confrontation in the Indian Ocean, but it has not minimized the regional conflicts and major powers' military presence in the Indian Ocean. In this scenario, we are likely to see increasing nuclearization of the Indian Ocean and perpetual threat to the economic security of the Indian Ocean rim states. Consequently, it could hinder the free flow of international trade through the Indian Ocean in the future.

Anticipatory and timely actions are essential for the Indian Ocean region's peace and security. It is imperative that India and Pakistan opt for an ahistorical, apolitical method(s) of articulating the right answers to their nuclear weapons related problems. They should settle their mutual differences by peaceful means and avoid mating of their nuclear warheads with delivery systems and deployment of these lethal weapons. At the same time, they should try and build mutual interdependence. A mutual interdependence approach would start to build stakeholders on both sides to exert pressure for co-operative peace rather than looking for ways to bleed each other to death. This is also where the international community could play a constructive role.

In sum, the great powers also take into account the economic prospects of creating Indian Ocean as a zone of peace and relinquish their struggle for power and military postures in the Indian Ocean. It is timely for users and littoral states to step up discussions on the concepts of Indian Ocean as a zone of peace and nuclear weapon free zone.

* Zafar Nawaz Jaspal is Assistant Professor at the Department of International Relations, Quaid-i-Azam University, Islamabad, Pakistan. (Re-printed with permission from Islamabad Policy Research Institute Journal, Pakistan, Winter 2004.)

Endnotes

1. Pervaiz Iqbal Cheema, "Conflict and Cooperation in the Indian Ocean: Pakistan's Interest and Choices", *Canberra Report on Strategy and Defence: No 23,* (Australia: Australian National University: 1980), p. 5

2. The United States military presence in the Indian Ocean could be traced to the end of World War II. In 1948, the Americans raised their own Middle Eastern Force.

3. Michael. T. Klare, "The New Geography of Conflict", *Foreign Affairs,* vol. 80, no. 3 May/June 2001, pp. 49-61.

4. V. S. Sheth, "Indian Ocean in a Globalising World", *Journal of Indian Ocean Studies,* vol. 10, no. 3, December 2002, p.348.

5. J. N. Dixit, "Role of Navies in Asia's Regional Security", *Journal of Indian Ocean Studies,* vol. 9, no. 2, August 2001, p. 175.

6. Kamal Kumar, *Indian Ocean as a Zone of Peace: Problems and Prospects* (New Delhi: A.P.H. Publishing Corporation, 2000), p. 15.

7. Today, the United States aircraft carriers constantly conduct surveillance while its submarines patrol the Indian Ocean's depth.

8. Chris Gagne, "Nuclear Risk Reduction in South Asia: Building on Common Ground", in Michael Krepon and Chris Gagne, ed., *The Stability-Instability Paradox: Nuclear Weapons and Brinkmanship in South Asia,* Report No. 38 (Washington, DC: The Henry L. Stimson Center, June 2001), p. 40.

9. "Pakistan N-power with assured delivery system", *The Nation,* January 9, 2003. Rana Qaisar, "Pakistan Army gets Hatf-V missiles" *Daily Times,* January 9, 2003. "Hatf-IV handed over to army", *Dawn,* March 7, 2003.

10. "Indian Pakistani Missile Activities, Accelerate As Bilateral Talks Continue", *Arms Control Today* (June/July 1997), p. 24.

11. "Agni-I ready for induction into Indian armed forces", *The Daily Times,* May 12, 2003.

    <http://www.dailytimes.com.pk/default.asp?page=story_12-5-2003_pg4_14>

12. Geoffrey Till, "Regional Naval Trends in the Indian Ocean", in *Indian Ocean: Security and Stability in the Post-Cold War Era* (Rawalpindi: The Army Press, 1995), p. 30.

13. In a modern international political set up not only the littoral states alone are maritime states, but also all the nations in today's world could be considered members of the maritime states club because of their dependence on the sea. Prabhakaran Palen, "Maritime Security and Concept of Ocean Property", *Journal of Indian Ocean Studies,* vol. 10, no.1, April 2002, pp. 18, 20, 21.

14. Ashley J. Tellis, "The Naval Balance in the Indian Subcontinent: Demanding Missions for the Indian Navy", *Asian Survey,* vol. xxv, no. 12, December 1985, p. 1187.

15. Honore M. Catudal, *Nuclear Deterrence—Does it Deter?* (New Jersey: Humanities Press International Inc., 1986), p. 40.

16. J. N. Dixit, "Role of Navies in Asia's Regional Security", *Journal of Indian Ocean Studies,* vol. 9, no. 2, August 2001, p. 175.

17. P. S. Das, "Indian Ocean Region in India's Security Calculus", *Journal of Indian Ocean Studies,* vol. 9, no. 3, December 2001, p. 320.

18. On 18 July 2003 the agreement was reached between China and Pakistan to conduct joint maritime exercise. It was reported that it would be for the first time that People's Liberation Army Navy would be conducting joint maritime exercise with any foreign navy. "Pakistan, China plan joint naval exercise", *The News* (Rawalpindi), 19 July 2003, p. 1. A short while later, China also conducted naval exercises with India.

19. *East Asian Strategic Review 2002* (Japan: The National Institute for Defense Studies, 2002), pp. 109, 110.

20. J. N. Dixit, "Role of Navies in Asia's Regional Security", *Journal of Indian Ocean Studies,* vol. 9, no. 2, August 2001, p. 168.

21. Colonel Gregory Allen Harding, "Implications of the Expansion of Indian Naval Power", *NDC Journal* (2000), p. 29.

22. *The Military Balance 2002-2003*, International Institute of Strategic Studies (London: Oxford University Press, October 2002), p 125.

23. Bharat Karnad, "India's Force Planning Imperative: The Thermonuclear Option", in D. R. SarDesai and Raju G. C. Thomas, ed. *Nuclear India in the Twenty-First Century* (New York: Palgrave-Macmillan, 2002), p. 107.

24. *East Asian Strategic Review 2002,* Op. Cit., p. 123.

25. Ibid., pp. 123, 124.

26. Rear Admiral Raja Menon, *A Nuclear Strategy for India* (New Delhi: Sage Publications, 2000), p. 225.

27. The test was not that successful with the missile travelling only 20-25 kilometers before plunging into the sea. See Ben Sheppard, "Ballistic Missiles: Complicating the Nuclear Quagmire", in D. R. SarDesai and Raju G. C. Thomas, ed., Op. Cit., p. 196.

28. Lt. General (Retd.) R. K. Jasbir Singh, edit., *Indian Defence Yearbook 2002* (Dehradun, Natraj Publishers, 2002), p. 359.

29. Ibid, p. 360.

30. Matin Zuberi, "Nuclear Oceans", *Journal of Indian Ocean Studies,* vol. 10, no. 1, April 2002, p. 12.

31. India is valued in the United States foreign and strategic policies because of its potential as a trade market, democratic values and above all as a hedge against China's prominence.

32. *The Military Balance 2002-2003*, Op. cit, p 126.

33. Rasul Bakhsh Rais, "Pakistan's Maritime Interests and Policy", in *Indian Ocean: Security and Stability in the Post-Cold War Era* (Rawalpindi: The Army Press, 1995), pp. 189, 190. For more details about Pakistan Navy see Pervaiz Iqbal Cheema, *The Armed Forces of Pakistan* (Karachi: Oxford University Press, 2002), pp. 97-99

34. Pakistan nuclear program has been developed almost exclusively as a counterweight to India's size and conventional military superiority and in response to India's own nuclear program. John B. Wolfsthal, "Asia's Nuclear Dominos?", *Current History,* vol. 102, no. 663, April 2003, p.172.

35. Since 1971 to date, despite some 450 meetings of the United Nation's Ad Hoc Committee on the Indian Ocean, the contemplated Zone of Peace still has to come up. Moreover, the key western members of the committee withdrew from this body in 1989, arguing that superpower rivalry in the Indian Ocean had been diminished with the end of the cold war and, therefore, creation of a Zone of Peace would be a purposeless exercise. Donald L. Berlin, "Indian Ocean Redux—Arms, Bases and Re-emergence of Strategic Rivalry", *Journal of Indian Ocean Studies,* vol. 10, no. 1, April 2002, p. 27.

36. Ibid., p, 32.

37. Matin Zuberi, Op. Cit., p. 3.

38. Akhtar Ali, *Pakistan's Nuclear Dilemma-Energy and Security Dimensions* (Karachi: Economic Research Unit, 1984), p. 34.

39. K. Subrahmanyam, "India and the International Nuclear Order", in D. R. SarDesai and Raju G. C. Thomas, ed. Op. Cit, p. 64.

40. Geoffrey Till, "International Maritime Trends and Indian Ocean in 21st Century", *Journal of Indian Ocean Studies,* vol. 9, no. 2, August 2001, p. 161.

41. Vice Admiral Arun Prakash, "Evolution of the Joint Andaman and Nicobar Command and Defence of Our Island Territories (Part 11)", *The Journal of the United Services Institution of India,* vol. cxxxiii, no. 551, January-March 2003, p. 23.

42. Mohan Malik, "High Hopes: India's Response to US Security Policies", *Asian Affairs An American Review,* vol. 30, no. 2, Summer 2003, p. 107.

43. The reason the United States has a legitimate and critical interest in seeing that Persian Gulf oil continues to flow copiously and relatively cheaply is simply that the global economy built over the last 50 years rests on a foundation of inexpensive, plentiful oil, and if that foundation were removed, the global economy would collapse. See Kenneth M. Pollack, "Securing the Gulf", *Foreign Affairs,* vol. 82, no 4, July/August 2003, p. 3.

44. The British had recognized these features early and set about exercising their suzerainty through a chain of naval bases, suitably garrisoned with adequate naval forces to ensure control. Once they withdrew, the Americans entered the scene and their bases in the Gulf and at Diego Garcia provide them power to transform the Indian Ocean strategic environment according to their will. P. S. Das, Op. Cit., p. 317.

45. South Africa renounced its nuclear weapons program. After dismantling its nuclear weapon, South Africa joined Nuclear Non-proliferation Treaty as a regime, non-possessor of nuclear weapons in 1991. For how long it would stick with this policy in a changed strategic environment is a matter of debate.

46. Japan does not possess nuclear weapons. However, it can easily develop them, once any such political decision is taken and in a very short span of time. The factor fuelling such suspicions are: Japan is continuing its research and development work on its 'Fast Breeder' reactors for power generation even after the majority of countries have given up the technology as impracticable, and it has been stockpiling plutonium that could be used in nuclear weapons. Secondly, the impact of domino theory - in case North Korea conducts nuclear tests and declares itself a Nuclear Weapon State. In sum, Japan has its capability ready in the basement.

47. Raju G. C. Thomas, "Whither Nuclear India", in D. R. SarDesai and Raju G. C. Thomas, ed.. Op. Cit., p. 11.

48. Donald L. Berlin, Op. Cit., p. 28.

49. China plans for a security and commercial alternative to the Pacific Ocean—an Irrawaddy corridor linking China directly to the Indian Ocean through Burma. For the relevant details about China's modernizing naval equipment and training its personnel see *East*

Asian Strategic Review 2003 (Tokyo: The National Institute For Defense Studies, June 2003), pp. 192-194.

50. An important Pentagon planning document stated in 1992, "Our strategy must now refocus on precluding the emergence of any potential future global competitor." See John J. Mearsheimer, "The Future of the American Pacifier", *Foreign Affairs,* vol. 80, no. 5, September/October 2001, p. 46.

51. Joseph S. Nye, Jr., "US Power and Strategy After Iraq", *Foreign Affairs,* vol. 82, No. 4, July/August 2003. For the United States and China relations see also Denny Roy, "A Late Honeymoon for Bush and China: Enjoy It While It Lasts", *Asian Affairs An American Review,* vol. 30, no. 2, Summer 2003, pp. 79-87.

52. Geoffrey Till, "International Maritime Trends and Indian Ocean in 21st Century", *Journal of Indian Ocean Studies,* vol. 9, no. 2, August 2001, p. 159.

53. Jasjit Singh, "Not a pipe dream", *The Indian Express*, July 23, 2003. *<http://www.indianexpress.com/full_story.php?content_id=28120 > accessed on July 30, 2003.*

Pakistan and India: Can NRRCs Help to Strengthen the Peace?

Rafi uz Zaman Khan

Pakistan and India are currently experiencing the worst phase of their relations since 1971. While their armed forces have recently demobilized, none of the underlying disputes have been resolved and the risk of adventurism remains. Any conflict has the potential to escalate into a full-scale war. Following the nuclearization of South Asia, the potential for renewed escalation between these two traditional enemies has assumed horrific significance. Conflict remains unpredictable and may not necessarily remain conventional. The concepts of limited war and pre-emption are fraught with danger and may no longer be applicable in South Asia. General Pervez Musharraf has said that let there be no doubt that the doctrine of pre-emptive strike does not apply in the context of India and Pakistan – at least not in the foreseeable future.[1] Admiral L. Ramdas, former Indian Chief of Naval Staff, and Arjun Makhijani, a US-based nuclear scientist, have argued that by going nuclear India has lost its conventional superiority over Pakistan. Consequently, both Ramdas and Makhijani have advocated a conventional and nuclear ceasefire plan for the two countries.[2] A number of military analysts have thus ruled out the option of a conventional war between India and Pakistan as a method of conflict resolution.[3]

Since the partition of the subcontinent, the Kashmir dispute has been the *raison d'être* for hostility between India and

Pakistan. The two countries have fought three conventional wars and one limited war in the past, and the level of animosity remains high. Numerous bilateral efforts, in the form of various confidence-building measures and nuclear risk reduction measures, have failed to bring lasting peace to South Asia. These measures, in addition to lacking certain key elements, have not addressed future conflict resolution or avoidance, nor have they dealt with the prime irritants. Kashmir is considered to be the "nuclear flashpoint" in the region. Following the nuclearization of South Asia, President Clinton described Kashmir as "the most dangerous place in the world."[4] India and Pakistan continue to teeter on the precipice of war.

In the subcontinent, CBMs and NRRMs have failed due to a lack of trust and of strong political will, as well as the marked absence of a dispute resolution mechanism and the means to enforce it. The possession[5] of nuclear weapons makes a resolution by force of the Kashmir dispute unlikely. As long as Pakistan can flatten India five times over, does it matter if India can flatten Pakistan twenty times?[6] The longer India and Pakistan remain estranged, the more distrust builds and the more both sides expect the worst from each other. Conditions for stable deterrence are absent, and an accident or miscalculation during a crisis has become increasingly possible. As both nations struggle to adapt to the "stability-instability paradox", should they be left alone at the nuclear brink to deliberately or inadvertently let out the nuclear genie, causing both nations to suffer the consequences?

CBMs and NRRMs assume great significance in such situations, but in the aftermath of South Asian nuclearization, and given the pathetic history of past CBMs in South Asia, a greater need exists for a concrete arrangement for building trust and preventing misperceptions. Besides introducing measures to resolve the Kashmir issue politically –without which no confidence-building or nuclear-risk reduction measures are likely to succeed it is imperative for the two nations to develop a renewed mechanism to consolidate and expand the current CBMs and NRRMs for uninterrupted and lasting implementation. The establishment of nuclear risk reduction centres (NRRCs) in India and Pakistan might help to realize these objectives.

NRRCs, serving as central message centers for all CBM/ NRRM notifications, would be effective, exclusive, and dedicated technical means of official communication for the rapid exchange of accurate and factual information. This could prevent unintended signals from leading to a crisis or inadvertent nuclear escalation. The centres could also facilitate the identification, negotiation and implementation of additional institutional and procedural arrangements, as well as technical measures intended to reduce nuclear risks. The NRRCs could thus provide technical experts with the means for instantaneous communication in the event of a tragic incident or unusual event. While taking concurrent measures for conflict resolution at the political level to reassure the people, both countries can begin immediately to negotiate the establishment of NRRCs, symbolizing a change of heart within the two governments. The verification and implementation mechanisms built into the NRRCs could help not only to consolidate measures for the implementation of existing CBMs and NRRMs, but also to build the trust and confidence that is essential to strengthening peace. Functioning under an already negotiated, preformatted system to exchange notifications, the NRRCs would not involve any kind of voice communication for crisis resolution, as that might transmit misleading or unintended signals. Also, the NRRCs would never function as a substitute for the political and diplomatic means of communication between the two countries.

The US has played a key role in introducing CBMs between the two countries since the administrations of Ronald Reagan and George W. Bush. [7] Given its active role in crisis prevention in South Asia, the US is still in a position to persuade the two leaderships to establish trust and to stabilize their relations, abandoning nuclear brinkmanship in the interest of their citizens and all of humanity.

In addressing the question of establishing NRRCs between Pakistan and India, one first needs to describe the existing CBMs and NRRMs. Then one needs to ask why these centres are needed, and why NRRCs would work when other CBMs have failed. Would NRRCs have any relation to the Kashmir issue? If so, how much progress on a settlement is required before NRRCs can be established? Or could the two occur simultaneously? Would the establishment of NRRCs help prevent dangerous military activities? Finally, are the NRRCs useful in preventing unintended escalation?

Another important issue relates to the US-Soviet coldwar experience with and arguments for NRRMs and NRRCs. Is that narrative still valid and is it relevant to the subcontinent's security paradigms? Further, what would be the goals of Indian and Pakistani NRRCs and how would they differ from their coldwar counterparts? Successful functioning of the NRRCs requires trust in the given communications. How can trust and confidence be established in this instance?

What are the merits and demerits of establishing NRRCs for South Asia and what could be the likely apprehensions of the citizens? Would NRRCs have a role in crisis management along with the existing political and diplomatic channels of communications? What purpose would the NRRCs not serve? Would they help to improve the poor record of CBM implementation? Given the dissolution of previous Indo-Pak security agreements, how can NRRCs be successfully operationalized? Would the NRRC become the central message centre for all the CBMs and NRRMs notifications to ensure their implementation? How would Pakistan's NRRC function and be organized? Where would it be located? This paper is an attempt to examine and address these questions.

What are CBMs?

CBMs can be broadly divided into three categories: political, military, and socio-economic. In the military realm they have been subdivided into conventional and nuclear CBMs. The latter are commonly known as NRRMs. Following the nuclearization of South Asia, NRRMs have attained greater significance. It is necessary here to define CBMs before making any further deliberations on their evolution and effectiveness in South Asia. According to Johan Jørgen Holst: confidence-building measures (CBMs) may be defined as arrangements designed to enhance assurance of mind and belief in the trust-worthiness of states confidence is the product of much broader patterns of relations than those which relate to military security. In fact, the latter have to be woven into a complex texture of economic, cultural, technical and social relationships.[8]

The concept of CBMs is generally believed to have originated in the 1970s in the backdrop of East-West confrontation. There is, however, sufficient evidence that the concept and process had already existed in various parts of the world, albeit undefined. The most comprehensive, elaborate, and successful model of CBMs to date is found in the Helsinki Final Act of 1975 that was essentially designed for conventional armed forces in Europe.[9] The introduction of transparency and verification elements increased the efficiency of CBMs. CBM terminology was first applied to India-Pakistan relations after the 1987 Brasstacks crisis. The process of CBMs, however, had already existed between India and Pakistan. The 1949 Karachi Agreement, the Liaquat-Nehru Pact of 1950, the India-Pakistan Border Ground Rules Agreement of 1960, the Indus Water Treaty of 1962, the Tashkent Agreement of 1966, and the Simla Agreement of 1972 are cases in point.[10]

The principal CBMs of the last 40 years are:

- Hotline between Military Operation Directorates (1965);
- Agreement on the Prohibition of Attack against Nuclear Installations and Facilities (1988, ratified and implemented in 1992);
- Hotline between prime ministers Benazir Bhutto and Rajiv Gandhi (1989);
- Agreement on Advance Notice of Military Exercises, Maneuvers and Troops Movements (1991);
- Measures to Prevent Air Space Violations and to Permit Over Flights and Landing by Military Aircrafts (1992).[11]

In the Lahore Declaration, the two prime ministers recognized that the nuclear reality of the subcontinent gives each nation the responsibility to avoid conflict. The document indicates that they were convinced of the need for mutually agreed CBMs to improve the security environment.[12] Seven of the eight points in the MOU signed by the foreign secretaries of India and Pakistan on that occasion concerned nuclear risk reduction, an issue that was being addressed for the first time.[13] An item alluding to the prevention of incidents at sea has added significance since India has announced intentions to nuclearize its navy[14] and Pakistan has established the Naval Strategic Force Command.[15]

Why Nuclear Risk Reduction Centers are Needed

Tension and animosity between India and Pakistan has been increased by lack of trust, perpetual suspicion of each other's actions, non-acceptance of co-existence from the day of Partition and, more importantly, a reluctance to solve and deliberate attempts to postpone a resolution of the Kashmir issue. The lack of compliance or implementation mechanisms, the lack of transparency and verification measures, and the lack of dispute resolution forums are the key reasons why the existing CBMs and NRRMs have failed to achieve the desired objectives. Michael Krepon has observed that India and Pakistan have used CBMs more as competition building measures than as confidence building measures.[16] He continued, "Most of the CBM proposals have instead been designed to capture the political high ground, not to solve problems."[17] He points out another important reason the juridical status of CBMs as "politically binding" rather than legally binding documents helps afford India and Pakistan the latitude to skirt proper implementation.[18]

During the critical periods of heightened tensions between India and Pakistan, CBMs have been either ineffective or absent. In fact, Pakistan and India have not yet moved beyond the first stage of the CBM process. Michael Krepon describes the three stages of the CBM process as conflict avoidance measures, confidence-building measures and strengthening the peace.[19] Dr. Maleeha Lodhi notes that: ... CBMs cannot stand-alone and can only work in a broader context. The presumption of priority for CBMs is that underlying problems are not resolvable, and therefore, by freezing the status quo, CBMs can somehow reduce tension and avert the danger of war meant to be a step towards conflict resolution, they can often be used as a substitute. They have frequently been pursued in South Asia under external prodding or pressure and at the expense of problem solving.[20]

The twin processes of confidence building and nuclear risk reduction between India and Pakistan stopped soon after the Lahore MoU, which did not explicitly address the core issue of Kashmir. In the drive to postpone the resolution of conflicts, we denied our people reassurance. Pakistanis perceive that Indian ideological chauvinism and jingoistic behaviour in Kashmir, and its coercive strategy of compellance has furthered mistrust and misperceptions by weaker neighbors. [21] President Pervez Musharraf has very explicitly conveyed to India, "We in Pakistan can not [sic] be frightened into compromising on our principled position on Kashmir."[22] Bilateral initiatives in the absence of conflict resolution are no longer workable in South Asia. CBMs and NRRMs have, thus far, failed to bridge the gap of mistrust and animosity between the two countries and therefore, have a poor record in the subcontinent. The remedy for both India and Pakistan is to follow a principle of sovereign equality and mutual respect during their interstate relations, to abandon belligerency, and also to follow a civilized method to resolve differences through political means. Pakistan has already proffered a genuine, sustained, and purpose-oriented dialogue in this regard several times. Pakistan has offered India a triad of peace: resolution of disputes, a no-war pact, mutual reduction of forces and de-nuclearization and economic cooperation.[23] Almost every world leader today, including Vajpayee himself, concedes, "there seems to be no rational alternative to dialogue".[24]

In any prospective dialogue, the establishment of NRRCs could be considered. They are genuinely needed, especially to alleviate the environment of mistrust and misperception between the two nations. Functioning as a central message centre for all CBM and NRRM notifications, they would help to serve as an effective, exclusive and a dedicated technical means of official communications for rapid and accurate exchange of factual information. Besides serving as a measure to consolidate and implement the existing CBMs through renewed consultation, dispute resolution, and legally binding implementation mechanisms, the NRRCs are expected to facilitate identification, negotiation and implementation of additional institutional and procedural arrangements. They should also possess the technical means to reduce or prevent misperceptions or actions that could lead to an unintended or accidental nuclear escalation. The conflict resolution measures, if addressed concurrently at the political levels, would help reassure and assuage the frustrations of the citizenry, and would help build confidence to ensure the success of the NRRCs.

Kashmir and the Nuclear Risk Reduction Centers

India and Pakistan are experiencing the most turbulent period of their relations since early 1999. Today, peace in South Asia has become hostage to one incident, one act of terrorism and one strategic miscalculation. Most analysts now opine that India and Pakistan have failed to resolve the Kashmir issue bilaterally. In fact the Kashmiris, on both sides, have experienced the worst kind of human suffering in their struggle for self-determination. However, many political figures, statesmen, and academics are still vibrantly optimistic about a political resolution of the issues and the viability of CBMs and NRRMs between India and Pakistan. Michael Krepon, Karl Inderfurth, Ambassador Teresita Schaffer, Bruce Blair, Robert Einhorn, Dr Zafar Iqbal Cheema, Dr Pervez Iqbal Cheema, Dr Rifaat Hussain, General (retired) Jehangir Karamat, Major General (retired) William Burns and Rear Admiral (retired) John Sigler, all recognize the significance of these types of measures during the current situation between India and Pakistan. [25]

There is almost a general consensus on the importance of the resolving the Kashmir issue, without which peace may remain distant from South Asia. Stephen P. Cohen argues: Kashmir is the most important single conflict in the subcontinent, not just because its territory and its population are contested, but because larger issues of national identity and regional power balances are imbedded in it. "Solving" the Kashmir dispute means addressing these larger concerns and they cannot be addressed without new thinking on Kashmir and Kashmiris.[26]

Given the fact that neither India nor Pakistan is in a position to resolve the issue through the use of force, it is difficult to understand why they do not pursue a pragmatic, political approach. The need for serious and sustained dialogue along with concrete measures to reduce nuclear dangers has never been greater. Therefore, until positive measures for conflict resolution and new initiatives for the prevention of escalation and nuclear risk reduction are worked out and implemented, nuclear-risk reduction in South Asia will remain rhetoric, just as the proposals for conflict avoidance have been for decades.[27]

It is therefore proposed that besides establishing an India-Pakistan Joint Commission on Kashmir and other measures for socio-economic and scientific cooperation, we should seriously consider the proposal for establishing NRRCs between the two countries. The commission would be composed of special envoys determined by the respective heads of state and may later integrate representatives from Kashmir. [28] To ensure transparency in this process, it may be worthwhile to include a group of facilitators, which could be composed of widely respected world figures (Jimmy Carter or Nelson Mandela, for instance), along with regional representatives from Asia (from Japan, for instance) and the European Union. The people of India and Pakistan would be strongly reassured if their governments decided to commence a meaningful and sustained dialogue with an expressed determination to resolve the Kashmir issue, along with establishing NRRCs for a lasting peace. Any preconditions to commence this process may not produce a positive outcome.

Following the commencement of a dialogue between India and Pakistan, the proposal for establishing NRRCs may be promptly negotiated and immediately activated. As the Kashmir issue may take several years to resolve, the establishment of NRRCs should not be delayed until a settlement is reached. The successful functioning of the NRRCs depends on concurrent measures being taken towards a resolution of the Kashmir issue. NRRC success may also help build the trust and confidence that is essential for strengthening peace in the region. If the people of India, Pakistan, and Kashmir are convinced of the sincerity of the two governments and reassured by the progress of their dialogue on Kashmir, dangerous practices and the conviction for armed struggle are likely to wane. As violence decreased, Pakistan would expect India to reduce the number of security forces in Jammu and Kashmir. However, it should be expected that the Kashmiris will continue to struggle indigenously for their self-determination until an ultimate resolution can be reached. The purpose of the NRRCs would be to avert mistrust and misperceptions and the consequences they could bring while the conflict resolution process occurred.

The US Cold War Experience and Nuclear Risk Reduction Measures

Before discussing the objectives and merits or demerits of establishing NRRCs between India and Pakistan, it may be appropriate to analyze the US-Soviet coldwar experience with nuclear risk reduction measures to determine their applicability and adaptability to South Asian security environments.

Michael Krepon and P. R. Chari have both argued that despite differences in the environments, the key elements of nuclear risk reduction during the coldwar are still applicable in southern Asia. To comment and enumerate them briefly: [29]

- A formal agreement not to change the territorial status quo by military means: we need to pursue the provisions embodied in the Simla agreement and other CBMs and NRRMs seriously.

- A tacit agreement to avoid nuclear brinkmanship: the rhetoric and threatening statements from the political and military leadership in both countries must be arrested. Jingoistic statements made by the leadership of both countries, particularly during crises, are fraught with danger. This trend must be avoided.

- A formal agreement to minimize or avoid dangerous military practices/exercises: it is widely believed that the people of India and Pakistan now understand the significance of this provision.

- Special reassurance measures for ballistic missiles and nuclear weapon systems: exchange of information on storage or deployment sites of their respective limited nuclear arsenals may be currently considered a security hazard by India and Pakistan. However, prior notifications for missile tests (presently being followed) and a non-deployment posture of nuclear weapons systems or notification of their movement during training and exercises may be formally agreed upon and implemented with some verification mechanism to add transparency.

- Trust in the faithful implementation of treaty obligations and CBMs: this needs to be addressed deliberately through conflict resolution and legally binding implementation mechanisms.

- Verification: India has rudimentary capabilities while Pakistan currently does not possess national technical means for verification. However, military attachés and/or a few inspectors could subsequently be incorporated to verify the military exercises or to confirm non-deployment of nuclear weapons on suspected sites after transparency measures had been established. A means to lessen misperceptions could be achieved by establishing Indian and Pakistani NRRCs that already integrate an element of verification.

- "Establishing reliable lines of communication across borders for both political and military leaders": the hotlines between the DGMOs are now functioning well and have remained intact even during the recent military standoff, which is a positive sign.[30] However, despite Pakistan's best efforts during the hijacking of a plane from Nepal, the Indian DGMO did not respond on the hotline and the Indian foreign secretary broke the communication immediately after the plane took off from Amritsar despite repeated Pakistani requests for this not to happen. The Indian media fueled further misperceptions. According to Brigadier Feroz Khan, this demonstrates Indian intentions to utilize the hotline/CBMs only when it suits their requirements.[31] Pakistani use of the hotline leaves much to be desired as well. The significance of the hotline channel between the heads of states needs no more evidence.

- Establishment of reliable and redundant command and control systems as well as intelligence capabilities: Pakistan has already declared its command and control arrangement through the establishment of its National Command Authority in February 2000.[32] However, a senior Indian defense official reportedly stated on June 6, 2002, that "India is in no haste to establish a nuclear command and control structure,"[33] an issue that should be addressed immediately.

- Upgrade and strengthen existing risk-reduction measures: this is a continuous process applicable both in crisis situations as well as in peace time. This provides the context in which Indian and Pakistani NRRCs would operate.

The following measures are recommended for consideration by both countries as soon as government-to-government interaction and the process of dialogue are resumed. The US may help to monitor, facilitate, and render necessary assistance as considered appropriate to make the CBMs and NRRMs workable:

- Revival of old CBMs and NRRMs with special reference to incorporating a India-Pakistan Dispute Resolution Forum and a Legally Binding and Implementing Mechanism as a policy instrument to support all CBMs and NRRMs. The forum may have annual or semi-annual meetings.[34]

- Bilateral channels of communication and revival of hotlines to stipulate expanded levels including the Navy and Air Force, directions and frequency of communication, and face-to-face meetings if stipulations are violated.[35]

- Reducing the danger from false alarms through prior notifications of certain activities, possibly including major military exercises, large troop movements, changes in the deployment of air forces or other strategic elements, and cooperative aerial monitoring efforts.

- Establishment of an India-Pakistan Joint Commission on Kashmir.

- A comprehensive nuclear restraint regime, which may include the following:
- Prior notification of missile tests including the direction of fire.
- Agreement not to conduct missile tests, even those that were pre-planned, during a crisis or while major exercises are being conducted.
- Notification of all exercises that involve troop movement out of garrisons at division or above levels.
- Notification of strategic force and/or equipment movement for training.
- Agreement not to deploy nuclear tipped weapon systems. A "zero alert policy" could also be explored and discussed.[36]
- Agreement for non-mating and separate storage of nuclear warheads and delivery vehicles.
- Negotiation for the establishment of Nuclear Risk Reduction Centers (NRRCs) between India and Pakistan.[37] An agreement to this effect may include and emphasize the centrality of these institutions for the communication and implementation of the confidence building and risk reduction regimes.
- A mechanism for cooperation while confronting a nuclear accident or an incident of nuclear terrorism.

The US Nuclear Risk Reduction Center

The US Nuclear Risk Reduction Center (NRRC) is a unique

government entity located in and staffed by the State Department. The concept of the NRRC originated in a working group organized by senators Sam Nunn and John Warner. The US's NRRC and its Russian (then Soviet) counterpart were formally established at a signing ceremony in Washington, DC on September 15, 1987. The two centers provided the first direct communication link between the two capitals since the presidential "hotline" was instituted in 1963.

Although used primarily for the exchange of notifications under existing bilateral and multilateral treaties, the NRRC has periodically proved its use in other areas as well. In January 1991, goodwill notifications were used to exchange information on the re-entry of the Salyut 7 space station. Later that same year the NRRCs served as a means of emergency communications during a major fire in the US Embassy in Moscow. In the last twelve years, eleven such goodwill messages have been exchanged.

From the first message sent in April 1988 to the most recent stage of multilateral arms control notifications, the NRRC has served as a dependable means of exchanging information. It is an integral player in arms control implementation, and meets communications requirements for almost twenty arms control treaties and agreements with over fifty countries in six different languages. Presently, 153 different types of notifications are being exchanged annually in accordance with various treaties.[38]

Nuclear Risk Reduction Centers for India and Pakistan

As stated earlier, the establishment of NRRCs between nuclear India and Pakistan would facilitate official communication for exchanging information to prevent misperception or unintended reactions leading to a crisis or escalation. It would be an additional but separate high-level technical means of official communication between the two governments. The hotline monitors and other electronic communication systems placed in the NRRCs would be used for advance notifications of various strategic and military training manoeuvers to prevent misinterpretation or miscalculation. Though exchanging information on the exact location of their nuclear missiles or storage sites may not be in the security interest of the two countries, the NRRC could greatly aid in the implementation of various arms control and force reduction measures through inspection and verification elements.

The existing hotline between the DGMOs, the heads of states, and other diplomatic channels of communication would continue to function as they have their own specific military, political and diplomatic roles. The NRRCs, under a senior diplomat or a political figure directly appointed by the head of state and with sufficient experience in handling security issues would coordinate with all relevant military, intelligence and diplomatic circles to perform its functions for the timely exchange of accurate information and notifications under various agreements. The NRRCs may thus become the highest central coordinating institution in the country for the exchange of information and notifications and for the implementation of various agreements. The director general, besides having his own reporting channel, would have direct communication access to the senior armed and strategic force commanders, senior bureaucrats and the heads of intelligence agencies.

NRRCs could help clarify an intended message or information with greater accuracy by using already agreed upon formats or through a goodwill message extended in an emergency. The NRRCs would, therefore, become an appropriate official channel for the exchange of information during crises to prevent misperceptions, which in a local conflict could prevent accidental or inadvertent escalation. The second element of the NRRCs may be a verification mechanism, essentially to build trust. It may consist of observers and inspectors to verify the authenticity of intelligence in case either country expresses doubt. These details are covered in the operational aspects discussed below. Thus, the NRRCs would work hard to establish the trust and confidence necessary to strengthen peace. They should not, however, be a substitute for the political and diplomatic channels of communication.

Objectives of the NRRCs

Much like the NRRCs established for the US and Russia, Michael Krepon believes that an agreement between India and Pakistan to establish NRRCs would indicate that they recognize the need for a separate channel of high-level communication and autonomous institutional arrangements dedicated to reducing the risks of conflict escalation. It is believed that most of the Indian political leadership generally agrees and is interested in the creation of NRRCs in principle, though Pakistan's leadership, while also believing in the merits of the idea, currently considers it difficult to pursue at the official level.[39] The centers would operate under the policy guidelines of their respective leaderships and in collaboration with various civil and military instruments of their governments.

The same spirit is relevant to the objectives of NRRCs in South Asia as was present during the Cold War. The US-Soviet objectives were:

- To facilitate negotiation and implementation of additional institutional and procedural arrangements, as well as technical measures intended to reduce nuclear risks;
- To create a buffer around nuclear risk prevention measures and to protect them from the vicissitudes of US-Soviet relations;
- To provide more latitude to national leaders during crises;
- To provide a means of instantaneous communications among technical experts in the event of unusual contingencies;
- To provide a mechanism for training skilled interagency crisis teams;
- To reassure the publics in both nations, and in third countries, that the two great powers were acting to reduce the risk of nuclear war.[40]

These objectives are pertinent to India and Pakistan as well and are discussed in the following paragraphs. The additional objectives for NRRCs could include:

- To institutionalize the implementation of unilateral, bilateral or multilateral measures for nuclear risk reduction, arms control, and/or force reduction in the region. Various proposals for a comprehensive restraint regime are already in the offing. The NRRCs may subsequently help to effect arms control and mutual force reduction measures.
- To provide a mechanism to build trust and confidence through an instrument of consultation to address disputes

and a system of verifications to nullify misperceptions. The elements of trust and confidence have been lacking in the security environments of South Asia. Mutual consultations, joint planning, and analysis to handle various contingencies, along with a verification mechanism would fill the existing vacuum to ensure the credibility of this institution. Incorporating technical experts into the NRRCs' staff to verify the information or notifications would help ensuring the same.

- A mechanism to consolidate and ensure implementation of the existing agreements through legally binding arrangements instead of politically binding systems. The NRRCs functioning as a central institution for the exchange of information and notifications in coordination with various segments of the government may automatically serve to consolidate and implement the existing CBMs and NRRMs. The verification and implementation mechanisms and the dispute resolution forum developed to make the NRRCs workable would renew the credibility of existing CBMs.

For effective functioning of the NRRCs, as established under the supervision of a senior government functionary selected by the heads of state, the two governments would be expected to spare adequate resources for its operation. Besides seeking guidance and technical assistance from the government and intelligence agencies, the center's director general would also have direct communication and access to the foreign minister and the president/PM.

The NRRCs, through their legal and institutional procedural arrangements and through a separate channel of communication between government officials would serve as a good buffer during crises. The staff of the respective NRRCs, having developed good working relations during peacetime, would be more likely to communicate positively during crises. By exchanging preliminary information and assessments of mutual intentions and implementing procedural arrangements, NRRCs may prove more successful than existing hotlines between the DGMOs and the head of states.

Troop movement, military exercises, and intelligence-gathering systems are means of sending important signals. However, even at the diplomatic level it becomes difficult to convey an intended message with precision. The messages transmitted or conveyed may appear to be muted or overdrawn and could be entirely misinterpreted by the other side. The establishment of NRRCs would permit the rapid exchange of detailed and accurate messages between officials and experts well before communication between political leaders and bureaucrats occurred, which is essential during critical periods. The NRRCs, during periods of deep crisis, would be able to evaluate and analyse the facts before the governments/political leaders decided to take a specific course of action. The benefits of real-time communications through NRRCs would provide more intelligence and latitude to the national leadership to make better-informed analyses during crises well before they decide to take action.

Instantaneous means of communication among technical experts could be very useful during air and naval operations or in a crisis situation through cooperative monitoring. The shooting of Pakistan's naval aircraft "Atlantic" by India and similar incidents could have been more easily defused or perhaps prevented if an NRRC-like system was in place and the director and staff had established good working relations. The NRRCs would be a good method of exchanging information following an accident. Goodwill messages between the US and Russian NRRCs are a testament to this observation.

The NRRCs would be staffed by a selective group of interagency experts and technically skilled personnel. The procedural functions would help train skilled interagency crisis prevention teams. The staff of both centers would have to discuss and coordinate measures to handle crisis situations during negotiations for the NRRCs, and also during their regular meetings and consultations. The need for cooperation is particularly important for defusing potential crises involving nuclear terrorism. The interactions between the multidisciplinary NRRC staff would have great potential to handle situations the moment crises arise. Given a well-developed understanding of each other's concerns, prior planning, analysis, and training to handle such incidents, NRRCs would not only help to prevent potential crises, but may also be a step forward towards cooperation for a joint action to fight nuclear terrorism.

Building Trust and Confidence

The establishment of NRRCs would help clear the clouds of mistrust and reduce the chances of conflict and nuclear war in the region. Their goal would be to introduce measures of trust and confidence between the two nations by incorporating consultation and dispute resolution mechanisms along with verification and legally binding implementation mechanisms. Besides reactivating the existing CBMs/NRRMs with renewed resolve to address conflict resolution through political means, the introduction of NRRCs would establish a rainbow of peace and reassurance for the people of the two countries as well as for the region as a whole.

By institutionalizing an additional, official means for exchanging accurate and factual information under already agreed procedural arrangements, the previously poor record of CBMs and NRRMs would see a radical improvement. The establishment of détente in South Asia is, however, essential and critical to commence the official process, while the establishment and successful functioning of the NRRCs depends upon concurrent measures taken for conflict resolution. Kashmir is now unanimously considered to be the core issue and a nuclear flash point. But the process to negotiate, establish, or activate the NRRCs should not be delayed until a resolution of the Kashmir issue, which could take considerable time given its own internal dynamics and complexity. However, positive measures taken to resolve the dispute through a sustained dialogue would serve as the fuel to operate the NRRCs effectively, and would form the basis of trust and reassurance for the people of the two countries including the Kashmiris. In the absence of these measures peace and cooperation would remain distant from South Asia. The economic dividends that could be achieved from consequent socioeconomic cooperation are self-explanatory and are expected to kick start the economy of the whole region. The US, therefore, has a definite role to play.

Risks, Likely Apprehensions, Merits and Demerits

There may be significant doubts and concerns in the minds of the South Asian leadership in establishing of Indian and Pakistani NRRCs. Some of these are similar to US and Soviet concerns during the Cold War. It is appropriate to list their concerns first and then discuss their application to South Asia in this regard:

- Creation of centers may increase Soviet opportunities for spreading misleading information and deception leading up to and during crises;
- Creation of centers may increase Soviet opportunities for spreading misleading information, including sensitive information on sources and methods;
- Creation of centers may increase Soviet opportunities for spreading misleading information by providing an additional channel of communication, creation of the centers could lead to confusion and mixed signals regarding US policy as well as interpretations of Soviet actions;
- Creation of centers may increase Soviet opportunities for spreading misleading information. Creation of the centers could prompt concerns by allies, friends, or third parties that the great powers would discuss problems in which they had a stake without adequately considering their interests. [41]

The first three arguments listed above are equally applicable to current Indo-Pak relations. The arguments in support of or against establishing NRRCs for India and Pakistan are discussed below:

- Creation of centers may increase Soviet opportunities for spreading misleading information. *The opponent's abuse of the NRRC for misleading or false information for deception.* The NRRCs are designed to serve as a separate, additional channel of official communication among technical expert officials. They would have to follow a specific method of exchanging notifications and information according to an already negotiated mechanism. In the prevailing security environment, the interest of both countries to resolve the dispute may override their conflicting positions on several issues. In some situations, however, instead of taking measures to defuse the crisis, the NRRCs might be used to convey misleading or false information, further exacerbating tension in an already strained political environment. The important thing to note here is that a decision to misuse this official channel for nuclear risk reduction would itself convey the myth of the opponent's dubious intentions. The opponent's ability to misuse the NRRC is directly proportional to the intelligence and capabilities of its own staff to identify the same. The staff may, therefore, be trained in such a manner to identify the disinformation techniques of the opponent and have additional training to practice their skills. These staff members would be expected to advise the senior government officials and the political leaders when the information received through the NRRC channel appear to be disingenuous or misleading. The ability and shrewdness of the NRRC officials and the real purpose and potentials of the NRRC would, therefore, help to prevent the potential misuse of the centers.

- Creation of centers may increase Soviet opportunities for spreading misleading information *Threat to national security.* This is considered to be the principal concern for anyone who understands the importance of establishing

NRRCs between India and Pakistan. Many might say that it would neutralize Pakistan's deterrent against India and is just another Indian strategy to counter our first, use strategy. It must, therefore, be understood that the centres are being created to prevent misperceptions of intentions or of actions that could initiate conflict or lead to an unintended or an accidental nuclear exchange. It would be possible through a mechanism provided by these centers for an accurate and rapid exchange of factual information between the two countries. Secondly, there was no perceptible change in the nuclear strategies of the US or Russia following the establishment of their NRRCs. Likewise the NRRCs would not affect our strategy at all. This aspect is related to the apprehensions for leakage of sensitive information or intelligence through the use of advanced technical systems or verification through inspections. This risk is strictly within the exclusive powers of the authorities to control as the government would decide which information the NRRC may communicate or verify in a particular event, just as it controls any other official communication system. The measures taken at the NRRCs in pursuit of national policy must also help prepare a highly trained coterie of multidisciplinary personnel with considerable technical experience to handle the security and strategic environments of South Asia. A trained group of special staff under the specific guidance of the respective government is expected to provide a further check in this regard, as they would exchange the required information under an already agreed upon mechanism and on a pre-formatted system. Intelligence agency officials may be asked to provide guidance on all related matters as deemed necessary. The functioning of the NRRC would therefore encompass an in-built mechanism to guard against unauthorized disclosure of potentially sensitive or damaging information.

- Creation of centers may increase Soviet opportunities for spreading misleading information. *The NRRCs may not prevent a crisis from potential or actual nuclear terrorism.* Some analysts might have doubts about the difficulties that may arise in cases of nuclear terrorism. While it is true that prevention of the incident itself may not always be possible, NRRCs could still avoid the escalation of an ensuing conflict. The quick exchange of information in such situations could lead to cooperation in nuclear safety measures to prevent and control nuclear radiation that could result from an accident or as a result of an attack on a nuclear installation. Both India and Pakistan may be willing to cooperate in such situations instead of creating a conflict, with the potential for inadvertent or accidental escalation to the nuclear level. Non-government experts are already in the process of addressing this issue. [42] If deemed appropriate, the two governments may later consider an agreement for dealing with these situations. The institutionalization of the NRRCs, by offering it an opportunity to act in such situations, may gradually make the South Asian security environment amiable.

- Creation of centers may increase Soviet opportunities for spreading misleading information. *The establishment of NRRCs could generate countervailing forces harmful to regional security.* Actors within both governments may be ideologically opposed to an improvement in India-

Pakistan relations. Further, there are many that financially benefit from the continuing hostile environment and conflict. It is not difficult to imagine that these actors would attempt to disrupt or impair the successful functioning of the NRRCs. Further, the Kashmir issue may also be exploited to pressurize the authorities. Given this countervailing pressure, it is still hoped that the leaders at both ends, in considering this proposal, would demonstrate pragmatism for the larger interest of their people and the region. They may have to simultaneously address outstanding conflicts with flexibility to make headway towards the eventual elimination of conflict and to bring a lasting peace and prosperity to India and Pakistan.

The Functioning of the NRRCs

- The NRRCs would be legally bound to remain open continuously. The centers shall, therefore, be manned around the clock.

- No malfunctions or breakage in the technical equipment or hotline monitors will be tolerated at any time. The redundancy may either be ensured through duplications or other technically feasible measures.

- It must be understood that the NRRCs are not a substitute to the diplomatic and political channels of communication. The center's hotline is also no substitute to that of the military commander. Thus, the NRRC staff does not have to perform the functions directly concerned with these personnel. Key staff members from both centers will meet once or twice a year to resolve problems and to seek improvements in the efficiency of the centers.

- The staff will not exchange any voice or telephone communications, because of the potential this mode of communication has for misperception. The centers shall exchange only written and preformatted notifications, the text and details of which shall be mutually decided and agreed upon by both countries during their meetings.
- Goodwill messages may be used only in cases of an emergency to prevent a potential crisis. No deviations will be accepted in this regard. The US and Russia have exchanged only eleven "goodwill" messages in the last 14 years.
- Any message other than the preformatted notifications could send a wrong signal and would be tantamount to a violation of the agreements. The multidisciplinary staff must use its skill to identify any institutional or procedural anomaly and prevent its recurrence.
- The staff must always rapidly submit notification to their counterparts and effect prior coordination with various departments accordingly. In case of any delay or lapse, the notification should still be forwarded with regrets on the failure to retain trust and confidence in the institution.

It must be noted that the NRRCs are not the panacea for crisis management and should not become involved in substantive negotiations during crises. The purpose of the center is to prevent misperceptions or miscalculations leading to an unintended or accidental nuclear exchange. Crisis management is the job of trained diplomats and the burden will continue to fall on political leaders. Therefore, it should be conducted through normal diplomatic channels or between heads of state.

The NRRCs could compliment diplomatic channels during crises only when political authorities believe that technical exchanges about military activities could be useful supplements to the main diplomatic discourse.[43]

Operationalization of the NRRCs

The NRRCs could be operationalized after well-planned negotiations led to an agreement between the two governments in this regard. The agreement would only be possible when the two governments decide to sit down for a dialogue. Keeping in view the current stand off between the two governments and the absence of official interaction, this proposal cannot currently be considered at the official level.

The Track Two efforts, however, cannot be neglected as a means of discussing this proposal. The US, having already attempted to persuade the two leaderships to sit down together, could play a significant role in asking the parties to consider establishing the NRRCs. Meanwhile, a trilateral working group consisting of senior civil and retired military officials from Pakistan, India and the US could be formed to study the feasibility of establishing NRRCs between India and Pakistan. The working group could meet anywhere outside of India and Pakistan to analyze the broad contours and policy directions in this regard. A short report with recommendations from the group may be presented to the political leadership for consideration upon the establishment of détente and the resumption of dialogue between India and Pakistan.

The working group may start its work as soon as possible and may publish a report by the end of 2003 at latest. The two governments may then discuss the feasibility for establishing

NRRCs and may negotiate an agreement accordingly. The US would have a critical and challenging role to facilitate a dialogue, to render necessary assistance in the negotiations, and to establish the NRRCs.

Smooth operation would be ensured by clear organizational concepts and avoidance of "the don'ts". The consultative and verification mechanisms along with joint planning and procedural arrangements to handle various contingencies under the supervision of a senior director general and a highly trained interagency staff would help to ensure their eventual success to prevent crises and inadvertent escalation in South Asia. It is important to stress again that the fuel to run these NRRCs will be provided by simultaneously addressing conflict resolution measures. This is a reassurance mechanism exclusively in the hands of the leadership of the two countries. Once the core issues are resolved, it would add impetus to the functioning of the NRRCs. Thereafter, the NRRCs may run automatically.

The Organization and Function of the NRRCs

The nuclear risk reduction centers would be established in Islamabad and New Delhi and would run constantly for 24 hours during any event with the potential to cause a nuclear crisis. These centers could be equipped with the latest computers and hotlines with high-speed data facsimile transmission links as agreed by the two governments. Double or dual monitoring devices for both conventional, nuclear and hotline systems may be established to assure reliable and redundant technical means of communication. Both countries can acquire separate channels on the same or different satellites to further ensure the redundancy. Developing ciphers would enhance the communication security between the two countries. A group of diplomatic, military, and intelligence personnel along with a few civil and technical experts would be required to work in the NRRC on both a temporary and permanent basis.

The staff should operate under previously agreed upon instructions and may be taken from various government departments and agencies. The President/PM, as considered appropriate, may nominate the director general of the NRRC who would report to the President/PM's Advisor or to the Foreign Minister. He could be a civilian with prior experience in security negotiations. The proposed organization for Pakistan's NRRC and a suggested diagram for its technical equipment is attached as Annex D.

The second important element of the NRRCs would be the Group of Inspectors or Observers consisting of technical personnel only. This is essentially designed to compliment trust and confidence through a verification element. The inspectors or observers would be used, under the provisions of the NRRCs, in case the other country desires verification of any information, for example large-scale military exercises or movement of strategic forces/assets for training, etc. Considering security issues, especially on nuclear and strategic assets, it may initially be practiced at a limited level to oversee large scale military moves and exercises such as Brasstacks or Zarb-e Momin, or to aid civil authorities during emergencies, and may later be expanded to confirm the training moves of strategic forces or other activities. It would set a precedent by adding the element of verification to build trust and confidence, and to alleviate misperceptions. The officials may work out the details during negotiations. The list of the visiting inspectors of the other country may, however, be processed by the government and intelligence agencies to verify their credentials, including the pilots by the civil aviation authorities to accord the necessary clearances.

The NRRC staff may be required to perform a wide range of functions in peacetime as well as during periods of tension and crisis. Despite the development of standard operating procedures, the centers may not initially be able to perform all the functions of the US and Russian NRRCs. However, these may be worked out on modest requirements or task-oriented functions acceptable to the two governments. Once inventories are in place, additional functions can be worked out and improved at a later date. Initially, the staff might face certain difficulties in view of some of the anomalies and irregularities in the CBMs and NRRMs. Through political will and concerted efforts the hurdles are likely to be eliminated progressively. Annual or semiannual meetings between the staff are essential to enhance the scope and functioning of the NRRCs. The US support in this regard could be critical. The US NRRC officials and non-governmental experts were all optimistic about the merits of NRRCs for South Asia and were willing to render necessary assistance in the light of their experiences.[44]

An important aspect for the smooth and successful functioning of the NRRCs is the need for certain agreements that warrant compliance through exchange of information, notifications, and verifications. Without such agreed arrangements, the advanced technical means of communication may not produce the desired results. NRRCs in the Middle East failed due to the absence of such agreements.[45]

Location of Pakistan's NRRC

Both the staff and inspection elements of the Russian NRRC are functioning quite smoothly in the MoD. The US debate on the issue in 1986 considered four locations: the NSC apparatus at the White House, the Department of Defense, the Department of State, and a new setting separate from existing bureaucratic institutions.[46] However, then-Secretary of State George Shultz's argument prevailed. He argued that since the new channel of communication was being created as an additional link between the two governments and that function of the government is overseen by the State Department, the NRRC should function under the direct support and direction of the US Department of State.[47] The US on-site inspection expertise, however, functions under the Pentagon. Certain bureaucratic hurdles and vested interests were reportedly cited as reasons for preventing their integration.

Pakistan may decide either to keep the NRRC under the Principal Secretary/Advisor to the President/PM or under the Foreign Minister. Keeping in view the channel of reporting, the NRRC may be housed accordingly. The GHQ has its own hotline channel and reports to the MoD, therefore, the NRRC could work as a separate channel exclusively under civilian control. Military-related information and notification may be sent to NRRCs by routing through their official channels and the Ministry of Foreign Affairs or External Affairs as applicable to both countries. The final authority to exchange the notification would be the NRRCs under intimation to respective ministries or headquarters. The military and the intelligence agencies, however, may be needed to render necessary assistance and for interaction with the Operations Section as per the organization of the NRRC (See Annex D).

Conclusion

An agreement to refrain from the use of force and for the peaceful settlement of disputes already exists between India and Pakistan. They have also reached an understanding for taking NRRMs and the creation of an appropriate consultative mechanism as well as a periodical review of existing CBMs. Therefore, besides observance of a ceasefire along the LoC and immediate cessation of human rights violations against Kashmiris, a dialogue must be resumed between India and Pakistan. Prime Minister Vajpayee and President Musharraf already agreed to a structure for talks in Agra. Only a sustained and meaningful dialogue between the two countries could lead us towards conflict resolution. The incremental approaches suggested by General Mahmud Durrani and General Talat Masood to achieve this objective, point towards commencing a dialogue and subsequently improve it through sustained consultation and conflict resolution measures.[48]

The proposal for creating NRRCs, though quite optimistic at this stage, might serve as a cornerstone towards a radical shift in the current security environments of Southern Asia. The concept of the NRRCs may thus form part of an agenda for dialogue between the two countries. It should be negotiated and implemented promptly without waiting for the outcome of the Kashmir dispute. However, the positive measures simultaneously taken to resolve disputes through a sustained dialogue would serve as the fuel to operate the NRRCs effectively and would form the basis for a rainbow of hope, trust and reassurance for the people of the two countries, including Kashmiris. In the absence of these measures, peace and cooperation will remain distant from South Asia.

The NRRCs, due to an inbuilt mechanism, would not only help to consolidate and enhance the scope of current CBMs/NRRMs between the two countries, but would also accelerate the conflict resolution track. The NRRCs, through formation of consultation and dispute resolving forums and implementation mechanisms would also lay the foundation for generating transparency, reassurance, and trust in Indo-Pakistani relations besides building confidence, tolerance and reconciliation, and strengthening peace in the region.

Endnotes

1. "Musharraf says India-Pakistan conflict unlike US-Iraq", *Deutsche Presse-Agentur*, 19 September 2002.
2. "India Loses Conventional Superiority", *Dawn*, September 18, 2002, http://www.dawn.com/2002/09/18/top13.htm.
3. Indian plans to attack Pakistan's nuclear facilities were thrice deterred/ dropped in the 1980s and in the early 1990s due to recessed deterrence. Indira Gandhi's last plan was dropped after her assassination and Rajiv Gandhi eventually signed an agreement not to attack on nuclear facilities. Since Brasstacks, and Pakistani implicit threats for first use, there were no attempts for a conventional war. The Kargil Conflict was also deliberately confined to that sector only due to the "Nuclear Deterrent". Please see *From Surprise to Reckoning: The Kargil Review Committee Report* (New Delhi: Sage Publications, 2000), pp. 178-212.
4. Michael Krepon and Chris Gagné (eds), *The Stability-Instability Paradox: Nuclear Weapons and Brinkmanship in South Asia* (Washington, DC: The Henry L. Stimson Center, June 2001), p. 41.
5. This line of analysis was presented in a *Times of India* opinion reprinted in, "India can no longer beat Pakistan in War", *The Nation* (Islamabad) (June 4, 1998).
6. See Krepon and Gagné (eds.), *The Stability-Instability Paradox.*
7. Michael Krepon and Mishi Faruqee (eds.), *Conflict Prevention and Confidence Building Measures in South Asia: The 1990 Crisis,* Occasional

Paper No.17 (Washington, DC: The Henry L. Stimson Center, April 1994), pp. 11-12.

8. Holst quoted in Naeem Ahmad Salik, "CBMs – Past, Present and Future," *Pakistan Defense Review* (Winter 1998), p. 70.

9. Michael Krepon, Michael Newbill, Khurshid Khoja, and Jenny S. Drezin (eds), *Global Confidence Building, New Tools for Troubled Regions* (New York: St Martin's Press, 1999), pp. 277–284.

10. Naeem Ahmad Salik, "CBMs – Past, Present, and Future," p.69.

11. Swati Pandey and Teresita C. Schaffer, "Building Confidence in India and Pakistan," *South Asia Monitor,* No. 49 (Washington, D.C: Center for Strategic and International Studies), p. 1. See Annexes A and B for additional CBMs.

12. Chris Gagné, "Nuclear Risk Reduction in South Asia; Building on Common Ground", in Krepon and Gagne, *The Stability-Instability Paradox*, p. 51.

13. Ibid., p. 52. The Lahore MOU was signed on February 21, 1999. For the text of the agreement see Annex B.

14. *Ibid.*

15. *Ibid.*; Naeem Ahmad Salik, "False Warnings and Accidents" in CISAC Workshop on *Preventing Nuclear War in South Asia* held at Bangkok (August 4–7, 2001), p.73.

16. Krepon, et al., *Global Confidence Building,* p.178.

17. *Ibid.,* p. 183.

18. *Ibid.*, p. 176.

19. Michael Krepon, "Conflict Avoidance, Confidence Building and Peacemaking" in *A Handbook of Confidence Building Measures for Regional Security*, 3rd Ed. (Washington, DC: The Henry L. Stimson Center, 1998), p. 2.

20. Dr Maleeha Lodhi, "Nuclear Risk Reduction and Conflict Resolution in South Asia," *The News* (Islamabad), November 28, 1998.

21. For more on compellance, see Gaurav Kampani, "India's Compellance Strategy: Calling Pakistan's Nuclear Bluff over Kashmir" (Monterey, CA: Center for Nonproliferation Studies, Monterey Institute of International Studies, June 10, 2002).

22. President Pervez Musharraf, "President of Pakistan's Address to the United Nations General Assembly on 12-09-2002," Internet: http://www.infopak.gov.pk/President_Addresses/president-UNGA.htm.

23. "India Piling Up Arms," *Dawn* (September 12, 2002).

24. Major General Mahmud Ali Durrani, retired, "India and Pakistan: The Cost of Conflict and the Benefits of Peace" (Washington, DC: The Johns Hopkins University Foreign Policy Institute, School of Advanced International Studies, 2000), p. 52.

25. Interviews with the author, July and August 2002.

26. Stephen P. Cohen, "Draft Case Study: The Compound Crisis of 2002," mimeo, p. 31.

27. Mr. Inam ul Haq, former foreign secretary of Pakistan, in a statement at the Conference on Disarmament at Geneva on January 25, 2001 has proffered a three-tiered comprehensive peace and security framework that includes simultaneous conflict resolution dialogue, a regional strategic restraint regime, and regional cooperation in economic, trade and social revival between the two neighbors. See Feroz Hassan Khan, "Navigating the Crossroads", *The Monitor* Center for International Trade and Security, University of Georgia Vol. 7, No. 3 (Fall 2001), pp. 10–14.

28. Major General Durrani, "India and Pakistan," p. 59. General Durrani suggests appointing an emissary from the heads of state.

29. Michael Krepon, "Nuclear Risk Reduction: Is Cold War Experience Applicable to South Asia?" in Krepon and Gagné, *The Stability-Instability Paradox*, pp. 1–14 and P. R. Chari, "Nuclear Restraint, Nuclear Risk Reduction, and the Security-Insecurity Paradox in South Asia," in Krepon and Gagné, *The Stability-Instability Paradox* , pp. 32-33. The author has added certain comments and suggestions to assert the application of these elements in South Asia.

30. The author's personal experience during a visit to GHQ in early July 2002 as well as confirmation of the fact by Brigadier Naeem Salik, Director of Arms Control and Disarmament Affairs, Strategic Plans Division, Pakistan on September 5, 2002.

31. Author's interview with Brigadier Feroz H. Khan, Washington, DC, September 1, 2002.

32. Naeem Salik, "False Warning and Accidents," p. 73.

33. "India in No Haste to form N-Command Structure," *The News* (Islamabad), June 7, 2002.

34. Pandey and Schaffer, "Building Confidence in India and Pakistan."

35. *Ibid.*

36. See Bruce Blair, *Global Zero Alert of Nuclear Forces* (Washington, DC: The Brookings Institution, 1995), pp. 78–108.

37. See Feroz Hassan Khan, "Navigating the Crossroads," p. 14. He has made a fleeting reference for establishing a 'Crisis Prevention Center' in his recommendations at the end of his paper.

38. Barry M. Blechman and Michael Krepon, *Nuclear Risk Reduction Centers* (Washington DC: Center for Strategic and International Studies, 1986), pp. 1-26, *Brochure on The US NRRC: 1988–2002* (Washington, DC: Department of State, 2002), and author's interviews with NRRC Director Harold Kowalski, Jr. and NRRC staff (August 22, 2002). See Annex C for more information.

39. Author's interview with Robert J. Einhorn at Washington, DC, August 2002.

40. Barry M. Blechman and Krepon, *Nuclear Risk Reduction Centers*, pp. 6–8.

41. *Ibid.*

42. Rajesh Basrur and Hasan Askari Rizvi, "The Nuclear Terrorism in South Asia" (Washington, DC: Presented at the Brookings Institution, September 13, 2002).

43. Blechman and Krepon, *Nuclear Risk Reduction Centers*, pp. 12–13.

44. Interview with US NRRC Director Harold Kowalski, Jr., August 22, 2002.

45. Interviews with NRRC director and staff, August 22, 2002.

46. Blechman and Krepon, *Nuclear Risk Reduction Centers*, pp. 22–25.

47. Interviews with NRRC director and staff, August 22, 2002.

48. Major General Durrani, "India and Pakistan," pp. 53-54, and Talat Masood, "Military CBMs in South Asia" in *CBMs in South Asia: Potential and Possibilities* (Colombo, Sri Lanka: Regional Center for Strategic Studies, 2000), p. 46.

Annex A
List of India-Pakistan Confidence-building Measures

Communication Measures

- Hotline between DGMOs since December 1971.
- Direct communication lines between sector commanders across the LoC since 1991.
- Hotline between prime ministers since 1997.

Measures Notification

- Agreement for prior Notification of Military Exercises involving ten thousand or more troops is in place since April 1991. It stipulates that at Corps level exercises must be held 45 kilometres from the border while at Division level exercises must be held 25 kilometres away from the border. No military activity is permitted within 5 kilometres of the border.

Transparency Measures

- Invitation to military observers to attend major exercises to confirm non-hostile intent. Indian and other military attaches were invited to attend Zarb-e-Momin in 1989.
- To defuse tensions resulting from its spring 1990 exercises India invited US observers to monitor the exercises and to confirm their non-hostile intent.
- Border Security Measures.
- Karachi Agreement of 1949 which established an 800 mile CFL which obligated the troops to keep a distance

of 500 yards from the line and froze the force levels along the CFL.

- The 1960 Indo-Pak Agreement on Border Disputes established "Ground Rules" to regulate the activities along the West Pakistan-India border.
- The Rann of Kutch Tribunal Award of 1966. It, however, left the demarcation of boundary in Sir Creek area, which is still disputed.
- Air Space Violations Agreement signed in April 1991 and ratified in August 1992, which stipulates that no combat aircraft shall fly within 10 kilometres of each other's airspace.

Consultation Measures

- India-Pakistan Joint Commission established in 1982 to facilitate discussions at ministerial level.
- Since 1990 the Joint Commission has been superseded by a series of foreign secretary-level talks.

Water Rights

- The 1962 Indus Waters Treaty brokered by the World Bank helped resolve problems regarding distribution of water resources.

Declaratory Measures

- The Tashkent Declaration of 1966.
- The Shimla Accord of 1972.
- Agreement on "Non-Attack" on each others nuclear facilities signed in 1988 and ratified in 1991.

- Joint Declaration on the prohibition of Chemical Weapons concluded in 1992 in which both countries agreed not to develop, produce, acquire or use chemical weapons. India however, declared having stocks as well as production and storage facilities as a consequence of its ratification of the CWC in 1997.

Source: *A Handbook of Confidence-Building Measures for Regional Security*, 3rd Ed. (Washington, DC: The Henry L. Stimson Center, 1998),

Annex B
Lahore Memorandum of Understanding

The following is the text of the Memorandum of Understanding signed by the Indian Foreign Secretary, K. Raghunath, and the Pakistan Foreign Secretary, Shamshad Ahmad, in Lahore on February 21, 1999.

The Foreign Secretaries of India and Pakistan:

Reaffirming the continued commitment of their respective governments to the principles and purposes of the U N Charter;

Reiterating the determination of both countries to implementing the Shimla Agreement in letter and spirit;

Guided by the agreement between their Prime Ministers of 23rd September 1998 that an environment of peace and security is in the supreme national interest of both sides and that resolution of all outstanding issues, including Jammu and Kashmir, is essential for this purpose;

Pursuant to the directive given by their respective Prime

Ministers in Lahore, to adopt measures for promoting a stable environment of peace, and security between the two countries; Have on this day, agreed to the following:-

1. The two sides shall engage in bilateral consultations on security concepts, and nuclear doctrines, with a view to developing measures for confidence building in the nuclear and coventional fields, aimed at avoidance of conflict.

2. The two sides undertake to provide each other with advance notification in respect of ballistic missile flight tests, and shall conclude a bilateral agreement in this regard.

3. The two sides are fully committed to undertaking national measures to reducing the risks of accidential or unauthorised use of nuclear weapons under their respective control. The two sides further undertake to notify each, other immediately in the event of any accidential, unauthorised or unexplained incident that could create the risk of a fallout with adverse consequences for both sides, or an outbreak of a nuclear war between the two countries, as well as to adopt measures aimed at diminishing the possibility of such actions, or such incidents being misinterpreted by the other. The two sides shall identify/establish the appropriate communication mechanism for this purpose.

4. The two sides shall continue to abide by their respective unilateral moratorium on conducting further nuclear test explosions unless either side, in exercise of its national sovereignty decides that extraordinary events have jeopardised its supreme interests.

5. The two sides shall conclude an agreement on prevention of incidents at sea in order to ensure safety of navigation by naval vessels, and aircraft belonging to the two sides.

6. The two sides shall periodically review the implementation of existing Confidence-Building Measures (CBMs) and where necessary, set up appropriate consultative mechanisms to monitor and ensure effective implementation of these CBMs.

7. The two sides shall undertake a review of the existing communication links (e.g. between the respective Directors-General, Military Operations) with a view to upgrading and improving these links, and to provide for fail-safe and secure communications.

8. The two sides shall engage in bilateral consultations on security, disarmament and non-proliferation issues within the context of negotiations on these issues in multilateral fora.

9. Where required, the technical details of the above measures will be worked out by experts of the two sides in meetings to be held on mutually agreed dates, before mid 1999, with a view to reaching bilateral agreements.

Done at Lahore on 21st February 1999 in the presence of Prime Minister of India, Mr. Atal Behari Vajpayee, and Prime Minister of Pakistan, Mr. Muhammad Nawaz Sharif.

(K. Raghunath)
Foreign Secretary of the Republic of India
(Shamshad Ahmad)

Foreign Secretary of the Islamic Republic of Pakistan

Source: http://www.indianembassy.org/South_Asia/Pakistan/mou(lahore 01211999).html

Annex C
The US Nuclear Risk Reduction Center

The principal function of the centers is to exchange information and notifications as required under various arms control treaties and other confidence-building agreements.

Brief History

As the result of a US initiative, President Reagan and General Secretary Gorbachev agreed at the November 1985 Geneva Summit to have experts explore the possibility of establishing centres to reduce the risk of nuclear war. The impetus for this initiative grew out of consultations between the Executive Branch and Congress, particularly senators Sam Nunn and John Warner. US and Soviet experts held informal meetings in Geneva on May 5-6 and August 25, 1986. In October 1986, at their meeting in Reykjavik, President Reagan and General Secretary Gorbachev indicated satisfaction with the progress made at the experts meetings and agreed to begin formal negotiations to establish Nuclear Risk Reduction Centers. Those negotiations were held in Geneva on January 13 and May 3-4, 1987. The negotiations resulted in the agreement that was signed in Washington September 15, 1987, by Secretary of State Shultz and Foreign Minister Shevardnadze.

Under the agreement, which is of unlimited duration, each party agreed to establish a Nuclear Risk Reduction Center in its capital and to establish a special facsimile communications link between these Centers. These Nuclear Risk Reduction Centers became operational on April 1, 1988. The American

National Center (known as the NRRC) is located in Washington, DC in the Department of State. The Soviet National Center became the Russian National Center with the dissolution of the Soviet Union and is located in Moscow in the Russian Federation Ministry of Defense. Consequent to the breakup of the former Soviet Union the four START Treaty successor states of Russia, Belarus, Ukraine and Kazakhstan have become involved in the notification process, and the NRRC has established direct communications links with each of those republics.

Scope of NRRC

The Nuclear Risk Reduction Centers do not replace normal diplomatic channels of communication or the "Hot line", nor are they intended to have a crisis management role. The principal function of the centers is to exchange information and notifications as required under various arms control treaties and other confidence-building agreements.

There are two protocols to the NRRC Agreement. Protocol I identifies the notifications the parties agreed to exchange. These include:

- Ballistic missile launches required under Article 4 of the 1971 Agreement on Measures to Reduce the Risk of Outbreak of Nuclear War.
- Ballistic missile launches required under paragraph 1 of Article VI of the 1972 Agreement on the Prevention of Incidents on and over the High Seas.

Since the Agreement was signed, the Parties have additionally agreed to exchange through the Centers inspection and compliance notifications, as well as other information, required under the INF Treaty, notifications called for under the Ballistic Missile Launch Notification Agreement, Vienna Document of 1999, the CFE Treaty, the Open-Skies Treaty and the CWC.

The centers may also be used for the transmission by either side of additional communications as a display of good-will and with a view to building confidence. For example, in January 1991, goodwill notifications were used to exchange information on the re-entry of the Salyut 7 space station. Later that same year, the NRRC served as means of emergency communications during a major fire in the US Embassy in Moscow. There has been an exchange of 11 goodwill messages in the last 12 years.

Organization

There are two major components of the NRRC; the Notifications and the Verification. Russia holds integrated units of the two components under MoD while the US hold them separately under the Department of State and the MoD respectively. Though an integrated unit may help in smooth functioning of the center, however, certain political and bureaucratic intricacies are stated to prevent its integration in the US.

An assistant secretary of state is appointed by the president to serve as the director of the US NRRC. The NRRC is divided into two units: a staff component and a watch operations component. Staff members represent the NRRC at interagency meetings, prepare and clear NRRC policy positions, and assist in planning for future activities. The watch officers staff the 24-hour operations center providing communications over six distinct international communications systems. Watch personnel are both Foreign Service and Civil Service officers, including those with proficiencies in Russian and other Organization for Security and Cooperation in Europe (OSCE) languages.

Miscellaneous

Existence of an agreement that clearly stipulates the requirement of what to communicate through the NRRC is a pre-requisite for its successful functioning. The Middle East process was an example of failure as there was no agreement related to it.

No voice communication circuit was embodied into the NRRC deliberately as voice communication could lead to misinterpretation by voice modulation. Crypto and ciphers are used for communication security to prevent interception of messages by any other state.

Annual consultative meetings are held to revise the standard formats for conveying notifications and to seek other improvements.

Source: Author's interviews with NRRC Director Harold Kowalski, Jr. and NRRC staff (August 22, 2002); Barry M. Blechman and Michael Krepon, *Nuclear Risk Reduction Centers* (Washington DC: Center for Strategic and International Studies, 1986), pp. 1-26; and *Brochure on The US NRRC: 1988–2002* (Washington, DC: Department of State, 2002).

* *Re-printed with permission from Islamabad Policy Research Institute Journal, Pakistan, Summer 2003. The views expressed are those of the author and do not necessarily represent the policy viewpoints or opinion of the Government of Pakistan, the Pakistan Army or the Strategic Plans Division, the organization where the author is currently working.*

Kashmir: Indian Strategic Initiative Since 9/11 and Imperatives for US Policy in the Region

Moeed Pirzada

The terrorist attacks of September 11, 2001, in New York laid the foundation for emerging new world order, to which both Pakistan and India reacted in haste. As Pakistan joined the US-led coalition against its former ally Taliban regime in Afghanistan, to safeguard its national interests in a radically altered international scenario. A series of apparently inexplicable happenings, both in the Indian controlled state of Jammu & Kashmir and Delhi soon brought South Asia to the brink of a nuclear confrontation.

Kashmir emerged in the centre of this conflict where the separatist militancy suddenly became so explosive that it barged its way into the eye of international media at a time when the media's undivided attention was focused on the war in Afghanistan. Before 9/11, relations between India and Pakistan were far from being warm and cordial but they were not actively hostile either. Since the stalemate at Agra Summit, a relatively placid atmosphere prevailed between the two nuclear neighbours. However, within a few days of the highly symbolic terrorist attacks on Indian Parliament, India had recalled its ambassador from Islamabad, banned its airspace to Pakistani air line, severed all land communications with Pakistan and with its troop mobilization, more than a million men faced each other, eye ball to eye ball, along the disputed borders in Kashmir.[1]

As international media discussed scenarios of a possible nuclear melt-down in the subcontinent, Indian experts and media commentators predicted – and were in turn quoted by Pakistani commentators – that in the event of an Indian attack and thus war between India and Pakistan, US forces based in Pakistan will have to take out Pakistan's nuclear capability to save the world from a nuclear Armageddon. [2] International emissaries from the US, the UK and EU paid a series of high profile visits to Islamabad and Delhi and pressure mounted on Pakistan to make concessions to India.

However, despite Pakistani concessions and promises to restrain the Kashmiri separatists and their Pakistan based supporters, India's coercive diplomacy continued. Finally elections were held in the Indian controlled state of Jammu & Kashmir on a time schedule, surprisingly parallel to the elections in Pakistan. These elections were widely welcomed by the international community and media and robust international belief was palpable – even before the start of actual exercise – that these will be held free and fair and will help bring out a solution to the disputed state. In certain instances western countries made appeals to Pakistan that she should not interfere to fail the elections giving – in indirect way – credence to the Indian allegations that things do not return to normalcy inside Jammu & Kashmir because of the Pakistani influence and interference.

Though reductions in troop deployments took place on both the sides after the elections in Kashmir, but the overall tension between the two countries is far from over.

This article examines the challenges faced by Indian strategic thinking after 9/11, vis-à-vis Pakistan; options available to it and responses offered. A detailed analysis of the sequence of events that appeared at propitious moments to help advance the cause of Indian strategy will be conducted to raise the question: "If there is something more to the nature of terrorism within India and Indian controlled Kashmir that meets the eye?" The response of international community notably US and UK will be also be examined.

Focus will develop on Kashmir, because the apparent aim of the Indian strategy was to win legitimacy for itself in the disputed Himalayan state where it is pitched against Kashmiri separatists for the last thirteen years. However, the paper will examine Kashmir in the broader contours of Indian diplomacy which, despite its apparent focus on the disputed Himalayan state, was actually threatened by the prospects of increased good-will of international community towards Pakistan. It was seen by New Delhi as disrupting the emerging Indo-US roadmap; Kashmir being only a part of this strategy albeit a very important one.

The paper will finally examine the convergence of external and internal imperatives that now drive US strategic alliance with New Delhi. Is there a way Washington can prevent it from becoming a "zero sum game" in South Asia? As US policy attempts to win tacit support for the Indian position that Kashmir is only its internal problem, does it realize the new challenges it creates for the Pakistani state especially in the wake of Muthidda Majlis-e-Amal (MMA) gaining prominence in 2002 elections?[3] Is there a way US can build a close strategic alliance with India without jeopardizing its long-term interests in this region?

Indo-US Roadmap After Kargil

Though the US "tilt" towards India, driven both by the changed geo-strategic perceptions and corporate interests, was becoming obvious throughout the 1990s but it was brought out sharply by the Kargil conflict in the summer of 1999.[4] From that point onwards, from India's point of view a clear roadmap emerged for the future of US-India relations, independent of Pakistan and devoid of any shadows of Kashmir or talk of "Kashmiri self-determination".

By that time, India had more or less managed to overcome negative fallout, resulting from the human rights violations of its "brutal counter insurgency" in Kashmir. With the withdrawal of JKLF from armed resistance against India and the emergence of certain celebrated terrorist acts like the abductions of five western tourists by an obscure group Al-Faran in 1995, India had found it increasingly convenient to paint the insurgency in Kashmir as mainly a foreign sponsored terrorism.

The orchestrated domestic and international media campaign on Kargil bolstered by fiercely nationalistic Indian diaspora in major US and European cities and the chain of events inside Pakistan that ultimately resulted into the removal of the government of Nawaz Sharif by Pakistani military. These events led to severe shrinking of political space available to Pakistan in international arena. In this context it will be helpful to appreciate that Nawaz was widely perceived to be supported by the Clinton Administration in his power tussle with a nationalistic military that would not compromise his "vision for peace" by coming to some sort of conclusion on Kashmir.

Whether Nawaz had any viable vision of Kashmir and whether India was serious in any dialogue with Pakistan on Kashmir are besides the scope of this paper. What is important here is to appreciate that Nawaz was seen to be having the good will of Clinton administration against his own military.[5]

And this apparent cleft provided immense happiness to Indian strategists who, for the first time saw a serious disagreement emerging between the civil military establishment in Islamabad and the administration in Washington. The suspension of Pakistan's Commonwealth membership, its difficult economic conditions and overall adverse image helped Indian strategist to believe that short-lived parity which Pakistan claimed at the eve of a nuclear South Asia in May 1999, has finally been managed – encapsulated within the new perception: nuclear but failed state and thus more dangerous for regional and international order. South Block visionaries that had spent greater part of their energies throughout 1990s in getting Pakistan declared a "rogue state", sponsoring terrorism naturally felt comfortable that now finally a multi-dimensional strategic relationship with US can emerge without the troubling shadow of Pakistan, clinging to it.

Indian Strategic Response After 9/11

Indian strategic thinkers were quick to assess the impact of terrorist attacks in New York and – with the Pakistani jump into a willing and needy American lap – its possible effects on the region. Increased political space for Pakistan would mean reduced one for India for two reasons: one, Pakistan will find new diplomatic and media support for the cause in Kashmir and secondly, US will be under pressure to balance its strategic tilt towards India out of deference for its new relationship with Pakistan. There are indications that before 9/11 Indians were expecting US President George Bush to visit India in the first quarter of 2002. With operation in Afghanistan and Pakistan's support against Taliban, the visit delayed and was a joint visit to both India and Pakistan – something which Indian strategy saw as a serious setback to the gains made during the last years of Clinton presidency.[6]

A day by day follow-up of Indian press in the immediate aftermath of 9/11 brings out that tremendous anxiety through which Indian decision-making elite, both within and outside the government, suffered at this critical moment. Cabinet Committee on security met on September 13, to lay out the bare bones of a response strategy and this meeting, among others, was attended by the Foreign Secretary, Chokila Iyer, and the Chief of Air Staff, Air Chief Marshal A.Y. Tipnis. The consensus that emerged was that it is a must for India to develop an active identification with US administration's counter-terrorism drive.[7] By that time, Prime Minister Vajpayee had already written a letter to the US President George Bush, saying India is "ready to cooperate in the investigations into this crime and to strengthen our partnership in leading international efforts to ensure that terrorism never succeeds again."[8]

But what will be the contours of that cooperation? There is overwhelming evidence that in the first week following 9/11, Indian political and bureaucratic elite were prepared to go a long way to be part of US-led coalition. Given the geographic and thus logistic needs of then potential US operations in Afghanistan, it is somewhat surprising that Indian elite expected to become, in one way or the other, a part of the military operations.[9] On September 15, in a two-hour meeting, chaired by the prime minister, the Opposition, barring the exception of CPI(M), was united on offering base facilities to the US. However, the leaders were informed that there was no formal request from the US for the use of Indian bases to carry out military strikes in the region.[10]

By that time, even the liberal press had openly come out with the argument that India's 'strategic card' is to bank on America's military might to try and silence the guns of Pakistan-sponsored militancy in Kashmir.[11] It was thus extremely disconcerting to the Indian elite and middle classes when, around this time, they learnt that they were probably not getting an important role in the US-led coalition because Pakistan had asked Americans to keep India and Israel out of this effort. In all probability, it was true, however, US officials took exceptional pains to soothe the Indian sensitivities on this issue.[12]

It was around this time that President Bush called Vajpayee to assure of the importance US administration attached to India's role in the war against terrorism. However, on September 18, the Indian legislators gave a tough time to PM and External Affairs Minister on the question of Americans pandering to Pakistani sensitivities. And it was second time in less than a week that cabinet was utterly disappointed to learn that the Indian government has not received any formal request of assistance from US. Later, in the evening, the Prime Minister also told reporters that, "no specific requests" for assistance had been made by the US but dismissed as "hypothetical" another question – whether India was prepared to give "all assistance" as and when the American requests came in.[13]

Indian anxiety was by then clearly palpable across the borders by the Pakistanis. On September 19, General Musharraf, in his famous "lay-off" speech said, "They have offered all military facilities to America. They want America on their side. The objective is to get Pakistan declared as a terrorist state and harm our strategic interests and the Kashmir cause." Though, he did not mention who they were but it was obvious, he was referring to India. In India, on the other hand apprehension was mounting as summed up in *The Hindu's* editorial of September 18, that "contours of a possible coalition are still far from clear." And again on September 20, *The Hindu* pointed out that "regardless of tacit American assurance that present tie-up between the US and Pakistan need not destabilize peace and politics elsewhere on the international stage, the plan of forming the nucleus of a globalised alliance against terrorism does not yet seem to have crystallized." [14]

However, the best summing up of India's apprehensions and interests in the changed scenario was offered to Americans by a prominent academic, Kanti Bajpai, of the School of International Studies at Jawaharlal Nehru University, Delhi. His views appeared in an op-ed, published in *The Hindu* of September 22 and are of such far reaching significance that they deserve a detailed treatment. Kanti argued that "storm clouds are gathering over India-US relations" because Indian middle classes are worried that US, out of its present needs, has struck a kind of deal with Pakistan, reminiscent of 1950s and 1980s and Indian concerns and anxieties are to Americans dispensable and that, "US has sold India down the Indus."

Kanti argued that US's need to get Pakistan in its "coalition of 'moderate Islamic influentials' is understandable" and it may be that benefit of having India in that coalition at this stage are unclear but Washington needs to take a long-term view. In the long-term, it is the large democratic and developing India that is to US advantage and India due to its conflict with Pakistan over Kashmir "has a stake in the outcome of US policies in the region. India, therefore, matters in a coalition dedicated to managing terrorism problem."

He then suggested the remedies; it is important to mention a few of them because they have since then seen the light of the day, though perhaps not without a jolt from the Indian administration. (This will come later.) First, the US should publicly emphasize that it will not make a deal with Pakistan inimical to India's interests. In a rather interesting fashion he pointed out that US ignored India in the first few days and Pakistan successfully created the impression that it has a special relationship with the US and a new deal is in the offing. In the same vain, he suggested that US should be seen doing something in cooperation with India. It may not be something big or dramatic but it should be visible enough to the Indian middle classes to reassure them.

Second, "Washington must, at least privately, tell New Delhi that it will go beyond the immediate terrorism problem focused on Afghanistan." Kanti did not agree with the thesis that US efforts in Afghanistan will automatically help India in controlling and bringing normalcy to Kashmir. He, then identified the fronts where US should move to allay India's concerns.

First of all, it should apply pressure on Pakistan to wind down fundamentalist influences. This means at the very least, redefining the role of *madrassa* education in Pakistan. In addition, it means rooting out fundamentalist elements in the armed forces. Finally, and most importantly, in the short to medium term, it implies shutting down the militant groups operating in Kashmir. The Lashkar-e-Taiba, the Jaish-e-Mohammed, and the Hizbul Mujahideen are the three most important outfits. Washington should get Islamabad to act hard and fast against these groups and at least disarm them.

The second front that the US should move on, quietly but firmly, is to bring Kashmiri groups round to participating in Kashmir's electoral process. Some Kashmiri factions and sections are interested in contesting the polls. But the APHC has not come out publicly in support of the idea. Washington should use its influence with these groups. Pakistan will oppose Kashmiris voting and participating in the elections. Here is where the US can again be helpful beyond just Afghanistan. George Bush said that it would be a long hard campaign against terrorist violence and that it would require the use of punitive as well as positive incentives, that any strategy would have to combine economic, diplomatic, and political instruments in addition to the military. This would be a vital test case of subtle, strong, and extended engagement with the issue of terrorism.

Kanti also warned that in the long run these groups may sequester in Pakistan or Kashmir and: If these groups intensify their operations in India or do something spectacular like September 11 against Indian targets, there will be fantastic pressure on New Delhi to retaliate massively. This could lead to a confrontation with Pakistan, the likes of which we have not seen, with nuclear weapons not far away. [15]

In hindsight, we now know that ultimately US was forced to take a stock of Indian apprehensions and it ended up asking Pakistan to oblige India on all these demands so neatly illustrated by Kanti on September 22, 2001. This also includes a US position favourable to India on the electoral process in Kashmir. So, can a cynic analyst argue that if US had been persuaded quickly enough then the world would have been spared of the spectre of a possible nuclear meltdown in South Asia? Perhaps yes, but then in the third week of September, Americans, though acutely aware of India's importance to their larger world view, did not appreciate the level of Indian desperation and kept on reassuring Indians at various levels, but could not satisfy them. Can one ask the question, "Something dramatic had to happen for Americans to sit up and take notice of Indian concerns?"

On September 25, Indian National Security Advisor and Principal Secretary to the Prime Minister, Brajesh Mishra, was in Washington, meeting senior Bush administration officials and law-makers who again assured that India is part of the coalition against terror at many levels and in different ways. However he found US administration obsessed with "get Osama" project and took pains to point out that in spite of all the immediate concerns and objectives, the long-term implications should not be ignored or brushed aside. In particular, Mishra is said to have drawn attention to the networking of the Al-Qaeda as it pertains to the ongoing terrorism in Jammu & Kashmir.[16]

Recording the impressions of his visit and reception, Washington correspondent for Indian paper, *The Hindu* observed, "To say that India is totally out of the loop in the fight against terrorism is exaggerating things. But at least in the short term, the focus here is quite limited as far as the Bush administration is concerned. Senior officials have made no bones of the fact that the prime attention right now is on Osama bin Laden, his network and training camps." He also noted, "Mishra is here also at a time when there has been a tremendous amount of support and political sympathy for the President of Pakistan, General Pervez Musharraf, for his decision to fully align with the US in targeting the Taliban and Osama bin Laden. The political support to Islamabad aside, Washington, along with international financial institutions are putting together a hefty 'goodies bag' as well."[17]

The last week of September 2001 is very important to this analysis, as things seem to be moving to a point of convergence, perhaps to their logical end. The American Ambassador to India James Blackwell, in his first press conference in India and first major public gathering since 9/11 sought to dispel the perception that since the terrorist attacks against America two weeks ago, Pakistan had once again become the main focus of US policy in the subcontinent.

Blackwell said the relationship between India and the US had been "transformed in many practical ways" since September 11. This would have happened in any case but the attacks against the US had "accelerated" the process. He told press that India and the US were now engaged in cooperation "unthinkable even a month ago." The envoy pointed to the "intensity, frequency and transparency" of exchanges between the two governments at the diplomatic, intelligence and military levels. However, on the Indian offer of support to the US military operations against Afghanistan, Blackwell said that Washington had not made any request so far. When the US made up its mind on the military strategy to be adopted, it could come up with specific requests. [18]

A different mood emerged in a parliamentary meeting on September 27 in New Delhi. In a sharp distinction to the earlier sentiments expressed by both the government and Opposition benches, government now set at rest speculation on the nature of India's involvement in the proposed US action in Afghanistan. Addressing the meeting, the Prime Minister, Vajpayee, made it clear that India had not given any assurance either "directly or indirectly" on the use of its airbases. India's role was limited to intelligence sharing with the US. "We have given no direct or indirect assurance on making available airbases," Vajpayee told the meeting. And while pledging support to the government, the Opposition sounded a note of caution against deviating from the long-standing policy of non-alignment. [19] This change of mood was remarkably different from the one that prevailed in the same house only 12 days ago on September 15, when, with the only exception of CPI (M), virtually all political opinion supported extending airbases to US for its operations in Afghanistan.

In an equally significant change of tone, the Parliamentary Affairs Minister, Pramod Mahajan, in a press conference immediately after the two-hour long parliamentary meeting, said the government had made it clear that it was not under any illusion and was not depending on anyone in its fight against terrorism. [20] In an apparently unrelated development but nevertheless of significance in hindsight, the newspapers one day earlier, on September 27, carried stories citing unnamed "top security official" that clarified that contrary to earlier reports, militants are not leaving Kashmir but are actually regrouping and are planning major strikes to register their presence on the ground. [21]

Militants Attack Srinagar's Legislative Assembly

Kanti Bajpai in his above mentioned op-ed had predicted the possibility that militants when flushed out of Afghanistan may sequester in Indian or Pakistani Kashmir and their terrorist activities may force India to react with force against Pakistan. It may be a little ironical that militants struck exactly one week after his prophetic comments. On October 1, an unprecedented militant attack on the Kashmir Assembly left 38 dead and many injured. The Chief Minister, Farooq Abdullah, and his ministerial colleagues had, however, left the venue sometime earlier. [22] India immediately pointed the finger at Jaish-e-Muhammad, a militant outfit based in Pakistan. An anonymous caller first called to take responsibility of the attack but subsequently the organization formally denied any link or responsibility.

The identity of this anonymous caller was not the only intriguing thing about this militant attack. It also happened at a very crucial juncture in the US-led war against Taliban. Indian External Affairs Minister Jaswant Singh was about to arrive in Washington, busy in the final stages of mounting an attack on Afghanistan and thus relatively disinterested in an Indian "wish list on Kashmir". Washington correspondent of an Indian paper observed that his "arrival barely caused a ripple". [23] A week earlier National Security Advisor could not get undivided attention from the administration. But now, with terrorist bombing of Kashmir assembly, situation had dramatically changed. US administration had to sit up, open its eyes and listen to an injured India; a democratic partner that may not have been of any immediate military or logistic support for war effort but could certainly wreck the game by opening up any kind of front on the western borders of Pakistan in Kashmir.

Citing the attack on the Jammu & Kashmir Assembly, the Prime Minister, Atal Behari Vajpayee, wrote to the US President, George Bush, bringing to his attention the need to urgently restrain Pakistan from backing international terrorists in Kashmir. "Incidents of this kind raise questions for our security which, as a democratically elected leader of India, I have to address in our supreme national interest." Pointing to the urgency of holding back Islamabad, he said, "Pakistan must understand that there is a limit to the patience of the people of

India." In the letter, sent hours after the car bomb attack, Vajpayee said, "I write this with anguish at the most recent terrorist attack in our state of Jammu & Kashmir... A Pakistan-based terrorist organisation, Jaish-e-Muhammad, has claimed responsibility for the dastardly act and named the Pakistani national, based in Pakistan, as one of the suicide bombers involved." [24]

Though many in the state department, confronted by the faceless monster of international terrorism, might have wondered on the nature of terrorists, who not only intervened at a most propitious moment to bolster the Indian cause, but also called to leave their exact names and details but this was not the time for such reflections. Within the subcontinent, India was furiously demanding, in a war like language, that Pakistan ban Lashkar-e-Taiba and Jaish-e-Muhammad the two organizations it alleged were freely operating from Pakistan and Pakistan controlled Kashmir. [25] And in Washington, an aggrieved and earnest Indian External Affairs Minister, Jaswant Singh, was breathing on their necks.

The US President, George Bush, then personally assured India that the US campaign against terrorism is global and not one-dimensional as seen through the prism of Osama bin Laden and the Al-Qaeda terror network. George Bush conveyed this to the visiting External Affairs and Defence Minister, Jaswant Singh, when President Bush not only dropped in at a White House meeting between Singh and the US National Security Advisor, Condoleezza Rice, but spent 45 minutes of a 75-minute discussion with him. Washington correspondent of Indian paper, *The Hindu*, reported that, "Mr Bush had good reasons for spending his time at the meeting in spite of his hectic schedule....New Delhi has been quite wary of the growing Washington-Islamabad nexus, especially as it pertains to fighting terrorism." [26]

Next day, as Jaswant Singh stood by the Secretary of State, Colin Powell declared, "The events that took place in Kashmir yesterday, that terrible terrorist act, that heinous act, that killed innocent civilians and also struck a government facility... It is the kind of terrorism that we are united against." In a message, General Powell reiterated, "And as the President made it clear... we are going after terrorism in a comprehensive way, not just in the present instance of Al-Qaeda and Osama bin Laden, but terrorism as it affects nations around the world, to include the kind of terrorism that affects India." But Gen. Powell would not comment on any specific allegations that Pakistan was behind the terrorists in Afghanistan or Kashmir.[27] It was certainly music to Indian ears but still inability of the administration to condemn Pakistan for the acts was disappointing. Powell's caution was also shared by Secretary of Defence, Donald Rumsfeld. It is important to mention here that this was probably the first time that administration openly used the word "Al-Qaeda" in the context of Kashmir. India wanted to hear "Pakistan" instead of "Al-Qaeda", however, later Indian government and media, often talked of Al-Qaeda and Pakistan as one and the same thing.

This discussion, at this crucial juncture, will remain incomplete if we do not make some brief comments on the "false alarm of hijacking" that took place between the nights of October 3-4. A Boeing 737 of Alliance Airlines, a subsidiary of the Indian Airlines, that took off from Mumbai at night bound for Delhi, was soon declared hijacked by the civil aviation authorities. International media treated the news with scepticism raising the question that why India was not more careful in the prevailing circumstances. Pakistan promptly closed its airspace and alleged citing its own intelligence sources of October 2 that this is a plan to implicate Islamabad to intensify the international pressure being created since the Kashmir Assembly bomb attacks. [28]

The plane had landed at Delhi, and crisis management team met under Union Minister L.K. Advani. Plane was surrounded by NSG commandos and media was watching the story for a live coverage. However, by 4 a.m. the civil aviation authorities finally declared that hijacking was a "false alarm" and was caused due to confusion inside the cockpit. Unfortunately the sudden happy resolution left many questions unanswered. To begin with, there was a call to the offices of Alliance Airlines informing of the hijack. And at the height of the crisis, the Civil Aviation Secretary, A.H. Jung informed the press that there are two hijackers on board who do not speak good English. A visibly embarrassed Vajpayee government ordered a high powered inquiry to investigate the origin of this false alarm but only six days later the 24-year-old young man who had received the anonymous call, and was, therefore, a crucial witness to this investigation, was found dead of a heart attack. [29]

In the following week, British PM Tony Blair visited the subcontinent and Vajpayee, now unfettered to blame Pakistan in front of international cameras, kept on rubbing in his mantra about Pakistani terrorism. In an obvious reference to Pakistan, Vajpayee said, "We discussed the sinister agenda behind the Srinagar bomb blast. Even while extending our whole-hearted support to the pursuit of the guilty terrorists of September 11, we should not let countries pursue their own terrorist agenda under cover of this action."[30]

It is time for us to take stock of the situation. This was second week of October 2001 and by now US Secretary of State, Colin Powell's visit to the troubled region, that is subcontinent, was already announced and US and British bombings to aid Northern Alliance had already begun. Pakistan was too deeply embroiled in this situation and was providing assistance of all sorts to the US-led coalition. The main goal of US and British diplomacy – after realizing the extent of Indian desperation – was to placate Indians in such a way that prevents them from creating trouble for their war effort.

Indians, it can be argued, fashioned and waged a successful strategy that helped them barge their way into a situation by creating nuisance for the US-led war effort. Indians knew their importance in the overall US worldview and knew they were taking calculated risks. Though US would not have ignored them in the long term anyway but they were apprehensive, as so clearly illustrated by Kanti Bajpai of JNU, on two major counts: one, Pakistan might develop a sustainable relationship that can put pressure upon them for some sort of dialogue on Kashmir. Second, in relative terms, the new US-Pak relationship may interfere with their already achieved but as yet nascent position in the emerging world order – that to a great extent depends upon Indo-US roadmap at least at this stage.

In hindsight, we can see that by the end of first week of October, they had successfully completed the first part of their strategy. They caused nuisance and were rewarded for it. And this exercise further helped them to understand and fine-tune the pressure they could bring upon Pakistan by threatening to upset the interests of US. By the second week, Pakistan's President General Musharraf, prodded on by the US and Britain, was talking to Vajpayee assuring him of conducting an inquiry into the whole matter. When Musharraf expressed his desire that the stalled process of dialogue between India and Pakistan should be reinitiated, Vajpayee reminded him that if Pakistani focus would remain on Kashmir then no progress would be made. A patient Musharraf, aware of the fast changing kaleidoscope, politely listened. [31]

In Washington on October 11, General Powell, when asked by CBS-TV whether the US was concerned that India might try to take advantage of the situation and ignite a conflict while the world is distracted, answered, "I don't think that will be the case. In fact, we have been in touch with both governments and they both realize the volatile nature of this situation and I think both of them understand this is not the time for provocative action, which would cause the situation in the region to become unstable." He further said, "Both countries had been very forthcoming in terms of the support in the US-led campaign against terrorism. Pakistan is on the frontlines of it, really, because of their proximity to Afghanistan, and President Musharraf has done quite a number of very important things. The Indians have also been very forthcoming with the support that they have given." [32] Perhaps what he meant was that Indians are helping by not opening another front in the west of Pakistan, in Kashmir.

In his subsequent visit to Pakistan and India, Powell was treading a careful path. He assured Pakistanis that US takes a long-term view on the region and will thus maintain its engagement with Pakistan beyond Afghanistan. In his press conference in Islamabad, he described Kashmir as central to Indo-Pakistan relations and encouraged dialogue between the two countries. "We believe a dialogue on Kashmir is important. We believe maintenance of the Line of Control and the exercise of restraint is also very very important and avoidance of provocative acts which could lead to a conflict of any kind," he said.[33] However, during his follow-up trip to India, Ministry of External Affairs promptly rejected that Kashmir is central to the conflict between India and Pakistan and further clarified that India wishes to address Indo-Pak relations only in a "composite manner".[34]

Militant Attack on Indian Parliament

Though the coercive diplomacy that India set into motion after the "mysterious attacks" on the Indian Parliament on December 13, remained the focus of intense press commentaries but it would only be fair to argue that Indian strategy had developed its basic skeleton, and won a tacit US approval for itself. By the middle of October and the six-month long duel that started two months later was only to accentuate and consolidate its dominant position. Pakistan no doubt, along with US, was at the receiving end of this campaign, but it could also be seen as a clear Indian declaration of "regional assertion" to the world at large. Strategists in South Block understand too well the importance of war fought on media to the emerging global consciousness.

The timing of the attack on Indian Parliament is worth examining. The Srinagar bomb blasts took place on October 1, at the very beginning of the US-led campaign in Afghanistan. By that time Northern Alliance struggle was well on its way and direct US air attacks were imminent. As we have seen the terrorist attacks in Srinagar brought India, which had hitherto felt ignored, into the centre of the things. From the second week of October onwards, when US and Britain understood Indian dilemma and made public and private efforts to assuage Indian fears, nothing of any significance, whatsoever, happened in India or Indian controlled Kashmir till the very conclusion of the war in Afghanistan. This was the time when an operation of somewhat unpredictable duration was undertaken in Afghanistan to which Pakistan provided a crucial launching pad. We can safely surmise that US would not have looked kindly on any distraction at this juncture – especially one with doubtful credibility.

Kabul had fallen on November 13[35], however, the struggle continued till Taliban surrendered Kandhar on December 8. [36] Hamid Karzai, the head of interim government, arrived in Kabul on October 10, and the struggle against remnants of Taliban was limited to Tora Bora caves. The US administration and media could now conceivably be persuaded to look on issues elsewhere. It was precisely at this time, and not before, that the unknown terrorists decided to attack Indian Parliament buildings in New Delhi on December 13. In terms of timing, terrorists provided a most propitious moment for the Indian government to draw world attention to their concerns regarding Kashmir. Could it be argued that things inside India have faithfully followed a decent and responsible timetable? After all everyone from London to Brussels to Washington was telling New Delhi, from September onwards, that its concerns about Pakistan sponsored terrorism in Kashmir are genuine and will be addressed at an appropriate time. What could have been more appropriate time than the end of war in Afghanistan?

India quickly claimed that "dead attackers" of the Indian Parliament were of Pakistani origin; it arrested their accomplices, and found out Pakistani markings on weapons employed. However, it refused showing the faces of the dead men to the press, twice refused Pakistani requests for a joint inquiry and turned down FBI offers for investigation into the crime. Pakistanis condemned the attacks, offered their help and cried "conspiracy" but their arguments, however, reasoned they might have been, were of little consequence. By December 20, Indian strike forces were on the move towards the borders.

India recalled its ambassador from Pakistan and terminated its land and road links. It was the first time since 1971 that India took the step of recalling its envoy back from Pakistan. Under tremendous pressure from US and Britain, and less pronounced sources from EU, Pakistan moved in steps and stages to arrest leaders of militant outfits operating in Kashmir and banned their organizations. US took the lead by branding Lashkar-e-Taiba and Jaish-e-Muhammad as "foreign terrorist organizations" and Pakistan followed suit. General Musharraf in a much awaited televised address to the nation on January 12, announced his decision to ban these militant organizations and invited Vajpayee for talks.

Elections in Indian Controlled Kashmir

Pakistani government's decision to ban these militant organizations was less of a physical consequence as they were not reliant on government support and hardly maintained bank accounts in their names. Also there is reasonable evidence to suggest that by end 1990s, militancy, barring the sudden inexplicable dramatic events that were helpful to Indian public relations strategy, had ceased to be of any serious consequence to Indian hold in Kashmir. However, Pakistani decisions under US pressure and India's coercive diplomacy were helpful to India as they sent powerful signals to change the overall context of the Kashmir struggle. It graduated ingloriously from a people's struggle into a foreign sponsored terrorism against a legitimate government. Kashmiris, pitched against a regional hegemony of the size and power of India, relied upon Pakistani support of sorts to balance the odds. Even the nationalists like Sheikh Abdullah and his followers, who have sought to find, at various stages, an autonomous expression in alliance with the Indian Union have relied upon "Pakistani threat" to further their agenda of extracting political concessions from Delhi.

Pakistani presence on their borders and its vocal support, then ensures a dream pipe of sorts for Kashmiris of all political opinion; it inspires disenfranchised poor masses with the romantic possibility of freedom, however distinct it may be; it offers moderate political forces, who realize the staying power of Indian Union, better chances of clinching a dialogue with Delhi and ironically it has helped a generation of non-entities like Bakshi Ghulam Muhammad and Farooq Abdullah to sustain a political profile by blackmailing Delhi – afraid of Kashmiri masses' romantic attachment with Pakistan.

The spectre of a Pakistan locked in a nut cracker, and being pushed to a corner under India's coercive diplomacy, perceived as being aided and abetted by a conniving Washington, sent the message to Kashmiris which India so desperately wanted to send; a besieged Pakistan cannot come to their aid. Indian strategy has to talk of "Pakistan sponsored terrorism" as it is a marketable commodity to western audience but in reality it needed to clip that Kashmiri "pipe line of hope" that "Pakistan stands at the border." Indian strategists correctly concluded that with this "hope pipe line" gone, Kashmiri political elements, across-the-board would clearly see the reality fate has prepared for them.

With the hindsight of the events that have unfolded, it can safely be argued that it was certainly a great victory for the Indian strategy as it set the stage for an election exercise that has given the US and EU blessings from the beginning. International media also extended its good will, and APHC was under pressure to remain at least ambivalent, if it could not extend its support. Whether India is prepared or even capable of producing a political formula that can satisfy thc aspirations of Kashmiri people, with or without the framework of Indian Union, is a different discussion, beyond the scope of this paper. However, one thing is getting clear that with this success of Indian strategy on the horns of a carefully crafted coercive diplomacy, Indian need, desire and even ability to enter into a meaningful dialogue with either Pakistan or Kashmiris has further declined.

Emerging Imperatives for US Policy

In order to better understand what attitudes US policy makers now take towards Kashmir, we need to appreciate the dynamics that govern Indo-US roadmap and how they are essentially different from those with Pakistan. US imperative to build a closer relationship with India stems from three closely related yet distinct factors. One, after the end of Cold War, and with the appreciation of China as a strategic competitor rather than partner, it increasingly sees India as a counterweight to China. Second, with the liberalization of Indian economy, US corporations see Indian corporate world as a partner and India as a large potential market. Third, Americans of Indian origin are now emerging as a potent force that has started to influence domestic US politics in myriad ways.

These imperatives in themselves are not new. India always enjoyed serious consideration in US strategic view of the region and the world. Even in the Cold War days when India either strongly criticized US policies as leader of the non-aligned movement or later as a pro-Soviet state, US remained conscious of India's importance and thus careful in handling India. And even otherwise, India had powerful voices inside US academic world and liberal circles that could instil some balance in its favour. Kissinger comments in his latest book: "Indian leaders....calculated correctly that, based on its democratic institutions and elevated rhetoric, it had enough friends in liberal and intellectual circles within United States to keep American irritation within tolerable bounds." [37]

However with the end of Cold War and India's need to grow out of the Russian camp, and its opening of economy to foreign companies, the various imperatives driving US policy have finally converged to provide a sort of roadmap for Indo-US relations. On the contrary, US relations with Pakistan, from the very beginning, developed within a limited bandwidth of government to government interaction. Pakistan never had any friends in academic or liberal circles that shape public opinion and policy within America. US administrations, one after the other, have looked upon Pakistan as a convenient policy tool; may be trusted and loyal but essentially disposable. Though this certainly cannot explain the ups and downs of Pak-US relations in entirety but can help to understand the unstable dynamics that govern it.

Another related factor, but of distinct importance on its own, needs to be understood. Though US after the Gulf War gradually emerged as a kind of de-facto global government and certain scholars have argued that with its control of multilateral institutions and media, it is in fact a new kind of empire,[38] the exercise of power and influence within the American society is if any thing very different from past empires. Much of public debate and policy formation, critical to foreign relations, at the level of Senate and Congress takes place in a context that is highly influenced by a topical consciousness inspired by media. [39]

Pakistan suffers from natural disadvantages in this kind of exercise. It had few friends – if any at all – within the popular media that shapes American consciousness and in turn policy making. Most of its support historically has originated from the old "realist" school of thought or from government agencies like Pentagon or CIA or those former US diplomats who have served in the region and have, therefore, a first-hand understanding of issues that confront US policy and affect US long-term interests. Such a small pocket of support would have mattered something in an old style British or Soviet empire, where matters of national interests, even at the periphery, were influenced by a coterie of informed opinion. But in a rapidly fluctuating sea of topical public opinion, influenced by powerful lobbies and in turn bearing upon policy decisions, this limited pocket of support amounts to little more than "nothing".

In the aftermath of Soviet withdrawal from Afghanistan, two factors then easily altered inherently unstable Pak-US relations. One, in wake of the fall of the Berlin Wall and emergence of East Europe from under the iron curtain, there was a sudden loss of interest of US policy makers and thus administration into this region in the north of India. Second, the struggle in Afghanistan also influenced the polity within Pakistan, and a society and administration emerged, that was more closely identified with causes in the Middle East. This shift towards the right of religious spectrum in itself would have mattered little if US, in yet another short-sighted policy reversal, had not imposed sanctions on Pakistan under the Pressler Amendment. These sanctions failed to achieve their stated objectives, however, they reduced goodwill for US in both Pakistani public and government. [40] The net effect was a reduced influence for US in this region as a whole and a streak of "anti-Americanism" never seen before.

It is essentially within this context that US policy towards Pakistan and Kashmir needs to be understood. Indo-US roadmap towards a strategic relationship of wider significance is not necessarily a threat to Pakistan, if both sides take a mature attitude. For Pakistan, it is important to appreciate the combination of imperatives driving US policy and for Americans it is important to prevent it becoming a "zero-sum game". During the phase of Indian coercive diplomacy, US policy makers have repeatedly tried to assure Indians that a Pak-US and Indo-US relation should not be looked upon as a "zero-sum game". That was when a belligerent India was threatening to disrupt US interests. The test of US maturity now lies in how it will interact with a Pakistan in which religious parties in the shape of MMA have swept western and north-western belts of Pakistan on a mix of aggrieved Pushtun sentiments and anti-Americanism. And as a consequence, Kashmir also remains a defining issue for large sections of Pakistani populace.

Given the strong imperatives inherent in Indo-US roadmap and the increasing influence of Indian lobby inside US, it is widely feared that US will pressurize Pakistan to accept LoC in Kashmir as a solution; in other words subscribing to the Indian position that Kashmir is an internal issue. The underlying assumption of US policy, as exhibited so far, is that one-sided pressure can be endlessly applied to Pakistani state to nudge it in a desired direction with some economic incentives on the way. This is a dangerous assumption because if this policy continued, it will radicalise Pakistani politics, strengthen the anti-American feelings and threaten the stability of Pakistani state and society by sharpening the wedge between the governing elite and the governed. Formation of non-state actors will then jeopardize US interests in a vital region where it has – despite a deep sense of betrayal – to this day enjoyed tremendous institutional goodwill.

What possible solution can emerge in Kashmir acceptable to both India and Pakistan is beyond the scope of this paper but to develop a roadmap towards it, and to prevent regional stress waves, US needs to persuade both states for a dialogue. And it needs to develop a comprehensive relationship with Pakistani state and society at various levels. This relationship needs to grow out of the much-repeated aphorism of Pakistan being "our frontline partner against terrorism" to a platform where Pakistan is perceived as a moderate Muslim country with strong institutional and public links with US. The best guarantee for that to happen is if Pakistan can develop cultural and business exchanges with US and can make it attractive for US investments. Though US administration cannot certainly persuade corporate America to take an interest in Pakistan, but it can help Pakistan improve its business climate to make itself more attractive. A number of steps are badly needed.

One, US should help improve Pakistan's judicial and court system by helping to develop a comprehensive blueprint and providing funds and technical support. Though, Pak-US cooperation to improve law and order situation is emphasized in a narrow sense but it needs to be understood that no lasting solution to this problem can emerge if court procedure and performance is not improved. An assertive and self-respecting judiciary that can uphold the spirit of law in a transparent fashion can provide the basis for a mature and realistic relationship for Pak-US relations. The US administration's decision not to bully Pakistan for the extradition of Omar Saeed Sheikh[41] was a mature decision [42] and in the same vein it may be said that the whisking away of Mir Aimal Kasi in 1998, without the transparent 'due process of law' was damaging to the judicial institution within Pakistan. [43]

An independent and strong judicial system will contribute in two distinct yet interrelated ways. It will help improve the law and order situation and it can instil business confidence by strengthening the exercise of contract law and increasing the predictability of business transactions. The row over the Independent Power Producers (IPP's) in late nineties severely damaged the investment climate and confidence needs to be restored if Pakistan has to attract US corporate interest.

Second, with the revival of democracy in Pakistan, US should now move forward to develop a multi-level relationship with Pakistani parliament. The best strategy for Pakistani parliament to acquire greater authority vis-à-vis military and civil bureaucracy will be by consolidating parliamentary procedure and US can provide valuable help to strengthen the committee proceedings. Third, the limited academic exchanges between US and Pakistani think tanks, universities and media need to be expanded. And this should include the programs for US scholars to visit and stay within Pakistani institutions. [44]

This can help create a better understanding of respective positions. It needs to be understood that anti-Americanism in Pakistan did not start from bottom upwards but has travelled down from the elite in government and media that felt betrayed by the American attitudes and sudden reversals of policy for examples Pressler Amendment.

Finally re-establishing the long abandoned training exchanges between US and Pakistani militaries and joint exercises will go a long way in assuring Pakistanis that far from being sacrificed in a "zero-sum game" they are part of US strategic vision for this region. Best hope for a Kashmir solution – satisfactory to both India and Pakistan – now also lies embedded in this kind of arrangement.

* *(Re-printed with permission from Islamabad Policy Research Institute Journal, Pakistan, Winter 2003.)*

Endnotes

1. Sundeep Dikshit, "Strike forces moved closer to the border," *The Hindu,* December 21, 2001. The movement involved troops from central India, along with tanks and bridging equipment as well as other armoured units towards the International Border with Pakistan along Rajasthan and Gujarat. The increase in military traffic to the western border was apparently, according to Indians, in response to Pakistan's deployment of its strike forces—Army Reserves (South) and Army Reserves (North); Pakistan saw it differently. It is, however, important to realize the speed with which forward deployment started to build up.

2. This scenario was first raised by Dr K. Subrahmanyam, a leading Indian strategic thinker (and principal author of the 1999 Draft Nuclear Doctrine) in an oral presentation at the University of California at Berkeley on October 8, 2001. Dr Subrahmanyam argued that in a future coup, Pakistani's nuclear assets can fall in the hands of religious fanatics and made it abundantly clear that New Delhi would expect the US to take out Pakistan's bomb in that case. Since

then, it has been used much more loosely in Indian and Pakistani press and discussed on US media.

3. Muthida Majlis-e-Amal (MMA), a combined electoral alliance of religious parties that swept Pakistan's north-western and western provinces in the 2002 elections on a campaign of anti-Americanism predicated on aggrieved Pushtun sentiments due to American bombings on Afghanistan.

4. See, for instance, detailed discussion of the US perceptions, interests and attitudes towards both India and Pakistan by Bruce Riedel in his paper "American Diplomacy and the 1999 Kargil Summit at Blair House" submitted in Policy Paper Series 2002 at The Centre for the Advanced Study of India, University of Pennsylvania. Riedel was special Assistant to the President and senior Director for Near East and South Asia Affairs in the National Security Council at the White House from 1997 to 2001.
<http://www.sas.upenn.edu/casi/reports/Riedel Paper 051302.htm>.

5. Ibid. A careful reading of Bruce Riedel's account in the above cited policy paper will clearly illustrate the point. This was also a common perception in Pakistani press and quoted in other places, for instance, see Tariq Ali, *Clash of Fundamentalisms*. In chapter 16th of this book, "Plain Tales from Pakistan" he writes, "Yes, it was another coup, but with a difference. This was the first time the army had seized power without the approval of Washington. In October 1999, Nawaz Sharif, with US support, attempted to remove General Musharraf as Chief of Army Staff of Pakistan Army. They chose to do so while he was in Sri Lanka on an official trip. The plan backfired." Tariq Ali, *Clash of Fundamentalisms* (London: Verso, 2000), p. 200. These comments are important as Tariq Ali, a die hard Marxist, has been a fierce critic of Pakistani military and in his controversial book, *Can Pakistan Survive?*, he severely criticized Pakistan military.

6. Chidand Rajghatta, "Jaswant to hard sell India in US," *The Hindu,* October 1, 2001.

7. Atul Aneja, "Government discusses fall out of the US attacks on the region," *The Hindu,* September 14, 2001.

8. *The Hindu*, September 13, 2001.

9. Atul Aneja, "US may turn to India if Pakistan refuses air bases," *The Hindu*, September 16, 2001. This detailed news report makes an interesting reading in the sense that Indian elite at that time seems to be making lot of emotional investment into the issue of bases to US.

10. *The Hindu*, September 16, 2001. "Proceed with caution," report by Special Correspondent. In this meeting the CPI (M) said, in a written statement, that it strongly opposed the Government's move to offer logistical facilities and participate in the proposed US military action. "We have reiterated this position clearly again in the meeting." This was the only note of dissent from the whole political spectrum.

11. See for instance editorial of *The Hindu,* September 16, 2001, "Seeking an active role," in which the most liberal of the Indian papers argued that India has to be clear and specific about its objectives in siding with the US led coalition.

12. *The Hindu,* September 19, 2001, "Reports of Pak. Conditions false," by special correspondent. US Ambassador to India, James Blackwell had to personally convey these assurances to Union Minister Mr. L. K. Advani.

13. Harish Khare, "Fears over US-Pak. Deal allayed," *The Hindu*, September 19, 2001. It is also helpful to read *The Hindu's* editorial of September 19, "An evolving anti-terror agenda." This discussion, like many others, help to understand the deep-seated anxiety that had started to grip the Indian mind on the issue of being left out from the US led campaign.

14. *The Hindu*, September 18, 2001. Editorial, "An evolving anti-terror agenda," and also see editorial of September 20, 2001, "Towards an Anti-terror Alliance."

15. Kanti Bajpai, "India-US ties after September 11," *The Hindu,* September 22, 2001.

16. Sridhar Krishnaswami, "Mishra makes his point on terrorism in J & K," *The Hindu*, October 26, 2001.

17. Ibid.

18. Raja C. Mohan, "Unprecedented Cooperation," *The Hindu*, September 27, 2001.

19. "No promises to U.S: PM, " *The Hindu*, September 28, 2001.

20. Ibid.

21. Shujaat Bukhari,"Militants not quitting the Valley," *The Hindu*, October 27, 2001.

22. Shujaat Bukhari, " Suicide bomber targets J & K Assembly," *The Hindu*, October 2, 2001.

23. Rajghatta, Chidand, "Jaswant to hard sell India in US," *The Hindu*, October 1, 2001.

24. Atul Aneja, " It is time to restrain Pak. PM tells Bush," *The Hindu*, October 3, 2001

25. "Rein in Lashkar, Jaish too, India tells Pak.," *The Hindu*, October 2, 2001.

26. Sridhar Krishnaswami, "Campaign Global: Bush," *The Hindu*, October 3, 2001.

27. Sridhar Krishnaswami, " J & K too on agenda: Powell," *The Hindu*, October 4, 2001.

28. Bhaduri Nilanjan Jha, "The Hijack that never was" *Times of India*, October 4, 2001. For step by step details see " A blow by blow Account" in *Times of India* of October 4 and details regarding the Pakistani assertions see " Hijack Drama aimed at Discrediting us: Pak.," *Times of India*, October 4, 2001. A good account is also available in "Alliance Air Plane Hijacked," by Harish Khare in *The Hindu* of October 4, 2001.

29. Ambreen Ali Shah, "Sudden death of a witness in Hijack Drama," *The Telegraph* (Calcutta), October 10, 2001. The witness, Shahnawaz Wani, was the supervisor on duty in the Alliance Airlines office in Delhi, who received the anonymous call informing that the plane was hijacked and he had then set into motion the security operation by informing his superiors. With his death, this lead was finished right at its origin.

30. "Check Countries sponsoring Terrorism; says Vajpayee," *The Hindu*, October 7, 2001.

31. Harish Khare, "Musharraf rings up Vajpayee," *The Hindu*, October 9, 2001.

32. "India won't ignite the conflict," *The Hindu*, October 12, 2001.

33. "Resume Dialogue," *The Hindu*, October 16, 2001.

34. "India raises Powell's remarks on Kashmir," *The Hindu*, October 17, 2001.

35. "Northern Alliance Forces enter Kabul," *The Hindu*, November 14, 2001.

36. "Taliban Surrender Kandhar," *The Hindu*, December 8, 2001.

37. Henry Kissinger, *Does America Need a Foreign Policy?* (New York: Simon & Schuster), p. 156.

38. The best assertion of this view comes from Michael Hardt and Antonio Negri's book, *Empire,* in which they argue that today's empire draws on elements of US constitutionalism, with its tradition of hybrid identities and expanding frontiers.

39. Stephen Walt, Professor of International Affairs at Harvard University's John. F. Kennedy School of Govt., pointed out in a far reaching article in *Foreign Affairs* that, "two thirds of the Republicans elected to Congress in 1994 reportedly did not possess passports and argued that due to decline of interest in foreign affairs the power of special interest groups who take strong focused positions has increased. For a detailed discussion see: Stephen Walt, "Two Cheers for Clinton's Foreign Policy," *Foreign Affairs*, March/April 2000 (Vol. 79, No.2), pp. 65-66.

40. The White House Press Briefing on April 11, 1995, immediately after Bhutto-Clinton meeting gives a fairly good idea that State Dept. did realize the negative fallout of Pressler Amendment and its implications for US interests in this region but remained stalled due to the complexity of legislative process. A question arises: The complexity of US procedures may be of relevance to academicians but does it help the people of Pakistan who see repeated US betrayals? Transcript of this briefing is available at < http://www.fas.org/news/pakistan/1995/950412-387114.htm>

41. Ahmed Omar Saeed Sheikh was awarded death penalty by a Pakistani court on July 15, 2002 in the trial related to the abduction and murder of the *Wall Street Journal* reporter Daniel Pearl. *Dawn,* July 16, 2002.

42. For details see, "Agreement on Omar's trial in Pakistan," *Dawn,* May 12, 2002. After Pakistan's Interior Minister, Moinuddin Haider visited

US in May, it was announced by States Dept. that Pakistani judicial system should go first. It was still not clear if US will like to try him later or will the trial in Pakistan will be considered sufficient.

43. Mir Aimal Kasi, a Pakistani citizen was convicted by a Virginia court of the murder of two CIA employees outside Agency's headquarters in Langley, Virginia on January 25, 1993. On June 15, 1997, Kasi was arrested in a remote tribal area inside Pakistan and was flown out of Pakistan without any due process of extradition. It was claimed that his extradition took place under the 1931 treaty concluded between the British Empire and US. However, later his lawyers, provided by the Virginia State, pointed out that his extradition was illegal, as the 1931 treaty did not apply to his case as it stipulated that extradition has to take place in accordance with the law of the land from which prosecution seeks to extradite the defendant. However, in reply, the Supreme Courts of Virginia and US maintained that Kasi was not extradited but was instead 'kidnapped' by the FBI and as such there was no violation of the treaty. Kasi was later executed by lethal injection on November 14, 2002. For details, see "Aimal Kasi to be executed on 14th," *Dawn,* November 6, 2002.

44. This is important because Pakistanis travelling and living in US are common and Pakistani scholars tend to understand US position much better than their American counterparts. Programmes similar to that, usually offered in India, which makes it possible for US scholars to live with universities and think tanks, should be created.

From Divergence to Convergence and Back Again: Some Structural Constraints on Stability in India-Pakistan Relations

Subrata K. Mitra

In retrospect, once the dust has settled on the embattled mountain peaks of Kargil, the four months that separate the Lahore Declaration and the first Indian air strikes will be remembered as a period of lost opportunities for lasting peace in South Asia. If the signing of the agreement between the prime ministers of India and Pakistan in the historic location of Lahore, signaled the maturing of a process of deliberation between India and Pakistan on the main points of conflict including Kashmir, then the discovery of the massive infiltration on the Indian side of the Line of Control, and the rapid Indian response including air strikes, not seen since 1971, were a return to the past when the two neighbours could conceptualize one another only in terms of violent conflict. The sheer rapidity with which the scene changed from diplomacy of Lahore to war in Kargil questions the foundations on which the former was based.

In their own ways Lahore and Kargil describe two different ways of conceptualizing India-Pakistan relations. The Lahore Declaration symbolizes a non-dichotomous model which suggests a substantive base of shared interests from which diplomacy could work towards the containment and solution of other conflicts. Now, the outbreak of war so soon after the fanfare with which the Lahore Accord was signed makes the peace process look irrelevant to the reality of India-Pakistan relations which is better described as a dichotomous model, one where the two countries are seen as locked in a zero-sum conflict which leaves no room for negotiation or co-operation. The objective of this essay is to enquire into the origin of the two models and examine their implications for regional security.

The Problem Stated

Both dichotomous and non-dichotomous models start from the premise that states are sovereign actors which act solely out of national interest. The dichotomous model which underpins the analysis of India-Pakistan relations for many observers of South Asian politics since the inception of the two states as a consequence of the Partition of British India. The non-dichotomous model conceptualizes the interests of the two states in non-zero-sum terms which allows for co-operation in some areas. There are other secondary differences between the two approaches as well. The dichotomous model is "backward looking" in the sense that it draws its main inspiration from the "two-nation theory" which conceptualizes the contemporary political scene in South Asia in terms of the unfinished history of Partition as long as Pakistan does not have control over the whole of Kashmir. The state of Pakistan, according to the advocates of this approach is locked against a more powerful strategic adversary. In consequence, as the sole actor capable of defending the integrity of the nation, the state can, if need be at the cost of democracy at home, take every measure including alliance and war, to protect its sovereignty.[1] The non-dichotomous mode, on the other hand, looks beyond the Partition of the subcontinent and postulates the foundation of the South Asian Association for Regional Co-operation as the point of departure and recognizes the national states as principal but not exclusive actors in regional politics. At a given point of time, the state is represented by specific interests though the representatives of the state typically speak in the name of the whole nation, and with an indefinite time horizon. The non-dichotomous model recognizes actors above and below the state and brings into analysis, interests that are not represented by the state. It casts binary conflicts as nested within larger, regional structures.

Drawing on the history of conflict in South Asia and the logic of two-person non-cooperative games, this paper suggests that lasting peace in the region requires both India and Pakistan to follow the non-dichotomous model. A temporary and fragile truce is possible when both follow the dichotomous model. But belligerency and low intensity war can be expected when one actor follows the dichotomous model and the other a non-dichotomous model. The paper examines the implications of these conjectures on the basis of the history of war and security dilemma in South Asia. It shows that though the dichotomous model has mostly dominated this relation, there has been an increasing realization that the maximization of interests in terms of this model could actually lower the interest of individual actors. These lost "peace dividends" nevertheless remain beyond the reach of the states locked in zero-sum conflicts because of the very logic of the nature of their conflict relations, akin to a prisoner's dilemma game. Drawing on Axelrod's model of recursive games and confidence-building measures the article shows how a non-dichotomous approach could enhance welfare of both sides. However, the return of violent conflict in Kargil shows the fragility of the process of transition from the dichotomous to the non-dichotomous model. On the basis of the analysis undertaken here, the article suggests that stable peace in the South Asian context requires the adoption of a two-track strategy by both actors and a triangular normalization which involves India, Pakistan and China. Before we look at the origins of the two models and the history of their interaction, we shall briefly examine their formal implications with the help of a two person, non-co-operative game.

A Formal Model of India-Pakistan Relations

The theory employed here is taken from two person non-co-operative games. For each party – India and Pakistan – there is a choice between two tactics:

a) maintain status quo, corresponding to a state of conflict.

b) arms reduction.

Both players make their choices independently (that is without negotiating with the other). The "pay-offs" to the players make no inter-personal comparison of utility. Thus, 0 implies the least utility to the actor concerned, that is, a least desirable outcome. Higher numbers in the cell entries imply more utility for the actor concerned, and as such, more preferable outcome. In the pay-off matrix presented below, the first figure in each cell denotes the utility to the player named on the left (that is, India) and the second figure the utility to the player named above (that is, Pakistan). In the game analysed below, the expected outcome in an end-game scenario is as follows:

If both players try to "play it safe", that is, maximize minimum gain, they end up at the status quo where each is individually worse off than the best outcome where both reduce arms. Players might realize that and try to move away unilaterally in the direction of co-operation, leading to unilateral, non-negotiated arms reduction. For this, they run the risk of being punished, as a result of attempts by the other player to take advantage of the window of opportunity to strike the fatal blow. As such, both will be weary and neither will move away from the status quo.

It can be shown that each player would reason from "how much it stands to lose" in each case and would calculate what could happen at the worst. They would then choose that option which brings the best of the worst possible outcomes. In the language of the game, they would try to maximize the security levels. For India it is 10; for Pakistan 5. They would thus unilaterally choose to be at the cell 1.1, with the 10,5 outcome, far less than the possible 50,60 outcome. Thus, a non-co-operative variable sum game produces a sub-optimal game in an end-game scenario.

The Genesis of the Two Models

Following independence, under the leadership of Prime Minister Jawaharlal Nehru, India adopted non-alignment and planned development as the cornerstone of India's domestic politics. In spite of three wars with Pakistan, a serious border conflict with China and the dispatch of Indian Peace Keeping Forces to Sri Lanka and their subsequent ignominious withdrawal, the average voter as well as the politicians of India remain relatively unconcerned about foreign policy. Panchasheela which was intended to provide a link between domestic and foreign policy was based on a non-dichotomous model that, however, lost most of its moral force in the perception of Pakistan because of its unstated assumption that Kashmir was a non-issue when it came to India-Pakistan relations.

The state of Pakistan, in contrast to India, started with different premises from the outset. As a state based on the two-nation theory, Pakistan saw itself as the defender of the Muslims of the subcontinent, and as such, locked in conflict with India on the issue of Kashmir whose Muslim majority should have logically made it a part of its own territory. The greater military resources at the disposal of India have made Pakistan look for an equalizer in the form of military alliances with the United States and subsequently with China. The tit-for-tat nuclear explosions in Pakistan in response to the Indian tests have proved once again the durability of dichotomous thinking in Pakistan. Within this perspective, the bus diplomacy of Vajpayee and Sharif and the Lahore Declaration were an aberration from which, with shots flying in Kargil, the system has retracted to its original state under the weight of the history of conflict and dichotomous thinking on the part of key actors. The cost of this strategy has, however, been enormous in terms of the economy and arms race in the region.

In order to maintain steady economic growth and credibility in the international market both Pakistan and India need urgently to invest in key sectors of the economy, infrastructure and education, and, at least give the appearance of being serious about solving conflicts with their regional neighbours. Crucial to the latter is a formal or even informal regional security arrangement. The South Asian Association for Regional Co-operation (SAARC), hamstrung by a Charter which explicitly forbids the public discussion of matters of "domestic" politics, is currently unable to play the role. It is further restrained by the likelihood of parties to conflicts within South Asian calling on the good offices of non-regional forces, lowering the legitimacy and effectiveness of any regional arrangement. Besides, it has not in the past received sufficient endorsement from India, the most important country of the region. While contextual factors such as the personal equations between the prime ministers of India and Pakistan from 1996-1999 have produced an informal environment of regional conflict resolution, developments in domestic politics in India appear to cast a shadow on the recent foreign policy gains with regard to the creation of a South Asian security framework. The analysis that follows looks at the ensemble of factors that impinge on Indian policy in the face of South Asian security dilemma.

South Asia's Security Dilemma

Since the departure of British colonial rule from the region, South Asia has witnessed a series of severe border conflicts leading to war as well as serious outbreaks of mass insurgency, riots and communal violence. India and Pakistan had a serious conflict over Kashmir in 1947-1948, a border war in 1965, a war on both the eastern and the western fronts in 1971 and a state of low intensity conflict in the 1980s. The India-China border war of 1962 saw the Chinese troops coming close to the North Indian plains. There have been mass insurgencies in Kashmir, Punjab, Assam and Maoist violence in southern and eastern India. Pakistan has had a continuous series of ethnic conflicts in Sind, Karachi and has faced massive influx of refugees from Afghanistan. Sri Lanka has been beset with insurgency and large-scale military operations against the Tamil rebels. Bangladesh has faced insurgency in the Chakma Hill Tract. The Maldives faced a coup which was diffused with Indian assistance. It is strongly, believed that South Asia's domestic conflicts are not entirely endigenous and that foreign help plays an important role in exacerbating them. South Asia's domestic and regional conflicts are linked, greatly complicating the issues and contributing to the financial and military burden of maintaining order. The security problem and the lack of a comprehensive regional security arrangement have had their repercussions on the military budgets. A brief perusal of the relevant statistics shows the imbalance of developmental and military expenses in South Asia. South Asia's states are quite heavily armed (Table 1).

Table-1

India and her Neighbours: Conventional Weapons

Country	Armed Forces (active)	MBT	AIFC/ APC	Artiller	Heli-copters	Combat Aircraft	War-ships	Sub mari-nes
India	1.265.000	3.739	1.057	3.585	36	864	25	15
PR China	2.930.00	8.000	2.800	14.500	76	5.845	55	50
Pakistan	587.000	1.950	820	1.849	36	434	9	6
Bangladesh	115.000	140	0	140	0	69	4	0
Sri Lanka	126.000	25	185	65	17	27	0	0
Nepal	40.000	0	0	25	0	0	0	0
Myanmar	286.000	56	20	276	10	91	2	0
Indonesia	276.000	0	647	20	38	103	13	2
Australia	61.600	103	771	355	48	155	12	4

Source: IISS: The Military Balance 1994-1995. London: Brassey's, October 1994.
Notes: MBT=Main Battle Tank
AIFV=Armoured Infantry Fighting Vehicle
APC=Armoured Personnel Carrier

Artillery includes self-propelled, drawn artillery and MLRS-systems. Helicopters include combat helicopters and armed helicopters. Combat Aircraft includes fighters and fighter bombers. Warships include major surface combatants from frigate upwards.

Their military burden during the post-cold war period has gone up in contrast to the trend in all developing countries taken together (Table 2).

Table-2
Post-Cold War Military Burden
(% change between 1987-94)

	Military expenditure		Armed personnel	Forces
Bangladesh	% change	1994	%	1994
India	1987-94	position	1987-94	(thousand)
Nepal	7.5	US$	12.4	115
Pakistan	4.2	million	0.0	1.265
Sri Lanka	43.0	380	16.3	35
South Asia	30.0	9.500	22.0	590
Develop.	108.3	40	294.2	126
Countries	12.4	3.500	7.5	2.131
Industrial.	-13.0	500	-10	14.917
Countries	-41.0	13.920	-24.2	9.215
World	-36.7	171.420	-16.0	24.132
		622.160		
		793.580		

Source: Mahbub ul Haq, *Human Development in South Asia 1997*. Karachi et. al.: Oxford University Press 1997, p.81 (Table 4.2)

Their per cent increase of 12.4 in military spending during the period between 1987-1994 is a sharp contrast to the decrease of 41.2 on the part of the industrial countries of the world.

Particularly striking is the increase of the military expenditure as a percentage of the GDP between 1985-1994, from 2.6 to 3.6 in India and 5.2 to 7.0 in Pakistan (Table 3).One can talk about a virtual arms "race" between India and Pakistan in terms of their military expenditure, which, in case of Pakistan, has almost doubled during the period from 1987-1996 (Figure 1). By all reckoning, however, the states of South Asia are among the poorest in the world (Table 4), a fact that gives great significance to the "peace dividends" (Table 5). It should be noted here that the military expenditure of South Asia to a large extent goes into the purchase of arms and technology from powers outside the region and thus, does not act as a multiplier to defence and related industries in the region itself. It thus constitutes a "net drain" on the resources of South Asian countries.

Such heavy military expenditure in South Asia might come across as a surprise in view of the overall poverty of the region. Since strategic thinking of countries is guided by security as well as welfare, it would not, therefore, be unrealistic to expect the decision-makers of the states of South Asia to be aware of the trade-off between the defence and welfare budgets. The question that arises here is why are they unable to go from "here" and reap the benefits of the peace divided by reducing military expenditure? The next section would analyse the question from the point of view of India by concentrating on the evolution of Indian policy during the period after independence. (Table 3)

Table-3

Burden of Military Expenditure in South Asia

	% of GDP		% of Central Gov. Expenditure		% of Education and Health Spending	
Bangladesh	**985**	**1994**	**1980**	**1994**	**1985**	**1990/9**
India	1.3	1.5	9.4	17.6*	n/a	1
Nepal	2.6	3.6	14.1	12.8	68	41
Pakistan	0.8	1.1.	6.7	5.9*	67	65
Sri Lanka	5.2	7.0	30.6	26.9*	393	35
South Asia	2.7	4.7	1.6	11.6	17	125
East Asia (excl. China)	2.4	3.4	15.1	14.7	113	107
China (PRC)	7.4	4.8	n/a	n/a	273	72
Develop. Countries	7.5	5.6	n/a	n/a	387	49
Industrial.	5.5	3.6	n/a	n/a	143	114
Countries	41.	3.1	n/a	n/a	97	60
World	4.3	3.2	n/a	n/a	104	33

* 1993 value. Source: Mahbub ul Haq, *Human Development in South Asia 1997*. Karachi et. al.: Oxford University Press 1997, p. 80 (Table 4.)

FIGURE –1
Military expenditure of India and Pakistan, 1987-1996
(Source: SIPRI Yearbook 1997, online)

The Evolution of India's South Asia "Policy" since Independence

This section will provide the historical backdrop to the present context by drawing on the earlier years, going back to Nehru. For the purpose of this analysis, the period can be divided into four phases:

a) Classic non-alignment (1947-1962)

b) War, alliance with the USSR and attempts at regional dominance (1963-89)

c) Contained dominance based on negotiation (1989-1999)

d) The return to conflict and the limits of the 'two-track' strategy (1999-)

a. Classic Non-Alignment (1947-1962) – the "Nehru Doctrine"

The first place after independence, starting with the first war with Pakistan over Kashmir (1947-1948) and ending with the totally unexpected Himalayan war with China in 1962, is characterized by India's self-perception as one of the leaders and co-founder of the Non-aligned Movement (NAM). This first phase also was clearly dominated by Jawaharlal Nehru, one of India's founding fathers. Under his leadership, the newly independent state ventured out onto the international stage, firmly determined to stay clear from any entanglement with superpower politics. Nehru retained a deep distrust of the superpowers and was weary of their designs on the newly emerging post-colonial societies. But Nehru the internationalist was also a great believer in the United Nations Organization and wished to strengthen it by India's active participation in it. Unfortunately for Nehru (and India), the Kashmir drama was unfolding just about the time that Nehru was seeking to find a just and honourable place for India in the world system[2]. Contrary to Nehru's internationalist aspirations, the Kashmir imbroglio and the conflict with Pakistan was to become the focal point of India's security politics.

Nehru's view on Kashmir, which amounted to a doctrine-like position, was based on his firm conviction that, thanks to a lawful and legitimate Instrument of Accession, the status of Kashmir, like the other regions of India, was that of an integral part of the Union. The application of this doctrine to the creation of specific policies to Kashmir as to other regions of India during the two decades following independence would depend on the specific circumstances of each. The resulting confusion and contradictions would, in the years to come, give an appearance of a certain fuzziness, to Nehru's position. At various points, and to different actors, the Nehru "doctrine" would appear inconsistent, indecisive and vulnerable to pressure. Nehru would by turns be perceived as a half-hearted bully and a naïve internationalist. But the power and the institutional strength of this policy consisted in its internal cohesion notwithstanding its apparent contradictions, and, its close links with the ideological basis of the state in India.

Nehru's Kashmir policy also resulted over the years in a larger paradox with regard to Indian foreign policy. While its rhetoric gave every appearance of being non-dichotomous with regard to Pakistan, thanks to its intransigence when it came to Kashmir it was perceived by Pakistan as essentially dichotomous but not necessarily equipped with the requisite force to reinforce its implied belligerence. The perceptions of Nehru's policy towards Kashmir which in turn affected the perceptions of India's overall policy by the key players in the region and in the world at large can be summed up as follows:

1. *Indecisiveness.* With Nehru as prime minister and as such, the de facto decision-maker of the dominion, India lost valuable time in air-lifting elite troops to defend Kashmir. When they were effectively employed in fending-off the tribesmen, and were poised to push them back to the frontier of Kashmir,

instead of pressing on the advantage, Nehru's India did not put the military success to political use. Instead, the military gains were lost in political manoeuvres.

The same is true for Indian diplomacy on Kashmir. Even when India repeated in every conceivable forum that Kashmir was an integral part of India and that the accession of Kashmir on the basis of the Instrument of Accession was final, India's decision-makers, nevertheless kept behaving as if this was not the case and channels of negotiation were kept open to settle the Kashmir issue.

The contradiction between India's principle intransigence regarding the status of Kashmir as an absolute and irrevocable part of India based on the Instrument of Accession and her willingness to negotiate the point when called upon to do so was perceived by Pakistan and the external world as Indian vulnerability to pressure[3].

2. *Half-hearted bully.* Nehru's India, while giving a formal commitment to provide a higher degree of autonomy to Kashmir than what was available to the rest of India, nevertheless took up a series of measures that diluted this in practice. Nehru, however, stopped short of a full integration of Kashmir to bring it in line with the other parts of India. India's military actions, against Goa in 1961 and Indian opposition to self-determination in Kashmir through a "plebiscite" are seen in this light.

Article 370 of the Indian Constitution was originally instituted as a guarantee of the autonomy of Kashmir in all areas except defence, foreign affairs and communication. This formal undertaking was compromised in practice through a steady chipping away as the legal safeguard through amendments of the Constitution and Presidential Orders. On the other hand, full integration was deliberately obstructed through the prohibition of the settlement of refugees through the allocation of evacuee property and a special provision for the return of those who left Kashmir for Pakistan in the future. In spite of the fundamental right to the freedom of movement within India, Indian's were not allowed to settle in Kashmir.

3. *Naïve Internationalist.* Nehru's India went to the Security Council with great fanfare, but then, had cold feet when it came to follow this initiative up with action. Nehru went to the Security Council hoping to get the endorsement of the international community for the Indian position on Kashmir without taking into account the fact that the realpolitik underlying the perceptions of the superpowers dictated otherwise. Nehru's policy decisions regarding Kashmir, drawn from the basic goals of secure frontiers and popular consent, were increasingly affected by his basic equation of Kashmir's integration with India as a moral guarantee of India's secularism[4]. Nehru clearly wanted the world to condemn Pakistan for trying to undo the integration of Kashmir by brute force[5]. When it became clear to Nehru that the world did not accept India's case as categorically as Nehru had hoped, he became bitter and disillusioned.

4. *Vulnerability to Pressure.* Above all, Nehru followed the traditional policies of the Indian National Congress which was to rule by consensus and accommodation. He was aware of the conflicting pulls of narrow self-interest and high principle and through a long experience of the Congress culture. But Nehru who was also intensely aware of the international arena,

was conscious of being constantly under observation[6] and had to find a solution acceptable to all parties concerned[7]. His policies were thus not entirely his choices but were influenced by local conditions in Kashmir; the jockeying for positions and power in India's national politics, and, the regional and international actors, such as Pakistan, China, Soviet Union, the United Kingdom and the United States. These conditions changed from one period to another, causing, in the process, Nehru's policies to fluctuate.

The quintessence of the Nehru doctrine was a moral vision, seeking to balance security with democracy and categorically opposed to the 'two nation theory' and the religious dogmatism on which it was perceived to be based. Convinced about the rightness of his cause Nehru believed that with persuasion, patience and enlightenment others in Pakistan and in India would also be able to see things from his point of view.

b. Attempts at Regional Dominance: the 'Indira Doctrine'

From 1947 to 1962, Kashmir was the focal point of India's – and Nehru's international politics. The 1962 Himalayan war with China drove home the point that there were other security problems, too. Nehru the internationalist was not willing to believe up to the last minute that his vision of "Hindi-Chini bhai bhai" (Indian and Chinese are brothers) was not shared by China and that a war, or at least an armed conflict, was imminent. Therefore, the Chinese attack on Indian position along the border hit the Indian army unprepared. It has been argued that had Nehru been more realistic and less idealistic (or simply less native), this war probably could have been avoided[8]. As a direct result of this war, India went on an international shopping spree to acquire – finally – all those sophisticated weapons the Indian armed forces had been lobbying for years. For Pakistan, the pace of India's armament gave cause for alarm. As Ganguly argues[9], the Pakistani government saw a window of opportunity for the capture of the whole of Kashmir, created through the humiliation and the weakness of the Indian armed forces, closing rapidly. In this very crucial moment. Nehru died, causing a perception of vulnerability on the part of India.

With Nehru removed from the scene, the probability of war increased. On the Pakistani side, the replacement of Nehru by Shastri, perceived as less assertive, reinforced the perception of Indian vulnerability. On the Indian side, on the other hand, the military-strategic initiative passed into the hands of a different group of decision-makers who saw in Kashmir not so much the symbol of India's commitments to democracy and secularism but, instead territory, power, national self-interest and security. The policies pursued by Shastri and subsequently Indira Gandhi provide some insights into the transformation of the Nehru doctrine, and to the subtle shift from position of interest with regard to the general directions of India's Kashmir policy. These new men in charge of India's security were a military-political complex whose commitment to Kashmir, compared to Nehru's, was simultaneously less doctrinaire and more realistic. While lowering the intensity of the political rhetoric they were willing and able to increase the stakes in military terms.

Shastri's succession, stage-managed by the Congress Syndicate – India's regional power-brokers – took place against a background of ominous developments in the international arena. The famous threat of Bhutto's thousand year war against India on the floor of the Security Council found much comfort in the statement of the British delegate Sir Patrick Dean, who, while stating the British case for self-determination in Kashmir, made the statement: "We consider it unrealistic to consider the status of Kashmir purely in terms of the legal effect of the Maharaja's Instrument of Accession"[10]. The American representative kept a low profile but in the background was the intense annoyance of President Johnson at what he perceived as Nehru's high profile moral posturing, coupled with the repeated requests from India for ever-increasing quantities of food aid[11].

Lacking Nehru's stature and probably acting out of a sense of interest (that is, territory as the basis of the power of the state) rather than position (that is, Kashmir's status as symbolic of Indian commitment to secularism), Shastri came out with a package of policies that held out the possibility of a dialogue with Pakistan. Srivastava, Shastri's biographer, sums them up as follows[12]:

a) India had no desire whatsoever to acquire even one square inch of Pakistani territory.

b) India genuinely wished Pakistan well and would be delighted to see Pakistan progress and prosper.

c) India would never allow any interference by Pakistan in Kashmir which was an integral part of India, and

d) India and Pakistan had to live together in peace and harmony as they were constituted without either side trying to do anything to destabilize the other.

On the basis of these policy statements of Shastri and the impression gathered by Ayub Khan after their first meeting, the recently constituted Kashmir cell of Pakistan came to the conclusion that the "new Indian Prime Minister was unlikely to loosen India's links with Kashmir and that it was time for Pakistan to take some overt action for `reviving' the Kashmir issue and, defreezing the Kashmir situation"[13].

Shastri's handling of the situation was entirely in keeping with his character which marked a significant departure from Nehru. He quickly established a personal rapport with the defence chiefs and the leaders of the opposition in the Indian Parliament. In the place of the combination of Nehru's personal aloofness and the conspiratorial style of Krishna Menon, Nehru's main link with the party and the country at the height of the Indo-China conflict, Shastri's method was to build up a strong national consensus to meet the Pakistani challenge in Kashmir. As his biographer puts it, "On the political side, Shastri was in control of the situation and never allowed it to get out of hand. He had shown firmness, self-confidence, self-restraint, wisdom and flexibility. He was in favour of peace, but not peace at any cost."[14]

Shastri was able to take the initiative in political as well as military matters, ordering the Indian army to cross the international frontier in order to march in the direction of Lahore to relieve pressure on the Chhamb sector in Kashmir which was facing a massive armoured attack, getting the air force to come into the battle right at the outset in spite of the risk of the superior Pakistani air crafts. On the other hand, as in the Rann of Kutch where there was a first trial of strength between the Indian and Pakistani forces, in Tashkent, Shastri showed flexibility, trading land against security. Of course the Indian response to Pakistan greatly benefited from the fact that the 'spontaneous' mass uprising in Kashmir on which the Pakistani strategy had heavily banked did not take place. Srivastava reports how the people of Kashmir cooperated with the Indian army in order to capture Pakistani infiltrators – a fact that was used effectively by Indian publicity both to present India's case internationally as an attempt by a nation to defend her legitimate interests, and, internally, to bring the war to Indians in their personal capacity. This equation led in 1965 to the birth of the famous Shastri aphorism – "Jai Jawan – Jai Kisan"- victory to the soldier, victory to the peasant – meant for projecting the production of food and defence of boundaries as two different but complementary methods of safeguarding one's self-respect and self-confidence.

In spite of their different styles, the essentials of Shastri's flexible style and military pragmatism were adopted by Indira Gandhi. Under her tutelage, in radical contrast to the tenor of domestic politics in Nehru's lifetime, India went on vigorously using Kashmir to generate power internally as well as by entering into alliances with the Soviet Union[15]. India's efforts were matched by the efforts of Pakistan – through border provocation, war and diplomacy aimed at the internationlisation of the Kashmir issue, particularly in the UN. Even the Simla Accord, where Indira Gandhi gives sufficient evidence of having moved from position of interest as compared to her father, barely managed to paper over the wide gulf separating the perceptions and policies of the two neighbours.

In view of the brevity of his tenure, it is difficult to say how Shastri would have sought to reconcile the needs for security and democracy in Kashmir. Indira Gandhi clearly opted for the former. The policy of surreptitious integration that saw the autonomy of Kashmir steadily whittled away during Nehru's second phase, became the explicit basis of policy under Indira Gandhi. Pakistan and possibly the US as well were slow to appreciate this change which came during 1969-71, which led to the brinkmanship of Pakistani forces in East Pakistan. The war of 1971 which we can call Indira Gandhi's war because, unlike her father, she stage-managed it with great dexterity and proclaimed the temporary abandonment of Nehru's doctrinaire commitment to the non-dichotomous model. No serious or sustained efforts were made thereafter to win the hearts and minds of Pakistan and Kashmir while maintaining the needs of secure frontier, democracy and secularism.

The period following the 1971 war can be called retrospectively the "golden age" of Indian international politics[16]. Pakistan was split in two, the Kashmir issue solved, at least militarily, in India's favour and the USSR had been won as powerful ally against the USA and China. It is not surprising, therefore, to see a triumphant Indira Gandhi formulating a kind of "Monroe-Doctrine" for India. Like its famous predecessor, the Indira "Doctrine" tried on the one hand to keep "foreign hands" off from South Asia, on the other to persuade the smaller states of South Asia that this was done in their own interest. With regard to the smaller South Asian states except Pakistan, the doctrine was not that difficult to implement: there was simply not enough interest from outside powers in these states[17]. Trying to keep foreign hands off the Indian Ocean proved to be very difficult, however. In the era of British dominance, the Indian Ocean had been a "British Lake". Now, after the termination of British military presence east of Suez, the US Navy was about to establish their own presence in this waters, which, from an Indian point of view, should be turned into a "Mare Indicum". Inspired by similar attempts in other parts of the word, India tried to establish a zone of peace, which would have virtually closed the Indian Ocean to foreign warships, especially those equipped with nuclear weapons. The ambitious plan misfired, at least partially because of India's neighbour's suspicion and their perception of being unduly bullied but basically because of the United States' interest in the Indian Ocean as a gateway to the Persian Gulf. The Indian Ocean as a Zone of Peace Plan (IOZOP) was a still-born child in the very moment the USA acquired Diego Garcia from the United Kingdom[18].

The single-most important event in the two decades discussed here, which still has repercussions today, is the so-called "peaceful explosion" of a nuclear device at Pokhran in 1974. India proved to the world that she had the capability to establish itself as the sixth nuclear power, but for several reasons she abstained[19]. Part of the explanation can be found in the Emergency from 1975-77 and the subsequent change of government. The newly inaugurated Janata government was not as keen for a status as a world power as Indira Gandhi's government had been. This hiatus in India's quest for power did not last long, however. The elections of 1980 saw a comeback to power for Indira Gandhi, who had not changed her political ambitions in the meantime. But she found herself more and more entrapped in the Punjab crisis, which culminated in 1984 in the Operation "Bluestar" and her assassination by two of her own Sikh bodyguards[20]. Her son, Rajiv Gandhi, carried on with the same set of international aspirations, but he, too, became a victim of his policies: he was assassinated in 1991 by Tamil extremists after the ill-fated Indian peace-keeping effort in Sri Lanka[21]. With him the Gandhi "Dynasty", as well as India's attempts to dominate the region through a coercive application of the dichotomous model, came to an end.

c. Contained Dominance Based on Negotiation (1989-97) – the "Gujral Doctrine"

The successive Indian governments after the demise of the Gandhi "Dynasty", all had one thing in common: the weakness of their domestic power base. This weakness necessitated complicated political manoeuvres of those in power to keep their fragile coalitions together. The weakness of the various coalition governments fell in a time of radical domestic changes. Communal riots of unparalleled violence swept through several parts of India, highlighted in December 1992 by the destruction of the Babri mosque by a Hindu mob. The rise of Hindu nationalism, supported by parties like the BJP, went hand in hand with an upsurge of terrorism in the Punjab, in Kashmir and in West Bengal. This forced the Indian policymakers to concentrate on domestic politics, which led to an introspective policy that tried to take international events in its stride.

Unfortunately, this was a time of sweeping changes in the very structure of international relations – the collapse of the Eastern Bloc and the Warsaw Treaty Organization, the process leading to the re-unification of Germany, the end of the Cold War and, finally, the end of India's most powerful ally, the USSR. These events in the nineteen eighties took India's policymakers, concentrating on their own domestic problems, by surprise. Obviously, it was very hard for the Indian government to come to terms with the new realities. This can be illustrated by the Indian reaction to the putsch against Michail Gorbachev in Moscow, where the Indian government chose to support the conservative communist elements which tried to save the already doomed communist system.

The Gulf War two years later again found the Indian government in disarray. India, still perceiving itself as one of the leaders of the Non-aligned Movement, first initiated an unsuccessful peace mission to Baghdad and then alienated the USA with first allowing, and then disallowing the refueling of US planes in Bombay. The Indian vote against the UN Security Council's call for Iraq's surrender which bracketed the largest democracy of the world with Cuba and Yemen completed the series of Indian diplomatic blunders during the Gulf War[22] .

In September 1996, India again found itself trapped between a rock and a hard place, this time because of her stance on nuclear weapons and the Comprehensive Test Ban. Only two states supported India in rejecting the test ban: Bhutan and Libya[23]. In this context, Ramesh Thakur blames the Indian government of being "caught in a time warp"[24] We will see in the "prisoner's dilemma" below, however, that it is not easy for India to change its politics on nuclear weapons without taking the "Pakistan factor" and the "China factor" into consideration. Nevertheless, India's position was hard to sell given the realities of an international "quasi taboo" against nuclear weapons.

The spectacular series of Indian diplomatic disasters and the upsurge of communalism and terrorism on the domestic front makes it very easy for the casual observer to overlook the first tentative steps towards peace in South Asia, also initiated by and large by various Indian governments after the end of the Gandhi "Dynasty".

The first factor conducive to peace which has already been mentioned was the internal weakness of the coalition governments from 1989 onwards. The political manoeuvres to keep the coalitions intact led to a process of accommodation between various interest groups. Getting used to politics of accommodation at home could lead to de-emphasising conflictual, dominance-based behaviour towards Pakistan. Illustrative of this point is the resumption of talks between the foreign secretaries of India and Pakistan and the talks between the Prime Ministers, I.K. Gujral of India and Nawaz Sharif of Pakistan, themselves in the Maldives in May 1997, and which, despite regime changes finally led to the Lahore Declaration.

A second factor conducive to peace is the process of liberalization and globalization of the Indian economy, which is rapidly picking up pace, and a similar policy in Pakistan, where the industrial and entrepreneurial class forms the power base of the Prime Minister Nawaz Sharif. Both India and Pakistan seem to be more interested in furthering their economic relations than with waging war against each other. The focus on economics could lead to a new life for the nearly defunct SAARC, which would certainly help India to improve the bilateral relations with her neighbours. India's new prime minister I.K. Gujral, sworn in April 1997, even went so far as to talk about unilateral and nonreciprocal concessions from India to her neighbours. His "carrot without stick-approach" has already been called the "Gujral Doctrine".[25]

A third factor conducive to the potential for a regional security arrangement is a renewed interest of the sole surviving superpower, the US, in the region. For the US, South Asia in general and India in particular, forms a region of possible economic growth, and, as such, a lucrative future market for American goods. Therefore, the government in Washington is very keen to sponsor peace initiatives and tries to encourage both India and Pakistan to follow up on their first steps. However, the next steps towards a regional security arrangement are far more sophisticated than one realizes.

There is a growing realization in India that the arms race simply cannot be financed any longer without neglecting economic development at home. The same certainty is true for Pakistan, which is, like India, weary of war[26]. Indicative of this trend is a new interest in confidence and security building measures (CSBM)[27]. The talks about CSBMs between India and Pakistan are perhaps the most important step towards peace in South Asia. Establishing CSBMs between India and Pakistan is the sine qua non for all attempts to solve the Kashmir problem or the nuclear weapons issue within the framework of a regional security arrangement.

While some of these developments created a case for optimism with regard to peace in South Asia, the "China factor" continues to be one major obstacle. Since the days of the Himalayan war in 1962, India has watched China with a weary eye. The possibility of a conflict with China was often put forward to defend Indian armaments and Indian positions on nuclear weapons. The appearance of Chinese warships in the Indian Ocean did not help to alleviate Indian fears, too. Improving Indian relations with China would of cause give the Indian government the chance to concentrate on South Asian problems. Other constraints can be found in the domestic problems of India. In a worst casescenario, the rising forces of Hindu nationalism could destroy all steps towards peace, and

India could embark on chauvinistic politics again[28]. Another worst case-possibility would be a divided India, rendered ungovernable by the forces of separatism and terrorism.

d. The Return to Conflict and the limits of the 'Two-track' Strategy (1999—)

We do not yet have any reliable information on the strategic thinking on the part of the Pakistani elite; on the Indian side, predictably, great recrimination between advocates of negotiated settlement of outstanding conflict with Pakistan and those who could see violent conflict with Pakistan as both natural and necessary, has already started in the earnest and will get more acrimonious as the elections to the Lok Sabha, scheduled for September, get nearer. Thinly disguised by the outpouring of patriotism, the political recriminations on the Indian side (and presumably on the Pakistani side, but possibly to a lesser extent) reveal two clearly different mind-sets that underpin the different schools of thought on how the structural differences of interest between India and Pakistan are organized and the political language in which they could be articulated.

Indian Opinion and its Implications for Regional Security: Results of an Opinion Survey, 1996[29]

India's domestic politics is an important constraint on her regional policies. In view of their implications for the potential support for the non-dichotomous model in the electorate, we have selected three questions from a survey of the Indian population. After the 1996 parliamentary elections in India, a post-poll survey was conducted in 108 Lok Sabha constituencies, where 10000 Interviews were held. Among the questions asked were several which enable us to shed some light on the security perceptions of the Indian citizens themselves. Because of the importance of the opinions expressed, the three questions and the answers given by specific subpopulations provide important insights into both India's problems an available alternatives.

The first important question deals with relations with Pakistan: Question: *India should make more efforts to develop friendly relations with Pakistan. Do you agree or disagree with this?*

Table-6a

Agree (%)	44.6
Don't know/no opinion	37.8
Disagree	17.6

As we can see, a majority of 44.6% favours a development of relations with Pakistan. The detailed levels of agreement, which are clearly connected with the level of education and religion, can be broken down as follows:

Table-6b

Agree	%
Illiterate	30.6
Female	36.6
Hindu	40.6
56 years or more	42.8
All	44.6
Up to 25 years	47.2
Male	52.23
Muslim	57.5
College and above	67.7

The high level of support for policies resembling those advocated by the Gujral doctrine among highly educated Indians is most significant. Related with that question is the next question, which covers the perception of the people on the Kashmir problem, the most contentious issue between India and Pakistan. Question: *People's opinions are divided on the issue of Kashmir problem. Some people say that the government should suppress the agitation by any means while others say that this problem should be resolved by negotiation. What would you say – should the agitation be suppressed or resolved by negotiation?*

Tale-7a:

Should be suppressed	11.1
Resolved through negotiation	33.5
Have not heard about the Kashmir problem at all	21.6
Cannot say	31.9
Other	1.9

It is very interesting to see that only a minority of 11.1% opined in favour of suppression, while a majority of 33.5% voted for negotiations. Again, there is a connection between the level of education and the willingness to negotiate:

Table-7b:

Negotiate	
Illiterate	15.1
Female	24.6
56 years or more	29.4
Hindu	31.1
All	**35.5**

Up to 25 years	37.6
Male	41.8
Muslim	45.4
College and above	62.3

A more hawkish position, however, is taken regarding nuclear weapons: those advocating that India needs nuclear weapons are more numerous than those who argue to the contrary: Question: *There is no need for India to make the atomic bomb. Do you agree or disagre e?*

Table-8a:

Agree	25.9
Don't know/no opinion	38.0
Disagree	36.1

The detailed profile of the 'peacemongers' is as follows:

Table-8b:

Agree	%
Illiterate	19.3
56 years or more	22.8
Female	23.5
Hindu	24.5
All	25.8
Up to 25 years	26.8
Male	28.0
College and above	29.5
Muslim	33.0

As for the advocates of nuclear weapons, table 8c provides the profile:

Table-8c:

Diagree	%
Illiterate	22.8
Female	25.4
Muslim	30.6
56 years or more	32.7
All	36.1
Hindu	36.8
Upto 25 years	39.8
Male	46.0
College and above	63.9

For the government it means that the resumption of talks with Pakistan and probably, the attempts towards establishing CSBMs, is buttressed by a majority of Indians. The nuclear issue, however, will be much more difficult to solve.

Divergence and Convergence in South Asia's Regional Politics

The analysis from the previous section shows that for the last decade, there has been a growing realization among South Asia's states of the importance and necessity of constituting South Asia as a region, and to look for solutions to the problems of resource and security management within a regional framework. In specific terms, this indicates a convergence towards a regional framework, from the earlier divergence away from the region in search of particular national strategies, often in alliance with non-regional powers. The indicators of this convergence are: attempts at negotiated solutions to outstanding regional conflicts, strengthening of SAARC, regional trade. CBMs are an evidence that some convergence has taken place. In terms of the arguments presented so far, the following factors could lead India towards convergence:

1. The Gujral doctrine as an evidence of elite awareness of the peace divided on the Indian side.

2. Liberalisation of the Indian market pushing towards the search for regional markets.

3. American encouragement towards conflict-resolution.

On the other hand, the following factors could hinder convergence:

1. Continued insurgency in Kashmir.

2. Residual opposition to a rapprochement with Pakistan in some sections of Hindu nationalists and a similar apprehension in the Jamat-I-Islamic in Pakistan.

3. The instability of India's current ruling coalition.

4. Resistance from the Pakistani military establishment to a peace deal by politicians.

5. The "China" factor, discussed at length below

The Need for a Triangular Normalisation that Includes China

The scenario depicted in the game theoretic model in the first section of this paper which showed the status quo synonymous with conflict as a far from an ideal situation. However, it at least suggests a wasteful but stable relation between the two neighbours. Unfortunately, that is unlikely to be the case in view of the China factor in South Asian politics. The problem we are facing in South Asia is that the India – Pakistan two person game is part of a three person non-co-operative game together with China (the "China factor"). The presence of China makes a stable relationship proportionality difficult.[30] The likely scenario which makes a relationship between India and Pakistan as stable adversaries is presented below.

Suppose that at the outset of play, India and Pakistan work out a ratio of 3:1 which guarantees their mutual threat perception. At the next step, India would demand an additional unit of power k to meet the Chinese threat. Since Pakistan cannot be sure that India would not divert the k units in an end game with Pakistan, for her security needs Pakistan would want an additional increase of k/3. At this point, India, to keep the proportionality, would demand (k/3) x 3, that is an additional k, leading to a total of 3+2k units which will send Pakistan on another round of arms procurement. As such, until China is brought into a triangular security nexus along with India and Pakistan, no stable relationship, even adversarial, is possible. (Table 9)

Table-9

	Pakistan	**India**
Sequence 1	1	3
Sequence 2	1	3 + k (+k being an Indian security against China)
Sequence 3	1+k/3 (k/3 is the additional security which Pakistan demands as proportional defence, since India can redeploy forces)	3 + k (+k being an Indian security against China)

Sequence 4	1 + k/3	3 + k + (k/3) x 3 = 3+2k (Indian seeks to match the Pakistani additional capacity through a proportional increase)
Sequence 5		3 + 2k +m (m is the new Indian security against China)
Sequence 6	.....	......

Conclusion: Where Do We Go From Here?

For those concerned with South Asia's security dilemma, the examples of the European Union and the ASEAN hold important lessons with regard to the policies that promote convergence to a regional solution for problems of security and welfare. These comparative cases also indicate the limits to the process of convergence in terms of endogenous and exogenous factors that constitute the boundary conditions of the process. In both the EU and the ASEAN, the presence of external enemies has been an important incentive towards convergence. The lack of radical asymmetries in size has been conducive to co-operation in both cases. The third main factor has been domestic ideology. The American presence on European soil after the war, the democratic constitution imposed on a vastly reduced Germany and the Marshall aid provided a firm basis for economic consolidation; the Franco-German Coal and Steel Community laid, the first groundwork towards regional co-operation. Anti-communism played a similar role in the coming together of the states and markets of Southeast Asia in a similar manner. These factors, as we have seen above, were conspicuous by their absence in South Asia.

In addition to these structural factors, convergence towards stable peace in South Asia has been further handicapped by the self-perception of the actors. As we have seen above, the self-perception of India as a country unequivocally committed to peaceful conflict resolution in the Panchsheela mode is not borne out by the perception by her neighbours who see her as a bully and a belligerent power. The mirror image is provided by Pakistan which has often portrayed itself as the wronged party and the occupant of the moral high ground, often neglecting to temper this image with the fear and anxiety that her position invokes in large parts of India's electorate and among her policy makers. This mutual self-misperception has produced the chronic Indo-Pakistan rivalry, to the point where the international arena perceives South Asia exclusively in terms of Indo-Pakistan rivalry. Following this is the solicitude of the outside experts to be even-handed between the two warring neighbours. This position is anathema to Indian policy makers who are more prone to speak about India-China rivalry and are at a loss to understand as to why the world cannot understand the legitimate security needs of India. Indian inability to abide by the terms laid down by the West (the crucial role of India's threat perception from China is not taken sufficiently into account by western policy makers) is seen as Indian equivocation, for which the West's preferred solution has been to cut-off aid under the assumption that nation-states can be prevented from going to war because they do not have the cash to start a war.

If we focus on India, we can see that India's impressive arsenal is not backed up with cultural cohesion, governmental stability or great economic might. Mobilisation on the issue of cultural nationalism, a phenomenon to which Huntington alludes in his concept of Hindu fundamentalism as a political force[31], is far from it, being both socially inchoate and politically fragmented. Survey data shows simultaneously a peaceful and sanctimonious self-perception but at the same time, the desire to arm on self adequately. The ambiguity regarding CTBT shows the same tendency. On the Pakistani side, on the other hand, there is weary perception of the enormous cost of the nonfactual status quo with India and the awareness of the lost opportunity of the benefits of trade and economic co-operation with India. But the uncertain power equations between the civil and military authorities make it difficult to develop a consensus behind the peace initiative.[32]

The nuclear tests of South Asia have radically altered the security perception of the region because the start of an accidental nuclear war remains high. The fact remains, however, that during periods of crisis and escalation of belligerency across the Line of Control in Kashmir, both the nations' armed forces are placed in a state of alert. India has nevertheless so far desisted from crossing the Line of Control. India, while undertaking a maximum mobilization of forces has nevertheless so far desisted from crossing the Line of Control. Pakistan, on her side, has made continuous efforts to involve other powers in this bilateral conflict, looking for the equalizer in international mediation. All along, unlike in the previous three wars, there has been continuous exchanges through the normal diplomatic channels. This two-track strategy – of defending the borders while negotiating – on the part of both the actors is perhaps the best strategy for peace in the region.

* *Re-printed with permission from Islamabad Policy Research Institute Journal, Pakistan, Summer 2001.*

Endnotes

1. See Anita Inder Singh, *The Origins of the Partition of India*, 1936-1947 (Delhi: Oxford University Press; 1987) for a succinct analysis of the conditions leading to the partition of British India. Some of the implications for India and Pakistan, respectively, can be found in Christophe Jaffrellot, *The Hindu Nationalist Movement and Indian Politics, 1925 to the 1990s: Strategies of Identity Building, Implanation and Mobilisation* (Delhi: Viking; 1993), and Seyyed Reza Nasr, *The Vanguard of the Islamic Revolution* (London: I.B.Tauris; 1994).

2. For a detailed analysis of this point, see Subrata K. Mitra, "Nehru's Policy Towards Kashmir; Bringing Politics Back in Again", in the *Journal of Commonwealth & Comparative Politics*, Vol. 35, No. 2, (July 1997), pp. 55-74.

3. Stanley Wolpert, *Zulfi Bhutto of Pakistan: His Life and Time,* Delhi: Oxford University Press; 1993), p.75.

4. For Nehru, Kashmir was crucial for the security of India as well. In his statement on Kashmir on March 1948, Nehru stated that India had only two objectives in Jammu and Kashmir state: "to ensure the freedom and the progress of the people there, and to prevent anything happening that might endanger the security of India". G.Parthasarathi, ed., *Jawaharlal Nehru; Letters to Chief Ministers, vol. 1, 1947-1064,* Delhi: Oxford University Press 1985, p 81, fn 15).

5. Nehru even went as far as comparing Pakistan with Nazi Germany: "It is extraordinary how these developments remind one of the technique adopted by Hilter. Indeed, the whole policy of the Muslim League during the past few years has been singularly reminiscent of the Nazi tactics.... Another feature of Pakistan's attack on Kashmir, which also reminds one of Nazi Germany, is the fierce, blatant and false propaganda that has been carried on by their radio and press." (G. Parthasarathi, ed., *Jawaharlal Nehru: Letters to Chief Ministers,* vol. 1, 1947-1964, Delhi: Oxford University Press 1985, p 6-7).

6. Gopal writes, "His Nehru's visit to London and Paris brought home to him how much India was being judged by her conduct in Kashmir and Hyderabad. (Nehru to Patel from Paris, 27 October 1948) He was forced to recognize that his policies did not appear as impeccable to others as they did to him." Gopal, op.cit., p 33.

7. Sarvepalli Gopal comments: "...whatever Nehru's romantic attachment to the mountains of Kashmir, it did not influence his policy, and the decisions on Kashmir were not, as has been frequently suggested, being taken by him alone in an overwhelming mood of sentiment." S. Gopal, op.cit. p.20.

8. A very convincing analysis of the war is given by D.K. Palit, *War in High Himalaya. The Indian Army in Crisis, 1962*. London: Hurst & Company 1991.

9. Sumit Ganguly, *The Origins of War in South Asia. Indo-Pakistani Conflicts Since 1947,* Boulder, Colorado and London: Westview Press 1986, p.78. According to this line of reasoning, the 1965 war with Pakistan was a direct result of the 1962 war with China.

10. *Asian Recorder,* 18-24 March 1964, p. 5726.

11. There is some controversy as to whether Johnson used food aid to pressurize India into taking a less intransigent view of the Pakistani claim to Kashmir. Srivastava, Shastri's biographer does not believe that to have been the case. See C.P. Srivastava, *Lal Bahadur Shastri,Prime Minister of India, 1964-1966: A Life of Truth in Politics* (Delhi: Oxford University Press; 1995), pp 174-176. But Lewis, who was Johnson's aide at that time, thinks otherwise. See John P. Lewis, *India's Political Economy: Governance and Reform* (Delhi: Oxford University Press; 1995), pp 96-98.

12. Srivastava, op. cit., p 186.

13. Ibid. p. 186.

14. Ibid. p 198.

15. Surit Mansingh, *India's Search for Power: Indira Gandhi's Foreign Policy, 1966-1982* (Delhi: Sage; 1984). See Bharat Wariavwala, "Security Issues in Domestic Politics" in Mitra and Chiriyankandath, eds., *Electoral Politics in India: a Changing Landscape* (Delhi: Segment; 1992) for an analysis of the use of security as an issue in domestic politics in what he calls the "plebiscitary politics" of Indira Gandhi.

16. See Ramesh Thakur, "India in the World. Neither Rich, **Powerful, nor** Principled", in: *Foreign Affairs* Vol. 76 No. 4, July/August 1997, **p. 20**

17. Kanti P. Bajpai emphasizes this point in "Regions, Regional **Politics, and** the Security of South Asia", in: Weinbaum, Martin/Kumar,, Chetan (eds.): *South Asia Approaches the Millennium. Reexamining National Security.* Boulder/San Francisco/Oxford: Westview Press 1995, 205-233, and p. 218/219.

18. The attempts to establish a zone of peace in the Indian Ocean are covered by Dieter Braun, *Der Indische Ozean: Konfliktregion order "Zone des Friedens"? Globalpolitische Bezuge und regionalspezifische Entwicklungen,* Baden-Baden: Nomos 1982.

19. Perhaps the most important factor for India's not going nuclear was the fall of Indra Gandhi and the unequivocal rejection of nuclear weapons as well as nuclear testing by the succeeding Janata government of Prime Minister Morarji Desai. See Smith, Chris, *India's Ad hoc Arsenal. Direction or Drift in Defence Policy?* New York: Oxford University Press (SIPRI) 1994, pp. 186 passim.

20. For a coverage of Operation Bluestar, see Nayar, Kuldip/Khushwant Singh, *Tragedy of Punjab: Operation Bluestar and After.* New Delhi: Vision Books 1984; Man Singh Deora (ed.). *Aftermath of Operation Bluestar.* New Delhi , Anmol 1992.

21. For a story of the IPKF in Sri Lanka, see Depinder Singh, *The IPKF in Sri Lanka.* Noida:Trishul Publ. 1991.

22. Ramesh Thakur, "India in the World Neither Rich, Powerful, nor Principled", in *Foreign Affairs,* Vol. 76, No. 4. July/August 1997, p. 15.

23. Ramesh Thakur, ibid.

24. Ramesh Thakur, op. cit., p.21.

25. The Gujral 'Doctrine' is publicly denounced as appeasement by the Hindu nationalist Bharatiya Janata Party. Gujral himself does not have an independent political base. The ruling coalition, dependent on the support of the Congress Party has recently received a severe jolt to its stability. See Khare, Harish, "Cong. (1) decides to give U.F. another Chance", *The Hindu,* Sept. 217, 1997, p.1.

26. Ramesh Thakur, op. cit., p.21, argues along the same lines.

27. On CSBM, see Sumit Ganguly/Ted Greenwood (eds.), *Mending Fences. Confidence-and Security-Building Measures in South Asia.* Boulder, Colorado: Westview Press 1996.

28. It is, of course, possible to argue in the opposite direction and suggest that the BJP, once in power, might jettison its aggressive posture and become an advocate of conflict resolution within a regional framework.

29. The results of this report, which was partially funded by the Konrad-Adenauer Foundation, are available in: Mitra, Subrata K. and Singh, Vijay Bahadur, *Elections and Social Change in India.* Delhi: Sage 1999.

30. Recent reports of Chinese incursions into Arunachal Pradesh and reactivation of the disputed 650 miles border in India's North-East known as the Line of Actual Control (LAC) denotes what Indian policy makers regard as the hostile presence of the Chinese. Luke Harding, reporting from New Delhi, comments: 'superficially polite, relations between New Delhi and Beijing are best characterized as mistrustful. India accuses China of helping Pakistan to stockpile a nuclear and missile arsenal much larger than its own – a claim backed by US intelligence'. Luke Harding, China accused of infiltrating into India, *The Guardian Weekly,* Oct 18, 2000, p 17.

31. Samuel P. Huntington, *The Clash of Civilizations and the Remaking of the World Order,* New York: Simon and Schuster 1996.

32. This fuzzy policy and equally diffused self-perception made sense in the world of superpower rivalry, cold war and non-alignment. The question: has Indian foreign policy got a cohesive goal today, gets no clear answer, because, I.K. Gujral, India's Prime Minister and author of the Gujral 'doctrine' is himself an embattled figure in domestic politics, which, in the eyes of India's South Asian neighbours reduces the whole policy to an unacceptable level of uncertainty. In Ramesh Thakur's words, "... 50 years after independence, India is neither rich enough to bribe, powerful enough to bully, nor principled enough to inspire Ramesh Thakur, India in the World. Neither Rich, Powerful, nor Principled, in: *Foreign Affairs*, Vvol. 70, No. 4, July/August 1997, pp. 15.

The US Balancing Act in South Asia

Andrew C. Winner

The history of US policies towards both Pakistan and India has involved both stated preferences for one state or the other as well as the perception, in Islamabad and New Delhi, that Washington is favouring one or the other through a variety of policy decisions. Perhaps the most famous instance of this was then-US national security adviser Henry Kissinger's tilt towards Pakistan during the 1971 war, as part of a larger policy of balancing the Soviet Union by opening to China.[1] The most recent instance is the concern in Pakistan that, in the wake of the 1998 nuclear tests and relatively short-lived outrage amongst nonproliferation advocates, Washington has begun courting New Delhi as a strategic partner against both anti-western radical Islam in southwest Asia and against China in east Asia.

The issue for the US in the coming decade is not one of whether to lean towards one side or the other but rather, how to balance a variety of US national security interests that are primarily global in scope but that have elements connected to South Asia. This is easier said than done. Even if the US does not explicitly express a preference for one state or the other over time, both states will perceive that favouritism exists. This will be particularly true in Pakistan, which views India as its primary security threat. India will be concerned not just about US policies towards Pakistan but also about US policy towards China. In fact, New Delhi has and will continue to push for a de-linking of US policy towards India from that towards

Pakistan in part, because of New Delhi's desire to be seen as a player on the larger global stage. Some key US think-tanks are also recommending that the new administration de-couple India and Pakistan policy.[2] While this type of recommendation appears sensible on the surface, it is too simple a construct to apply. In some interest areas, US policy will indeed have to treat India and Pakistan differently. The US simply has different interests to pursue with each country in areas such as democracy, terrorism, and stability in the Persian Gulf. However in other areas, such as nuclear non-proliferation and particularly in crisis stability, policies towards the two must be inextricably linked. Again, the difficulty is in balancing these various interests and the policies pursued in advancing them. This article outlines US interests that have relevance for South Asia over the coming decade. It then analyses their intersections and speculates on what the Bush administration's priorities will be in pursuing these various interests.

US Interests and Strategy since the End of the Cold War

The end of the Cold War competition with the Soviet bloc forced the US to consider anew its national security interests, the potential threats to those interests, and its grand strategy. In large part, two events in the early 1990s set the tone for this reconsideration. The first was Iraq's invasion of Kuwait, the US assembling and leading a coalition to reverse that invasion, and the discoveries by the UN Special Commission (UNSCOM) of the extent of Iraq's weapons of mass destruction (WMD) programmes. The second event was the ongoing turmoil in the Balkans, culminating in the Dayton peace accord and the deployment of US military forces, under a UN mandate, as part of a peace-keeping force in Bosnia. More recently, the use of NATO airpower and the deployment of peacekeepers in Kosovo have underscored the fact that the US will continue to be drawn into regional conflicts in certain areas of the globe.

The reassessment resulted in a newly articulated US national security strategy that eschewed a clear list of national interests. Instead, it put forward a laundry list of challenges to US national security, including ethnic conflict, proliferation of WMD, large-scale environmental degradation, and population growth. Under the rubric of "engagement and enlargement", the strategy sought to sustain American security with military forces that were ready to fight, bolster America's economic revitalization, and promote democracy abroad.[3] As might be expected in such a public document, hard choices were not identified, nor were conflicts noted among particular goals. The long lists of areas of interest and policies in the succeeding documents made identification of priorities difficult.

However, the military strategy (which emerged from a first-year defense review) that supported this national security strategy was clearer. It focused, in the first part of the 1990s, on two sets of issues. The first was preparedness to fight and win a major regional war in both the Persian Gulf (basically a repeat of Iraq's invasion of Kuwait) and on the Korean peninsula. The assumption in these scenarios was that potential adversaries would consider early and extensive use of WMD to offset US conventional military prowess, given the lessons of Operation Desert Storm. The second set of issues was a preparedness to assist in lesser contingencies, often involving peace enforcement, peace-keeping, and/or the delivery of humanitarian assistance. These missions were considered secondary and would be dropped, if necessary, if both major regional contingencies occurred simultaneously or required assets tied up in peace-keeping activities.

Throughout the course of the 1990s, it became clear that requirements for fighting and winning two major theatre wars, at least within acceptable risk levels, exceeded existing capabilities, particularly if the pace of secondary operations such as peace-keeping was high. The second Clinton administration defense review, the Quadrennial Defense Review made four significant changes to US military strategy. First, it lowered requirements. US forces were required to fight and win two major theatre wars (MTWs) nearly simultaneously; in other words, sequentially. Second, it de-emphasized US involvement in peace-keeping missions. Third, the strategy began to include the potential of a near peer competitor arising that could challenge the United States directly in the mid-term against which the United States must hedge with research and development. Although not stated explicitly, this potential competitor is widely assumed to be China. Finally, it began to emphasize more starkly the dangers of asymmetrical warfare against the United States in both the potential regional contingencies and other instances as well.

Basically, the strategy recognized what potential adversaries of the United States realized following the Gulf war–that no state in the near to medium term could match America directly through force of conventional arms. Potential adversaries, therefore, began concentrating even more heavily on developing asymmetrical strategies, including terrorism, the use of WMD, and the possibility of using cyber attacks to counter the United States' high technology edge. The US experience in Mogadishu in 1993, where it lost eighteen of its most highly-trained soldiers to militias in a highly chaotic street battle, also heightened awareness in Washington that high technology and airpower would not suffice to meet all the challenges in the future.[5] It also lessened the US taste for engaging heavily in multilateral peace-keeping and peace enforcement operations, causing strategists to look elsewhere for new missions for the US military. Of course, despite this dislike for such missions, the US continued to become involved due to its own view of the requirements for global leadership and, in cases like Kosovo, the need to preserve the credibility of the NATO alliance.

Once beyond the two major theatre wars, the focus of national military strategy has become one of countering asymmetrical threats, including attacks on the US homeland. Terrorist attacks on US forces abroad, like the bombing at the Khobar Towers complex in Saudi Arabia in 1996, heightened awareness of how exposed US forces and installations were when conducting forward presence missions. Improved ballistic missile capabilities by potential adversaries who might be involved in MTWs–namely Iran and North Korea–heightened concerns about proliferation of both WMD and missile delivery capabilities. As mentioned above, the continuing revelations by UNSCOM throughout the 1990s about Iraq's capabilities shocked even the United States.

On the diplomatic side, the end of the Cold War and improving relations with Russia gave impetus to both the arms control and nonproliferation agendas, complementing in many ways the military concern with WMD. The end of the Cold War competition meant to many that strategic weapons in the arsenals of both the United States and Russia could be reduced significantly, thereby living up to the requirement in the Nuclear Non-proliferation Treaty for nuclear weapons states to take effective measures to end the nuclear arms race.[6] In addition, the demise of the Soviet Union brought about a renewed concern about proliferation of nuclear weapons capabilities because Ukraine, Belarus, and Khazakstan all had the potential to become nuclear weapons states by retaining portions of the arsenal of the former Soviet Union that were deployed on their soil. The success in getting these three states to forgo retention of nuclear arsenals encouraged non-proliferation advocates in Washington, leading them to push the broader non-proliferation agenda more vigorously.

This focus on non-proliferation was kept at the forefront of US foreign policy for much of the Clinton administration. However, a rigorous non-proliferation policy has not commanded enough bipartisan support in the US to make it the singular focus of US foreign policy. A quick example of countervailing pressures can be seen in the case of China. While Beijing was clearly engaging in activities that ran counter to US non-proliferation policies, including the transfer of both missile and nuclear technology to Pakistan, other US interests with China, such as trade and the desire for strategic stability in the Taiwan Strait, kept this issue from dominating the relationship. Moreover, despite the longstanding US interest in non-proliferation, it is a difficult policy to pursue in a universal manner.

In fact, historically the US has never pursued an undifferentiated non-proliferation policy, particularly on the nuclear front. While initially the US had some moments of high-mindedness, such as the placing of all nuclear capabilities under international control through the Baruch plan in the early days of the Cold War, realpolitik has always been part of non-proliferation policy. In fact, some analysts and historians argue persuasively that the Baruch plan was not as high-minded as it seems in retrospect and was in fact designed to constrain Soviet and nascent Chinese nuclear capabilities while preserving the US monopoly on the technology to produce nuclear weapons.[7]

US Interests and Strategy–Priorities of the Bush Administration

After an extended dispute over the US presidential election, Texas governor George W. Bush was ultimately declared the winner. Now sixteen months into his administration, the broad outlines of a new US national security and foreign policy are emerging. The extended transition initially slowed consideration of many issues, but the Bush team now appears to be on track. However, like many new administrations, including those who take over from a different political party, the Bush foreign policy team is discovering that there are limits to how much it can break from the policies of its predecessor. Despite the constraints of budgets, allies, and difficult situations in various parts of the world, the Bush administration has articulated some clear and clean breaks from the past.

The first area of emphasis for the Bush administration is on developing and deploying a missile defense system designed first and foremost to protect the US from what Washington sees as a growing ballistic missile and WMD threat from a small number of hostile states including Iraq, Iran, and North Korea. Over the past sixteen months, the administration has broadened this vision and begun talking about a missile defense system that could also cover US allies and perhaps even friends. As part of this effort, it has been made clear that the United States will either withdraw from or substantially modify the Anti-Ballistic Missile Treaty of 1972. This indicates continuity with the Clinton administration in terms of the focus on WMD but a different way of approaching it–through an emphasis on unilateral military capabilities vice multilateral regimes or agreements.

Second despite some false starts and protests from friends and allies, the Bush administration has continued to say that it will reduce, to the degree possible, US military involvement in operations other than war—in other words peace-keeping and peace enforcement operations.[8] Instead, in the near-term the military will focus its energies on deterring major theatre wars and preparing to fight and win them should deterrence fail. Interestingly, the focus on major theatre wars remains for the near-term, but the Clinton administration requirement to fight two nearly simultaneously has been dropped, in large part to free up resources for missile defense and what has been termed "transformation"–the changing of the military to be better prepared to deter and fight future conflicts.

This is the third difference – an increased focus on reorienting the US military, in terms of both strategy and capabilities, for future contingencies. While all of the official reviews are not yet done and a formal, Congressionally mandated defense strategy document is yet to be published, the outlines of such a reorientation are becoming clear. Again, missile defense as part of a broader emphasis on defending US territory is going to reap many resources in the revamped strategy and defense budget. This will be part of a focus on countering asymmetrical threats (seen as the threat of the future), ranging from weapons of mass destruction to terrorist strikes to cyber attacks. In addition, the military is going to focus on developing capabilities that would enable it to deter and, if necessary, dominate any strategic competitor that could arise in the medium to long term. The claim by President Bush during the campaign that the military is going to skip a generation of weapons systems now appears to be a bit hyperbolic, but the Pentagon will be devoting significantly more resources to research and development on new capabilities and systems.

As outlined briefly above, under a Bush administration countering WMD is seen primarily as a defense task, and a critical one in three areas of concern: MTWs, use by rogue states or non-state actors, and potential use by a future peer competitor. WMD should be deterred, countered, defended against. Non-proliferation policy, while a complement to what in the US Pentagon has termed "counter proliferation" is not likely to command as high a priority in a Bush administration. As part of the refocus, the Bush administration has made it very clear that it does not support certain elements of the global non-proliferation regime pushed by the Clinton administration and associated arms control agreements, including the Comprehensive Test Ban Treaty (CTBT) and the US Russian Anti-Ballistic Missile Treaty. While a Bush administration understands, like all US administrations since World War II, that it serves US interests for fewer states to have nuclear weapons, broad non-proliferation policy is being supplanted by one that focuses on states that have ongoing quarrels with the US and are seeking to acquire nuclear capabilities. Iraq, Iran, and North Korea top this list.

In sum, the national security strategy of the Bush administration, with its underlying military strategy, is focusing on preparing for a major theatre war, countering asymmetrical threats to the US, its deployed forces and its allies, and preparing for a future peer competitor. In all of these areas, weapons of mass destruction are an important component. Such a set of strategies is being accomplished by changing the focus of military spending and operations to de-emphasize US participation in peace-keeping and crisis-management operations. In addition research and development on countering weapons of mass destruction and other asymmetrical threats is being increased, even at the expense of replacing current generations of weapons that are becoming obsolete. On the diplomatic front, the administration is emphasizing relationships with traditional allies (although not without some setbacks in areas such as the environment) and appearing to promote unilateral action, or at most action in concert with a few traditional allies, when crises occur. It is, putting less stock in arms control treaties and multilateral legal undertakings, preferring unilateral adjustments of capabilities perhaps combined with broader transparency measures.

Implications for US Policy Towards South Asia

While the above is an admittedly broad brush outline of US interests and strategies under the Bush administration, it is not difficult to see how such a set of interests and policy priorities will affect US relations with both Pakistan and India. Obviously, the US has ongoing relations and interests that are specific to both Pakistan and India, and these will not suddenly be forsaken. However, they will be pursued in the context of, and be influenced significantly by, these higher order interests and policies.

On the military side, the US will focus on deterring and preparing for a major theatre war, either one on the Korean peninsula or in the Persian Gulf. Neither India nor Pakistan plays a significant role in the US focus on these near-term contingencies or preparations to address them. Korean contingency is remote both geographically and politically from South Asia, and the only connection would be the use of US assets prepositioned on ships based in the Indian Ocean or the transit of the Indian Ocean by US navy forces on their way to the Pacific theatre.

In a future conflict in the Persian Gulf, neither Pakistan nor India is likely to be a direct player. While an improved overall relationship with Pakistan may assist the reputation of the US with Islamic countries generally, other variables will have a much greater impact on that issue including progress in the Israeli-Palestinian peace process (should it ever resume). It could be argued, perhaps, that Pakistan's support for the Taliban in Afghanistan keeps Iran off-balance and reduces the likelihood that they would directly challenge US interests in the Gulf, but again other factors (US military capabilities, Iranian domestic politics) will have a much greater influence on decisions in Tehran. Finally, the prospect that Pakistan could or would provide military capabilities in the Gulf that would cooperate with US forces in deterring adventurism by either Baghdad or Tehran is highly unlikely. First, the US Pakistani relationship is simply not at that point currently and has many issues to resolve. Second, given other concerns, particularly India, Iran, and instability in Afghanistan, it is unclear whether Islamabad would have any interest in filling this role. Finally, it is unclear whether the Gulf states would currently be willing to have substantial numbers of Pakistani troops on their soil for extended periods of time.

India's role in either preventing or participating in any future Gulf conflict is unclear at best. While India has a growing economic interest in seeing that the free-flow of oil from this region remains steady, its political and military ability to contribute to this goal is extremely small in the near to medium term. Indian development of a true blue water navy capability is years off, and even if the next cruise of the Indian aircraft carrier were to the Persian Gulf, it would not have a measurable impact on stability in the region. In terms of US policy, relations in the region are complex and strained enough without Washington bringing in another player with potentially divergent points of view and an ongoing antagonistic relationship with an Islamic country – Pakistan. The US has a complex enough task in figuring out how to achieve its goals vis-a-vis Iran and Iraq, keep relations on keel with Saudi Arabia and other key GCC states, and facing down the political challenges from Baghdad and Tehran without adding New Delhi to its calculations in the Gulf.

For the US, the other link to Pakistan and India that relates to a potential major theatre war in the Persian Gulf region is the concern about terrorism in the Middle East. As noted in the US State Department's latest publication on terrorism, Washington is concerned about terrorism emanating from two regions – South Asia and the Middle East.[9] The trail of evidence on the bombing of the USS Cole has only reinforced this concern, as it appears likely that the perpetrators have links back to Osama bin Laden, who is currently residing in Afghanistan.[10] As noted in the State Department report, increasingly terrorist organizations from the two regions are linked. The issue of terrorism for the US is twofold. First, it is an asymmetric strategy that adversaries can use against the US homeland and against deployed forces and US installations worldwide. Second, terrorist attacks against US forces deployed in the Persian Gulf region are a direct attack on the US strategy for deterring and preparing to fight a future war in that region.

While terrorist attacks, like that on the Cole, will not drive the US from the region, they may threaten host governments enough to cause them to rethink their willingness to allow US forces to be based on, or deployed to, their territory.

Therefore, combating terrorism is likely to remain at the top of the national security and diplomatic agenda for the Bush administration. For Pakistan, this means that the US will continue to press it to be less sympathetic to the Taliban in Afghanistan. It will also expect Islamabad to use whatever leverage it has to press for the extradition of bin Laden to the US or a third country were he could be prosecuted. For India, the focus means that Washington and New Delhi will have a topic that at least generically they can discuss – terrorism in and emanating from South Asia. However, this discussion will not become a core element in US-Indian relations and practical limits to US-Indian cooperation on this topic will quickly become evident. On the US part, its focus is on terrorist activity that may be based in South Asia (specifically Afghanistan) but that is carried out elsewhere. New Delhi's focus, not surprisingly, is on Kashmir. While it will delight in US pressure on Pakistan on any and all issues, New Delhi will limit Washington's involvement in events on the ground in Kashmir.

A second US focus in the coming decade, preparing for a potential peer competitor in the medium term, could potentially have an impact on Washington's relations with both India and Pakistan. Since it is widely recognized that this potential competitor is China, the relationship of both Islamabad and New Delhi to Beijing will come into play. This focus, however, should not be over-emphasized. While a Republican administration will likely be somewhat tougher on

Beijing in certain areas such as relations with Taiwan and proliferation, it will not be declaring China an enemy or be constructing a containment policy anytime soon. No consensus exists on the proper policy towards China in the United States. Even with a Republican-controlled White House and (half of) Congress, China policy will remain a mix of engagement, competition, and some defense preparation for something worse. For this reason, hopes by some analysts in both Washington and New Delhi that the two will work together to contain China is fanciful at best.[11] In fact, if the United States ever decided to attempt to contain the growth of Chinese power, then East Asia (Japan, South Korea, Taiwan) would be the focal point rather than South Asia.[12]

For India, this US policy of engaging but also hedging with Beijing may prove frustrating. Washington is going to have significant issues with Beijing in the coming decade, not least of which are Taiwan and the construction by the United States of a missile defense system. Those front-burner issues, combined with the worry about China's potential as a global adversary, will mean that Washington will continue to consider Beijing more important than New Delhi. It will continue to consider the impact of its policies on China before it will consider their impact on India. For example, in the case of missile defense decisions, the US understands, and may take some minor steps to ameliorate, Chinese worries about missile defense deployments. The fact that Chinese responses to a US missile defense deployment, including modernization and expansion of its nuclear arsenal, has a domino affect on India's nuclear thinking will be recognized but will be much lower on Washington's list of worries, if it appears at all. All of this despite the relatively kind words that New Delhi had about President

Bush's statements on missile defense and the highly publicized trip by US Deputy Secretary of State Richard Armitage to India to consult on these issues.

For Pakistan, Washington's policies on China are likely to continue to be focused on technology transfer in the WMD area. The Bush administration will be tougher rhetorically on Beijing about the transfer of either nuclear or missile technology to Pakistan and elsewhere. It will draw brighter lines about what is acceptable and what is unacceptable, and it will be less likely to accept vague assurances from Beijing. That said, it will still remain a difficult issue, and Washington's leverage with Beijing will continue to be limited. In particular, however, the Bush administration will be eager to ensure that China does not proliferate missile capabilities that could defeat future US theatre or national missile defense systems. This means that any suspected future transfer of missile technologies to Pakistan will come under significant scrutiny. If evidence of such transfers is found in the future, it is likely to be harder on Pakistan than on China simply because of the disparity in US interest in the two states and because the US has more potent sanctions it can apply to Islamabad without significant repercussions in the US.

The more general US concern about weapons of mass destruction in South Asia under the Bush administration will have two areas of focus. The first area will be ensuring that the nuclear and missile capabilities in both Pakistan and India do not proliferate further, either to other states or to terrorist organizations. This means that the focus will be on the export control policies of Islamabad and New Delhi and on the physical safety and security of their nuclear arsenals. This concern meshes nicely with the second likely area of focus – that of lowering the chance that nuclear weapons would be used in any future conflict. Achieving both of these goals requires more detailed discussions with both countries about the development of their nuclear doctrines and arsenals and a corresponding lowering of pressure on them to reverse their programs and give up their nuclear capabilities. Bush administration official have suggested that the US should change its focus and cease trying to get India to eliminate its nuclear arsenal.[13] This does not mean that a Bush administration will openly accept India and Pakistan as nuclear weapon's power, but will, however, be less shrill in its denunciation of the 1998 tests and more pragmatic in its approach to nuclear developments on the subcontinent. This will all come as part of a policy of renewed engagement with both India and Pakistan and a further easing of sanctions that were imposed after the 1998 nuclear tests.

Conclusions

Despite sixteen months in office, the Bush administration has yet to outline a comprehensive and coherent set of foreign policy goals for South Asia. However, statements by incoming officials who will be responsible for the region and actions like Chairman of the Joint Chiefs of Staff General Henry Shelton's July 2001 visit to India show that it will have at least, a different tone from that of the Clinton administration. In fact, General Shelton followed up hints by other administration officials that the US sanctions on India initiated after the May 1998 nuclear tests might be lifted in the near future.[14] It is likely that similar sanctions may also be eased for Pakistan although the issues for Islamabad are a bit more complex because of the coup and some US policy and legal requirements for a return to democracy before certain restrictions can be lifted. This is in line with statements by key administration officials that sanctions will not be utilized as frequently as a tool of policy and that they will be applied only when they have a good chance of success.

Taking as a starting point the broad goals, interests, and strategies laid out by the Bush administration in its first seven months, one can begin to see how US interests and strategies will affect US relations with Pakistan and India. Despite early visits to India and diplomatic interaction with Pakistan, both states should not expect that they would be among the highest priorities for the Bush administration. They it is likely will be dealt with in the context of higher priority interests areas, including concern about major theatre wars, countering asymmetrical threats to the United States, and preparing for a potential future global adversary. This is not to say that India and Pakistan will be ignored or that a Bush administration will not be mindful of the unique historical, cultural, and political context in which Washington relates to Islamabad and New Delhi. It simply means that Islamabad should not expect some renewed special relationship like that during the Soviet occupation of Afghanistan, and New Delhi should not expect a Bush administration to attempt to build a new strategic partnership between the United States and India. In this sense, it is unlikely that any actual tilt will occur towards either state.

Washington will be taking a more traditional view of national security and foreign policy over the next four years, focusing on issues that fundamentally affect the security of the United States, its treaty allies, and its traditional friends. For Islamabad, this means a continuing focus on international terrorism and what the government of Pakistan can do to address Washington's desire to get at Osama bin Laden and hem in terrorist training and planning activities that take place in

Afghanistan. A return to democracy will be a continued requirement due to legislative strictures, but a Bush administration is likely to be relatively less concerned about a continuing behind-the-scenes role for the military once civilian rule is restored. On proliferation, the Bush administration will likely shift the focus to one of preventing further horizontal proliferation and possibly beginning to address crisis stability measures. For New Delhi, there will be interest by the Bush administration in seeing what broader cooperative activities can be started that address Washington's interests in both the Persian Gulf region and southeast Asia. However, the Bush administration is going to want specifics on what India can do for it before moving too far. As with Pakistan, Washington will likely be less concerned with pressing India to reverse its nuclear course and be more concerned with preventing further horizontal proliferation. Although New Delhi is likely to be less interested than Islamabad in discussing these issues, the Bush administration may also try to engage India in discussions about stabilizing measures to reduce potential problems of crisis stability in the future.

All of these areas, however, will come in the context of higher priority goals and interests for the United States. For good or for ill, South Asia is more likely to remain an object of policy than a subject of policy under the Bush administration.

* *(Re-printed with permission from Islamabad Policy Research Institute Journal, Pakistan, Summer 2001.)*

Endnotes

1. George Perkovitch, *India's Nuclear Bomb: The Impact on Global Proliferation* (Berkeley: University of California Press, 1999), p. 164.

2. Frank Carlucci, Robert Hunter, Zalmay Khalilzad, *Taking Charge: A Bipartisan Report to the President Elect on Foreign Policy and National Security,* The Rand Corporation, available at www.rand.org.

3. The White House, A National Security Strategy of Engagement and Enlargement , February 1995. Various versions of this strategy were issued by the Clinton administration, but all had these central characteristics and themes.

5. The lessons of the battle of Mogadishu for US security strategy were numerous and hotly debated in the United States. To this day no consensus exists. One immediate outcome was a pull-back from even greater US participation in multilateral peace enforcement and peacekeeping missions and an increased suspicion, rightly or wrongly, of UN-led operations. A more long-term consequence was a heightened suspicion of missions that went beyond simple peacekeeping principles and began engaging in what was termed "nation-building."

6. The text of article VI is as follows: "Each of the Parties to the Treaty undertakes to pursue negotiations in good faith on effective measures relating to cessation of the nuclear arms race at an early date and to nuclear disarmament, and on a Treaty on general and complete disarmament under strict and effective international control." The full text of the treaty is available on the Web at http://www.state.gov/www/global/arms/treaties/nptI.html

7. Richard Rhodes, *Dark Sun: The Making of the Hydrogen Bomb*, (New York: Simon and Shuster, 1995), pp. 239-240.

8. Michael R. Gordon, "The 2000 Campaign: The Military; Bush Would Stop US Peacekeeping in Balkan Fights," *The New York Times*, 21 October 2000.

9. Office of the Coordinator for Counter terrorism, United States Department of State, Patterns of Global Terrorism 1999, April 2001.

10. Vernon Loeb, "Planned January 2000 Attacks Failed or Were Thwarted; Plot Targeted US, Jordan, American Warship, Official Says," *The Washington Post*, 24 December 2000, p. A2.

11. Jim Mann, "India: Growing implications For US," *Los Angeles Times* 17 May 2000, p. 2. Victor M. Gobarev, "India as a World Power Changing Washington's Myopic Policy," Policy Analysis, 11 September 2000 (Washington: The Cato Institute).

12. Ashley Tellis, "Sino-US-South Asian Relations: Report of the IPCS Seminar of 6 June 2000," *JPCS Bulletin* Vol. 3, No. 11, 2000

13. Richard N. Haass, "Clinton Should Try to Cool South Asia," *Newsday*, 17 March 2000, p. A5 1.

14 Agence France-Presse, "Sanctions on India May Be Lifted, Joint Chiefs Chairman Suggests," *Washington Times*, July 20, 200 1, p. 15.

Index

B

D

L

Q

R

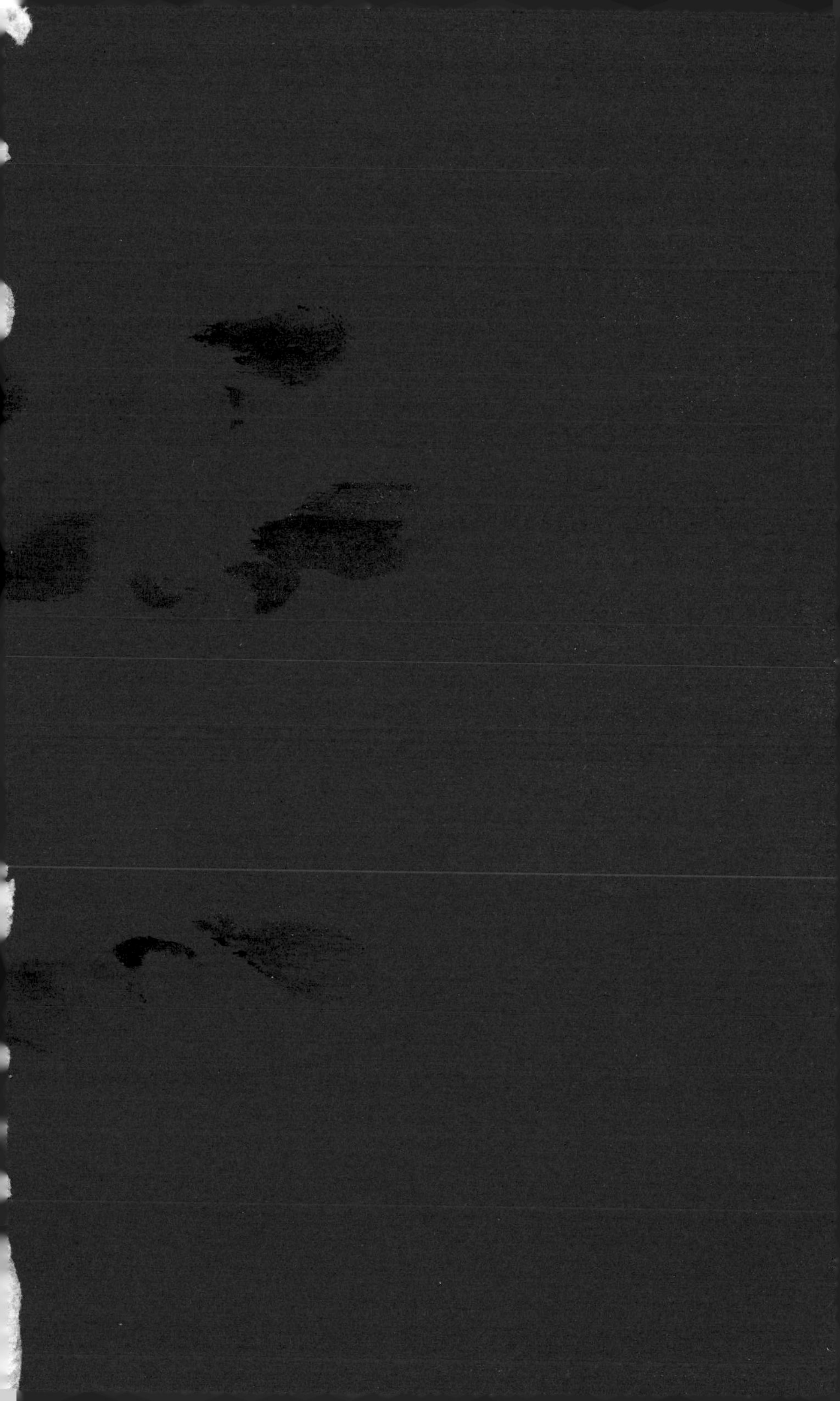